Virtualism
A New Political Economy

Edited by
James G. Carrier
and
Daniel Miller

BERG

Oxford • New York

First published in 1998 by
Berg
Editorial offices:
150 Cowley Road, Oxford, OX4 1JJ, UK
70 Washington Square South, New York, NY 10012, USA

Berg is the imprint of Oxford International Publishers Ltd.

Library of Congress Cataloging-in-Publication Data

A catalogue record for this book is available from the Library of Congress.

British Library Cataloguing-in-Publication Data

A catalogue record for this book is available from the British Library.

ISBN 1 85973 237 2 (Cloth)
1 85973 242 9 (Paper)

Typeset by JS Typesetting, Wellingborough, Northants.
Printed in the United Kingdom by Biddles Ltd, Guildford and King's Lynn.

Virtualism

Contents

Introduction

James G. Carrier

When the Berlin Wall was breached and the Soviet Union dissolved, the world came to look very different in very many ways. We saw attempts at a New World Order and proclamations of the End of History. But while the end of the Cold War changed our world, its very disappearance enabled us to see differently what was already there. Whatever the gains, losses and passions of the Cold War, it was also a tremendous distraction. It so dominated our perceptions of the world that it diverted attention from other things that were going on; things that would, in more normal times, have demanded more of our notice. One of those things is the continuing evolution of Western capitalist economic thought and practice. That evolution is the focus of this collection; my purpose in this Introduction is to sketch the nature of that focus.

Much about capitalism changed in the second half of the twentieth century, the time when the Cold War fascinated the Western world. For instance, we saw (or thought we saw) the end of the Keynesian consensus and welfare capitalism, the strengthening and spread of the competitive and innovative Free Market (Carrier 1997). Although the Free Market is often taken as a central element of the genius of the West, frequently these changes were discussed as signs of the growing sovereignty of the consumer. People increasingly were to be free to make their own choices, and those organisations that could not cater to that choice were the inflexible dinosaurs of economic and commercial history. In this relatively common view of the changes that occurred, attention was focused increasingly on market transactions between individual purchasers and commercial suppliers of commodities of different sorts.

Like the Cold War, however, this view of changing capitalism has distracted our attention from other things that have been going on, and have been going on in other parts of our economic lives. These other changes occurred not so much in the realm of transaction between firm and consumer as in the internal operation of firms and in the ways that different, influential sets of people have thought about, organised and carried out economic activity. We have glimpsed these changes from time to time over the past decade or two, though they have not been as consistent a theme in the mass media as has the image of the increasingly powerful consumer. For example, the rise of the market-driven, flexible firm has been accompanied by a demand for market-driven, flexible workers. In practice, this has meant those who can be hired and fired easily and cheaply. Similarly, concern to promote economic growth has in many places been manifest as the promotion of greater freedom of international trade, just as the desire of many firms to increase their profits has been manifest as an expansion into international markets. In the view of many, this combination has threatened to reduce productive work in central Western, developed countries, as firms move aspects of their operations 'off shore', to poorer countries with lower wages and more tractable workers. These sorts of changes are part of a process that is the focus of this collection.

That process is the growing abstraction of economy in the West and, because of Western power, in the world more generally, a process that appears to be culminating in what this collection calls 'virtualism', a trend that is only beginning to become apparent. As 'abstraction' is a nebulous term and 'virtualism' a novel one, it is important to explain what they mean in the context of this collection.

The core of economic abstraction is the process that Karl Polanyi (1957a) described as 'dis-embedding': that is, the removal of economic activities from the social and other relationships in which they had occurred, and carrying them out in a context in which the only important relationships are those defined by the economic activity itself. In essence, economic activity becomes abstracted from social relations. This abstraction occurs in practical activity, what Polanyi (1957b) referred to as the realm of substantive economy, which is the ways that people, firms and other agents organise and carry out their activities of the production and circulation of objects and services. It occurs as well at a conceptual level, what Polanyi refers to as the realm of formal economy, which is the ways that people think about and understand their economic lives.

Abstraction at this formal, conceptual level leads at least some people to adopt an abstract-economic world-view. Here, the world is seen in terms of the concepts and models of economic abstraction, which are taken to be the fundamental reality that underlies and shapes the world. Those who adopt this view of the world can be said to perceive a virtual reality, seemingly real but dependent upon the conceptual apparatus and outlook that generate it. Perceiving a virtual reality becomes virtualism when people take this virtual reality to be not just a parsimonious description of what is really happening, but prescriptive of what the world ought to be; when, that is, they seek to make the world conform to their virtual vision. Virtualism, thus, operates at both the conceptual and practical levels, for it is a practical effort to make the world conform to the structures of the conceptual.

I have sketched briefly two complex notions, abstraction and virtualism, that operate at practical and conceptual levels. It is worth spending some time to elaborate the notions, which are central to this collection. I do so through a consideration of economic abstraction at the practical and conceptual levels.

Practical Abstraction

It is perhaps easiest to describe economic abstraction in the practical realm with a somewhat simplified example. Imagine an English weaver who ceases producing at home on his own account (English weavers historically were mostly men) and takes a job in a textile mill, as many did in England in the eighteenth century.

When weaving at home, that weaver was carrying out the economic activity of producing cloth for sale, and thereby earning a livelihood. He was doing so, however, in the context of familial relations, for while the man may have been the weaver, his wife and children were likely to have had important parts to play in this economic activity. These relationships existed outside of and prior to his weaving: if he ceased to be a weaver and became a huckster or carter he would still have had the same wife and children and would have been likely to have incorporated them in his new economic activity. When our weaver took a mill job, he continued to produce cloth for sale and earn his livelihood thereby. However, he did so in the context of a different set of relationships, those centred on the mill. These differ from the relations surrounding his weaving at home, for he entered into them only as a part of his economic activity, and they owed their existence to the economic activity carried out within them: if the mill shut down, his relationship with his co-workers, superiors and inferiors would end. In short, when our cottage weaver took a job at a mill, cloth production became that much more abstracted from people's social and other non-economic contexts. Jonathan Parry's (1986: 446) statement summarises this historical process nicely: '[T]he economy becomes disembedded from society, . . . economic relationships become increasingly differentiated from other types of social relationships.'

As this simple example suggests, the growth of practical economic abstraction that occurred in the second half of the twentieth century and that is a focus of this collection was hardly a novel process. (Equally, criticism of this economic abstraction has also been around for some time; see O. Harris 1989: 234–239; Kahn 1997.) At least some economic activities in the West appear to have taken place in relatively dis-embedded realms since the ancient Greeks had market-places (Agnew 1986), just as relatively dis-embedded economic realms are fairly common in non-capitalist areas around the world (Bloch and Parry 1989). However, it is the case that in the West the abstracting has been accelerating over the past century and more, and especially since the Second World War. Predominantly, however, the relationships from which economic activity has been abstracted in the more recent past have not been those of the family, but of other forms of social life. For instance, with the spread of free-trade areas, economic activity becomes increasingly abstracted from pre-existing political contexts and relationships, which is to say, from countries, for this is one purpose of free-trade arrangements. Similarly, with the decline of fair-trade laws and of regulation of industries, economic activity becomes increasingly abstracted from state political contexts. Likewise, it is not too far-fetched to see the disaggregation of firms and the increasing use of out-sourcing and temporary workers as a kind of dis-embedding, for economic activities that had occurred within the structure of the firm and the durable employment and institutional relations contained within it, move outside and are acquired through relatively more impersonal and transient market relationships.

In pointing out that free trade and out-sourcing are a kind of practical economic abstraction, I am noting that this abstraction is unlikely ever to be absolute. This is so for two reasons. First, practical economic abstraction is a matter of degree. Certainly our weaver in the mill is engaged in economic activities that are more abstracted from their social and other contexts than is the same man working at home. However, the mill belongs to a company that has an identity (which can be important; see Chapman and Buckley 1997: 239–240) and an organisational structure. These things may be creatures of the economic activities that they contain, but they can and do provide for more durable relationships and interactions than are available to the person hired on a short-term contract to do a specific job.

The second reason that practical economic abstraction is unlikely ever to be absolute is that people seem prone to socialise and complicate their economic relationships when they can. In spite of David Schneider's (1980) stylised description of American views of the workplace, relationships in modern firms are not totally impersonal, for employees form sociable groups, and interactions between superiors and inferiors become entwined with social expectation and personality (see, for example, Halle 1984; R. Harris 1987; Mars 1982; Salaman 1986). The same seems to be the case at the level of the firm. As Ronald Dore (1983) and Mark Granovetter (1985) have argued, companies that start trading with each other at the classic arm's-length of the market often find that their relations can come to take on a moral air. However, it is important not to assume that the persistence of people's socialising and complicating tendencies means that things, in the end, remain the same. Socialising and complicating can be more or less urgent, easier or harder, depending on the institutional environment, and the secular trend over the past few centuries has been in the direction of greater urgency and difficulty as people's institutional environments have become less promising socially, at least below the level of senior management (see, for example, Kanter 1977). People have had to work harder at injecting sociality into their economic activities, and that sociality has become more purely symbolic as its direct and legitimate influence on economic activity has declined, so that it has become increasingly fragile or even spurious (Carrier 1990; Carrier 1992: 551–552).

But practical economic abstraction is only part of what this collection is about, and it is a part that contains few, if any, surprises for those who have reflected on changes in economy over the past few centuries. It is only part, because economy is an object of contemplation as well as an aspect of life. The two are not, of course, separate. Economic practice shapes economic thought. Moreover, and more central to this collection, economic thought shapes economic practice. This is because people are driven by ideas and idealism, the desire to make the world conform to the image. This process is the virtualism of this Introduction's title; the tendency to see the world in terms of idealised categories, a virtual reality, and then act in ways that make the real conform to the virtual. Because this influence of thought on practice is much less studied than is abstraction, the comments that follow are necessarily more tentative and exploratory, in line with the orientation of the contributors to this collection.

Conceptual Abstraction

> Between what does naturally take place, and what ought to take place, there is indeed some difference; but it is a difference which moralists are apt enough to overlook, which they constantly overlook as often as they talk of the law of nature.

> — Jeremy Bentham, *The Defence of a Maximum*
> (quoted in Hutchison 1994: 37)

I turn now to the second meaning of my intentionally-ambiguous phrase, 'economy in the West', 'economy' not as economic action but as economic thought. It is in economic thought that the move to greater abstraction and virtualism is especially apparent. Even here, however, the trends of the second half of the twentieth century are not wholly new. In the middle of the nineteenth century, for instance, many English cotton-mill owners promulgated a viewpoint that abstracted economy from its social context and advocated policies that would bring the world into line with their viewpoint. They did so when they sought to abstract cotton, and hence their firms, from the social and political contexts in which it was cultivated. 'The motto of the Cotton Supply Association was "Cotton knows no politics" and Henry Ashworth [a Lancashire mill owner] declared that the cotton spinners would buy cotton from anywhere and "they asked no questions as to whether it was slave-grown or not"' (Boyson 1970: 233).

Almost a century previously, Adam Smith, and other thinkers of the Scottish Enlightenment, argued that life was becoming differentiated into two spheres because a distinct economic realm was emerging, in which people were motivated predominantly by material self-interest rather than by the ties of social relationship and obligation. 'It is not from the benevolence of the butcher, the brewer, or the baker, that we expect our dinner, but from their regard to their own interest' (Smith 1976: 18). Marx and Engels made the same point more gloomily when they said that the emergence of modern capitalism has pitilessly torn asunder the motley feudal ties that bound man to his 'natural superiors', and has left no other bond between man and man than naked self-interest, than callous 'cash payment'. It has drowned the most heavenly ecstasies of religious fervour, of chivalrous enthusiasm, of philistine sentimentalism, in the icy water of egotistical calculation (Marx and Engels 1948: 11).

From the foundations of modern Western economic thought, then, there has been a tendency to construe people in their economic guise as autonomous individuals motivated by internal springs rather than interpersonal relations, to dis-embed them from the social relations and structures within which they exist.

While this strand may run deep in Western economic thought, it gained significance in the twentieth century for at least two reasons. First, within economics itself older and more institutional and political models of economy yielded to the marginalist revolution and were transmuted into neo-classical economics, which is striking in its methodical fixation on the notion of the autonomous, asocial and apolitical individual who rationally calculates how to achieve his or her best advantage. Thus, while Adam Smith may have portrayed a world of self-regarding economic actors, he was concerned to locate those actors in a larger frame, the frame indicated by the very title of his classic work, *The Wealth of Nations*. Such larger frames were and are important to perhaps the most durable alternative construction of economy, that of Marxian economists, who have been concerned with the importance of political and social institutions, and have consistently criticised the presuppositions of economic models that portray a world of abstracted individuals (see, for example, Hollis and Nell 1975). Similar criticisms are found as well in Keynes's work, which was probably the most powerful alternative to classical and neo-classical economics in the West in this century (see, for example, Heilbroner and Milberg 1995).

However, by the second half of the twentieth century these models, which understood economic activities in terms of the non-economic framework in which they operated, increasingly were swept aside by neo-classical economics, which understood economic activities in abstracted, dis-embedded form, often presented in economics journals as mathematical formalism that takes little or no cognisance of empirical economic activity (see McCloskey 1986). The fate of a name may help illustrate the nature of this change. The period of the opening decades of the twentieth century saw a variety of thought called 'institutional economics', associated with writers like Thorstein Veblen (1927) and John Commons (1934). Here, economy was seen as an aspect of the institutions of social and political life, inseparable from them. The period of the closing decades of the twentieth century saw a variety of thought called 'new institutional economics', associated particularly with the writer Oliver Williamson (especially 1975). Here, the institutions of life, social and political as well as economic, were explained in terms of the rational calculation of the costs of transactions within and between them. In short, where institutional economics had seen the economy as a creature of its institutional framework, for new institutional economics the direction of influence is reversed: the institutional framework is seen as a creature of the economy, populated by autonomous, rational calculators (see Chapman and Buckley 1997; Hodgson 1988: 154–156).

The second reason this theme of economic abstraction gained significance in the second half of the twentieth century is the growing influence of the discipline of economics itself. What had been a rather arcane academic discipline, made visible by the presence of occasional representatives who, like Keynes, engaged in public debate, has become more prestigious and pervasive. Not only is there now a Nobel prize awarded in economics (the only social science so treated); economists who have won that prize, together with their less exalted fellows, write columns in popular periodicals (for example Becker 1996) and lecture the public on the fallacies of government policy (for example Krugman 1994). Similarly, economists have increasingly visible and powerful positions in a range of organisations that deal with money. The World Bank is a striking example, an institution that appears to be dominated in important ways not by bankers but by economists (Wade 1996), a situation analogous to having an aircraft design company dominated not by aerodynamic engineers but by physicists.

With the growing influence of the discipline of economics and the growing dominance of neo-classical economics within the discipline, more and more people and institutions have adopted the abstract economic viewpoint that I have described. Such a viewpoint seems to produce something like a virtual reality. As with the much-touted, machine-generated virtual reality of computer games, this form of perception produces a synthetic picture that shapes so much of the beholder's perceptual field that it appears real. Thus, to continue the metaphor, the individual confronts a real-seeming world that is in fact not so, but is an artefact of the logical structure of the computer program that generates it. Being so generated, it displays a uniformity and logicality that necessarily departs from the uncertainty of the real world, with its unanticipated influences and unknowable future, not to mention the factors that can be known and anticipated but are ignored in the governing program. This sort of virtual reality is not, of course, unique to abstracted economic viewpoints. Rather, to a degree it is common to all disciplined, rigorous viewpoints, be they theological, philosophical, physical or chemical. What Thomas Kuhn (1970) describes as a scientific paradigm, for instance, illustrates this. The paradigm, after all, is a set of research practices and theoretical structures that define what things are significant in the world, endow them with meaning, tell us the appropriate ways to interact with them and predict the results.

Those who see their world in such a way will act in terms of their perceptions: indeed, who can do otherwise? The results of their actions will contain those perceptions and so, to a degree, recreate the world with the perceptions embedded in it, transforming 'nature' into what Kenneth Burke (1966: 15–16) calls 'second nature'. What distinguishes the economic abstraction of the latter part of the twentieth century, then, is not just that it is a way of seeing the world that tends to generate among its adherents a virtual reality. Cold War ideologues, after all, lived in just as virtual a reality as neo-classical economists. Equally, it is not just that those who see the world that way tend through their actions to re-shape the world in terms of that way of seeing. Rather, what distinguishes economic abstraction from most such perspectives on the world (though not from Cold War ideology) is the combination of its institutional power and its tendency to slip into virtualism. This is the conscious attempt to make the real world conform to the virtual image, justified by the claim that the failure of the real to conform to the ideal is a consequence merely of imperfections, but is a failure that itself has undesirable consequences.

Such attempts reflect this abstracted, economic view of the world, and hence are rooted in neo-classical economics. However, they can not be laid wholly at the feet of professional economists, for that discipline's messages about the nature of the world have to persuade an audience if they are to have an effect. And they have found an audience. Since the end of the 1970s a growing number of governments, international agencies and trade associations have been listening and being persuaded. The results have included efforts to reduce government control over international trade in a range of objects and services, to de-regulate different industries in various countries, to turn different sorts of collective property into commodities that can be bought and sold freely, to encourage or oblige governments in various places to reduce or eliminate programmes of support for public goods and services, to encourage international standards that make it easier for international investors to place and profit from their money, and so on and so forth. It is in programmes and policies like these that the word is made flesh, the virtual becomes the blueprint for the real.

About the Chapters

While the purpose of this collection is to sketch the lineaments of the abstraction and virtualism that have been gaining strength late in the twentieth century, doing so also requires sketching its lineage. Thus, the first chapter, my 'Abstraction in Western Economic Practice', is concerned with the period from the eighteenth century to the middle of the twentieth. Moreover, it deals with changes in economic practice, and so helps make the point that the processes of concern in this collection are not just cultural webs in Clifford Geertz's sense (1973: 5), but spring from and shape people's practical experiences. Indeed, one of the points of this collection is the way that economic abstraction and virtualism are not just webs of meaning, but also practical webs, in which many people can become ensnared.

In my chapter I present a familiar tale. In both production and circulation there has been a continual process of the removal of economic activity from the social relationships in which it had previously existed, a process instituted by some and imposed upon and experienced by others. The older frameworks included the household, where much commercial production and circulation took place, and groups of artisans, occasionally constituted formally as guilds but more often not. Both household and artisanal group were commercial institutions; but they had a strong social aspect. This is because the commercial activity that occurred within them took place in sets of relationships that were structured by, as they were understood in terms of, identities and values that were not unique to commercial activity, but were important generally in people's lives: kinship, gender, religion and the like.

In the case of production, the weakening of these earlier forms of the organisation of commercial activity was coupled with the emergence of a relatively free market in labour, one in which capitalists increasingly were able to treat labour as a commodity and increasingly were predisposed to locate cheap and secure sources of labour. Associated with this, the identities, relationships and values that emerging entrepreneurs sought to impose on their commercial organisations came increasingly to reflect a set of concerns that were more purely rational and economic. As a consequence, people's experiences of paid work increasingly were shaped by identities, relationships and values that were distinct from those that were important in the rest of their lives. In short, the economic activity of production became more abstracted from social life generally. A similar set of changes occurred in the realm of commercial circulation. The period covered by my chapter saw the gradual decay of the pre-eminence of direct trading between those who produced and those who consumed, people who tended to be linked by and who tended to trade within an enduring set of social relations that their transactions expressed. This older system was displaced slowly by mass, anonymous retail trade, governed by a logic increasingly distant from the sociality of buying and selling and increasingly dominated by the abstract imperatives of capital and labour markets.

While the focus of this first chapter is retrospective, it is clear that the kinds of changes it describes continue late in the twentieth century. One instance of this is the separation of commercial activity from the visible and public centre of town and city life, which has taken different forms at different times. Around the beginning of the eighteenth century in England it meant removing markets from open sites in the centre of towns to enclosed market halls (Borsay 1989: 107, 294). In the nineteenth century it meant central commercial areas became devoted to retail shops and other service functions as manufacturers moved elsewhere (Brown 1986: 55; see also the description of Chester in Mitchell 1981: 46). In the second half of the twentieth century it meant the spread of the shopping centre and the shopping mall, relatively isolated commercial sites placed on the edge of urban areas. Equally, and as has been noted already in this Introduction, the abstraction of work relationships from other, non-economic relationships has continued as firms, increasingly global in aspiration if not in actuality, have become more and more willing and able to remove their production from the localities and even countries that form their leading markets, seeking pliable and cheap labour elsewhere. For those who work in the foreign plants owned by those firms, the ordering of their economic life is governed by concerns almost wholly alien to the pre-existing relationships and institutions of those workers (see, for example, Comaroff and Comaroff 1987; Ong 1988). Those at home, on the other hand, confront a corporate rhetoric that increasingly invokes necessities and constraints that are global in origin or scope, rather than being local or even national, as it increasingly invokes economic forces rather than the social and political concerns to which those forces are self-consciously opposed.

The discussion in the first chapter in this collection provides the necessary background and complement to the chapters that follow. These are arranged in terms of a sequence that moves from concern with the formal to concern with the substantive economy. It begins with conceptions of the economy among the pre-eminent modern conceptualisers, economists. It moves then to the ways that these conceptions are made manifest and debated in economic policy and programmes. It concludes with a discussion of the ways that these conceptions and policies affect and are affected by firms and those who control and are controlled by them. These chapters clearly demonstrate the nature and importance of the economic abstraction, virtual reality and virtualism that are the concern of this collection. However, and as these chapters make clear, the processes of concern in this collection are not straightforward. Indeed, as various contributors make clear, the virtual reality of abstract economic life is flawed in important ways, as are attempts to make the world conform to that virtual reality. Thus, if the world is coming to resemble the virtual economic vision, it may be for reasons not adequately comprehended by either those who expound the abstract models or those who seek to bring the world into conformity with them.

The first concern is, I said, conceptions of the economy among economists. The first chapter that deals with this is Ben Fine's 'The Triumph of Economics; Or, "Rationality" Can Be Dangerous to Your Reasoning'. Fine describes a prime example of the way that neo-classical economics, which dominates the discipline, abstracts economy from its social and political contexts, and constructs a virtual reality of autonomous, rational individuals. Fine's example is the work of Gary Becker, one of the economists who has been awarded a Nobel prize. As Fine notes, Becker is exemplary not simply because he is pre-eminent in the field. In addition, Becker's is something of an ideal type of neo-classical thought, carrying the methods and presuppositions of neo-classical economics to their logical extreme, an extreme that is further than even some economists are willing to go.

In his more recent work, Becker has pursued to its logical extreme the methodological individualism that is central to neo-classical economics. While this pursuit is carried out technically in terms of the formal, deductive models of economic theory, the essence of this pursuit is the methodical denial of significance for economics to any level of existence other than the individual. Becker accomplishes this by reducing people's environments to interior states and predilections. Collective norms and relationships, historical debates and com-promises, ethical systems and social structures – all are reduced to the attributes of the individuals who populate the collectivity, a reduction that grants priority to those individuals and relegates the rest to the status of epiphenomenon. Like Marx's peasantry, Becker's economic individuals are potatoes in a sack, a concatenation of individuals rather than parts of a larger whole.

The vehicle for this is Becker's notion of the extended utility function, a pseudo-mathematical formulation that echoes the concern with abstract formalism common in the more prestigious branches of academic economics. Becker demands that all human activity be rendered as individual choice, itself guided by the rational pursuit of the greatest possible utility. This extended utility function allows Becker to dissolve the social into the individual, because one element of the function is the consequence of people's experiences. The person, for example, who sees an advertisement that says that the young and the sexy consume a particular product is, to put it rather simplistically, acquiring an experience about that product which, when incorporated into that person's extended utility function, affects the utility gained by consuming it. Likewise, other aspects of our lives among our fellows are reduced to factors that feed into the extended utility function, and so affect our future utility and through that the choices that we make. Becker's economic genius, then, is his abstraction of a rational, autonomous, utility-maximising core from each person, and with this the abstraction of these individuals from the social worlds in which they live.

I said that Becker's vision of humanity is of asocial, rational individuals. Equally, however, that is linked to another vision, that of the asocial, rational knower, the objective, scientific thinker who, when he thinks about the economy, is the scientific economist. And I use 'he' advisedly, for the gender of this pronoun is part of the point of the second chapter that considers formal economics, Julie Nelson's 'Abstraction, Reality and the Gender of "Economic Man"'. She is concerned with two, linked limitations in neo-classical economics: limitations in its construction of the knower and limitations in its virtual reality, its construction of the known.

Nelson points out that the autonomous individual of neo-classical economics is not itself an autonomous concept, but one that is embedded in and that draws significance from a broader set of Western cultural values and social arrangements.

The ones that particularly concern her are those that revolve around gender and moral valuation. When Nelson locates the idea of the autonomous individual within its broader context, we can begin to see its limitations. Thus, for instance, autonomy exists in the context of its opposite, dependence; the former being valued positively and typically construed as male, the latter being negative and female. Such a view makes it easier to separate the dimensions that frame autonomy and dependency, and so easier to see the presuppositions that underlie the idea of the autonomous individual. These presuppositions make it difficult to see the ways that autonomy is a mis-conceived ideal, whether it is expressed in an economic model of how people are, or expressed in a methodological model of how economists ought to approach and know the world.

Nelson's chapter helps to show the way that the neo-classical autonomous individual rests on a basic misperception of humanity. We are not, after all, autonomous in any real sense. We depend on, shape and are shaped by others throughout our lives, both as economic actors and as knowers. To claim that we ought to be autonomous, to construe people as though they were autonomous, is to accept a particular gendered, evaluative view of people, and one that simply conflicts with the reality of human existence. Thus Nelson produces a dual criticism of the neo-classical project exemplified by Becker. First, it is simply wrong in its systematic refusal to consider the ways that people are linked to each other. Second, it is misguided in its assumption that the scientific ideal that underlies economics is the only way to generate knowledge. Becker's project may dazzle or dismay, with its technical apparatus and its dispassionate view of human life; but equally that project is wrongly conceived, and its results are suspect.

Nelson criticises neo-classical economics not because it abstracts, but because of the way it does so. Its virtual reality is flawed in systematic and important ways. Such criticism is important for helping us to see economics' basic limitations and inadequacies. However, as there is more to this collection than abstraction, so there is more to economics than its view of the world. In addition, there is virtualism, the ways that different sets of people attempt to make the world conform to the virtual reality, whether that reality is misconstrued or not. The next pair of chapters deals with just this practical, institutional face of economic abstraction.

The first of these is Philip McMichael's 'Development and Structural Adjustment', a discussion of perhaps the most visible virtualism of economic abstraction, international aid policies that seek to make national governments re-order their countries' polities and economies to bring them into line with the virtual reality of economics. Like Nelson, McMichael shows how that virtual reality contains a fundamental flaw – a flaw with profound consequences.

The processes that McMichael describes begin where Karl Polanyi left off, at the completion of the great transformation that saw the promotion and subsequent taming by states of national markets in land, labour and capital. It is appropriate, therefore, that McMichael approaches those processes in terms of Polanyi's classic analysis. McMichael observes that after the Second World War the dominant institutional approach to economy involved national governments shaping and protecting their national economies under the general framework of the Bretton Woods agreement, which limited the international flow of capital and produced a regime of fixed rates of exchange tied to the American dollar. Under this system, the growing number of independent former colonies were encouraged to develop their economies in ways that emulated the pattern thought to characterise those countries that had developed in the nineteenth century: endogenous development resulting in a mature and diversified economy generating and meeting most of its own needs. McMichael calls this strategy the 'development project'. Its conception and execution may have been flawed, but it provided a framework that encouraged countries to develop relatively consensual political systems in which a range of social groups were brought into the project and were to benefit from it: nation-building.

However, in the 1970s the development project unravelled. While the reasons are complex, the immediate cause was the abdication by the United States of its central role in the Bretton Woods system. The consequent collapse of that system was associated with reduced restrictions on the international flow of money and the growth of offshore dollars. This combination of events led to something like a free international market in capital and, as with the earlier free market that Polanyi described, the result was uncertainty and disorder, exemplified by the debt crisis of the 1980s and the currency crises of the 1990s, which threatened central financial institutions in the developed countries. McMichael says that the response to the debt crisis of the 1980s was the adoption of a set of practices and policies by developed countries and the international agencies that they dominated that sought to secure the place of international capital movements as financial flows rather than as productive investments, so that finance capital, exemplified by hedge funds, unit trusts and mutual funds, became separated from investment capital. These changes destroyed the development project.

Under the rhetoric of *laissez-faire* economics, countries in the Third World were put under increasing pressure not to develop, but to re-order their domestic political, economic and social policies in order to repay their debts, and so protect international finance capital. This meant reducing government deficits, and hence investments in the infrastructure that the development project required. It meant reducing the social welfare systems that nation-building required. It meant reorienting economic policy away from the goal of broad-based endogenous development and toward production that would generate foreign exchange. These pressures are most apparent in the increasing use of structural adjustment loans, intended to oblige countries to change their domestic political, social and economic arrangements. Through these loans, the IMF and the World Bank have led the way in taming the free market in international finance, and so exposed the fundamental flaw in the economic rhetoric that justifies these very policies. The virtual reality of free international markets, like the virtual reality of the free market in England that Polanyi describes, requires not freedom but institutional control.

Structural adjustment policies reflect and draw legitimacy from the economic belief in the virtue of free trade, unhindered by national variations in social or political practice. That is, this particular attempt at economic virtualism seeks not just a freedom of trade, but trade in a world of units that differ only in their narrowly-economic advantages and disadvantages. It appears that, were they to adjust their structures properly, the countries of the world would be very much alike, each the 'level playing field' evoked so frequently in discussions of international trade or, more accurately, evoked so frequently by companies seeking to expand their international business.

The figure of the level playing field is an interesting one, and not simply because of the things that, as McMichael notes, it hides from view. In addition, it evokes nicely one important aspect of the virtual reality of neo-classical economics. The metaphor is of a space in which all things and all economic actors are freely accessible to each other; a space in which there are no political or social hills or valleys that could impede or channel economic activity and the pursuit of economic gain. This spatial metaphor informs Agnar Helgason and Gísli Pálsson's 'Cash for Quotas: Disputes over the Legitimacy of an Economic Model of Fishing in Iceland'. Like McMichael's, their chapter is concerned with economic virtualism, though the field that concerns them is not international but internal; the hills and valleys are not national policies of internal development but the social beliefs and practices that resist the spread of commodity transaction itself.

Their concern is a common phenomenon: the conversion of access to the natural environment, which hitherto was not treated as something to be bought and sold, into a commodity like any other. Perhaps the most renowned example of this is the making into a commodity of access to the air and to rivers and the sea as places for disposing of waste: pollution rights. This commoditisation of access to the natural environment is not, of course, new. The enclosure of the commons in England is an earlier manifestation of what Helgason and Pálsson describe. The particular instance of this general phenomenon that concerns them is the conversion of fishing rights in Icelandic waters into commodities through the imposition of a system of individual, transferable quotas that entitle the owner to a share of the total Icelandic fishing catch: the ITQ system. In the 1980s, a quota system was introduced as a temporary conservation measure, with quotas awarded to individual fishing boats, based on the catch of each boat in the preceding few years. In the 1990s the system was modified to allow the sale and purchase of the quotas, so that quotas originally attached to boats and based on historical performance became fully-commoditised ITQs.

The transformation of boat quotas into ITQs was justified by the rhetoric of neo-classical economics, and with this transformation the world of Icelandic fishing was recast to make it conform to the virtual reality of economic abstraction. With the ITQ system, with access to the sea made a commodity, the less efficient fishers would abandon their fishing either voluntarily or through bankruptcy, to the benefit of the more efficient. The overall efficiency of the Iceland fisheries would improve. Also, because the market in quotas would be free, transactions would occur only if at least one party were better off and none worse off. The playing field would be levelled and all would gain. What autonomous, rational calculator could object to such an arrangement?

The response was less positive than the economic virtual vision anticipated. Icelandic fisheries workers revealed their preferences by a national strike that ended only when special legislation forced them back to work. They revealed their preferences again later with another national strike. Their disaffection, and a broader public disaffection, revolved around a number of points, including the ways that the system benefited large-scale fishers, especially those with several deep-sea boats and those with processing plants. More importantly in the context of this collection, disaffection also sprang precisely from the commoditisation of access to the sea, from the levelling of the playing field.

Historically, access to the sea had strong cultural and political meanings in Iceland. The idea of Icelandic waters as a common resource for the nation was an important aspect of that country's successful attempt to gain independence from Denmark, and hence was a part of the national self-conception. Equally, many people inside and outside the fisheries argued that fish became commodities only when people caught them, and that they belonged only to those who had caught them. The ITQ system, these critics argued, made commodities of fish not yet caught or even spawned. These responses were not rejections of commercial fishing. Iceland survived by its commercial fisheries. Rather, those who objected did so because they did not want their world reconstructed as a social, cultural and political featureless plain, populated only by abstract economic actors and commodities.

The two chapters I have described suggest that there may be practical and theoretical limits to virtualism, limits to the degree to which the world can be made to conform to economic virtual reality. As Helgason and Pálsson describe, people may organise to reject the featureless plain; as McMichael notes, the IMF and the World Bank are slowly coming to see the need for a social order as well as an economic one. Of course this growing interest is motivated by a desire to assure the political will to adopt and implement structural adjustment policies; but it is still a recognition that economic prescription by itself is not enough. To an extent, then, Julie Nelson's rebuttal of Gary Becker's project may be justified. But it remains a possibility that large parts of the lives of many people will end up resembling the abstract economic view of the world. This may not come about because of the influence of rigorous, self-conscious models of the sort envisaged by Becker; it may not reflect policies like structural adjustment quotas or ITQ systems. It may be significant even so.

The final pair of chapters in the collection explore different aspects of this possibility. They do so by moving us back from a virtualism driven by economic views of the world to one driven by more practical and inarticulate forces: those that arise from the activities of the firms that operate in and shape competitive capitalism. It may not be proper to call this 'virtualism', for it lacks the guiding vision and intentionality that the term connotes. The practical results, however, may not be all that different. This practical virtualism is appropriate, however, for a collection concerned with economic abstraction. It is so because it makes visible the ways that neo-classical economics is a bourgeois economics, a vision of the world that attains a significant part of its force by making appear natural the ascendant commercial practices of powerful capitalist firms in the closing decades of the twentieth century. In a sense, then, economic abstraction of the neo-classical sort may contain just the 'vision' that Robert Heilbroner says that economics now lacks (Heilbroner and Milberg 1995).

The first of the two chapters that deal with this question helps root practical virtualism squarely in contemporary capitalist dynamics. It is Leslie Sklair's 'The Transnational Capitalist Class'. This chapter seeks to establish the ways that a class is emerging that corresponds to the ownership and control of transnational corporations. These are not simply corporations that do business in many countries. Rather, they are corporations that see themselves as located in no particular place; in other words, as abstracted from the pre-existing political structures of states and the pre-existing economic structures of national and even regional markets.

The transnational corporation is a relatively recent phenomenon, rare before the 1960s and not common before the 1970s or even the 1980s. But the spread of transnational corporations is not the only tale Sklair tells, or even, perhaps, the most important one. In addition, he describes a growing transnational class, which he sees as having four main elements: the executives of transnational corporations; the employees of national and international governmental and quasi-governmental organisations who deal with and promote a global economic order; the politicians and professionals who have a similar orientation; and the transnational individuals and organisations who control media and other consumer-oriented firms and agencies. As Sklair describes them, the elements of this class are decreasingly likely to see themselves as rooted in any particular place and are increasingly likely to see themselves as 'citizens of the world', abstracted from the contexts of nationality and state – though the world of which they are citizens is, of course, rather different from the world the rest of us inhabit.

These four fractions of the transnational capitalist class are not driven by a neo-classical vision or the logic of the IMF. Rather, Sklair says, they are united in a common orientation toward a commercial realm and a social life that is global. And as part of that orientation they are increasingly able to facilitate the further spread of an abstracted, transnational institutional reality – ultimately, a level playing field in which all markets are open and all things are marketable. They do so through obvious avenues such as corporate political influence on states. They do so also through less obvious avenues, such as the business schools that increasingly are seen as a necessary prerequisite for a successful corporate career, and the international agencies and professional bodies that encourage standardisation of economic and commercial practice throughout the world and so increase the ability of transnational firms to exploit new markets.

As Sklair observes, the transnational capitalist class also promulgates its abstracted view of the world when transnational firms and agencies support organisations that propagate that view. These organisations, such as the Business Roundtable and the Trilateral Commission, address themselves not only to high-level corporate managers, but also to senior politicians and government and international functionaries. Such organisations convey a number of messages to a variety of different audiences. Most of these messages, however, presuppose a conception of a global economy, abstracted from place and state, and so can be seen as virtualising institutions. They encourage those in a position to influence the policies of national governments and international organisations to make the world a more profitable place in which to exist, a world that, for these expansionist firms, looks like a level playing field. Following Sklair, then, the members of this class are practical virtualisers, not theoretical ones. Although their practical actions may produce a world that converges with the economists' virtual reality, those actions themselves spring from a class embedded in complex social and institutional structures and relationships. If you will, Sklair suggests a kind of embeddedness for the powerful, abstraction for the weak.

The second of this final pair of chapters looks at a different way in which economic virtualism is generated from the practical concerns of firms. The chapter is 'Virtual Capitalism: The Globalisation of Reflexive Business Knowledge', in which Nigel Thrift lays out what Sklair touches on only in passing. That is the ways that firms, transnational and otherwise, are governed by a logic that not only is less formal and articulate than the logic of neo-classical economics, but also is shaped by the embedded practicalities of business life: the practicalities of things like calculation and record-keeping, the management seminar and a reflexive management orientation. In short, he argues that there may well be a virtualising capitalism, but that it is grounded on practical capitalism.

Thrift starts by distinguishing between theories *of* capitalism and theories *in* capitalism, and he says that the latter do not look much like the former, for four main reasons. First, although economists, like Becker or Oliver Williamson, may produce economic theories that seek to account for the operation of firms in a capitalist system, people in business do not in fact use economic theory very much (see, for example, Chapman and Buckley 1997). Second, unlike formal models, capitalist firms operate in an environment of irreversible time and confront the unavoidable task of shaping that time, of answering the question 'What do I do on Monday morning?' Third, the theories that exist in firms are not pure theories, but are inevitably linked to and partly dependent upon an elaborate material culture that ranges from computer-based accounting programs through seating arrangements at meetings to the layout of offices and factories. Finally, theory in the firm is not intended to explain the world, but is instead intended to help clarify the perception of practical problems and suggest solutions for them. One point that Thrift is making, then, is that even if firms act in ways that, as Sklair argues, lead to a more transnational economic order that looks like Helgason and Pálsson's featureless plain, they are not driven by abstract, featureless models of the neo-classical sort. Rather, they are driven by models that are embedded in a complex history and a web of social and institutional relationships and practices.

This embedding does not mean that there is no abstract dimension to theory in business. There is, and Thrift shows that the abstraction has become more pronounced since the Second World War and especially since the 1970s. Again, however, this abstraction is not the sort associated with neo-classical economics. Rather, it is the consequence of the spread of what Thrift calls 'reflexive capitalism': the spread of business schools, management consulting firms, business literature and the management fad, embodied in the business guru. Through this reflexivity, people are encouraged to reflect on the organisation and practices of their firm in order to improve its operation. While these are intensely practical concerns, in an important sense this reflexivity is abstract because the different models and theories that are promulgated are generic models, reflecting the latest word on the best way to run a business, whether that be a steel mill in Osaka, a software firm outside Bath or, indeed, a management consulting firm in Boston. This very abstraction, moreover, springs from very concrete roots. Most notably, Thrift says, it springs from the spread of degree programmes in business administration: students are inculcated with this reflexivity; graduates expect it of themselves, their superiors and subordinates.

In their different ways, then, Thrift and Sklair tell similar tales. There does seem to be an increasing abstraction of the economic order from pre-existing social and political frames. However, this may not be the result of virtualism, of the conscious attempt to re-create the world, or at least the economy, to bring it into conformity to an abstract model. First, the spread of abstraction appears more strongly in relations between firms and their customers and suppliers than it does within firms, as it appears more strongly within firms at the lower levels of employee than it does among the higher. This is not, then, a thoroughgoing attempt to re-fashion the world. Second, the forces that lead to this abstraction are not themselves abstract.

They spring from the practical circumstances of firms seeking to improve their operations, which means increase their profits; they are guided by changing, practical models of how firms ought to organise themselves and carry out their activities; they reflect the web of institutional, social and practical relationships in which firms and those who govern or seek to influence them exist.

The six chapters that form the core of this collection make different arguments. Generally, however, they agree that in many important ways the economic realm is becoming more abstracted from its pre-existing social and political contexts, even if types of social and institutional context remain important. Similarly, they agree that there is a virtualising rhetoric that helps justify and further this abstraction. In his concluding chapter, 'A Theory of Virtualism', Daniel Miller takes this conjunction of abstraction and rhetoric seriously, as a sign of an important reorientation in public thought and economic practice. His interpretation of this conjunction locates the specific issues raised by the various chapters within an encompassing narrative of changes in the contemporary world. Emulating Marx's critique of capitalism, Miller sees the changes in public thought and economic practice as part of the regeneration of capitalism, one that transforms and turns to its advantage some of the forces that emerged as a criticism of and constraint on some elements of capitalism. These changes can, then, be seen as a part of a more general historical transformation: as Marx saw capitalism in the nineteenth century as a dialectical movement towards abstraction, so contemporary virtualism, whether the practical variety or that based on an articulated economic theory, can be seen as a similar dialectical movement, one that supersedes the previously-existing abstraction of capitalism.

Miller says that the abstraction of the capitalism that Marx described generated an opposition to it, one that brought about a degree of re-contextualisation in the economy. An aspect of this is the way that workers, who had been reduced to mere units of labour power, were able to reclaim a degree of identity and autonomy. Often this was through practices of consumption that allowed them to create relatively stable and humane domestic and social worlds that were distinct from the mass anonymity of the market and the state. For Miller, then, consumers are not merely the impersonal, final adjudicators of a firm in the way that they are often portrayed in economics, any more than they are merely the site at which the cycle of commodity production ends, and begins again. In addition, they are people who seek to impress a social identity on aspects of their world that capitalism had made abstract, people whose actions are generated as a response to capitalism and amount to a criticism of it.

Miller argues that in the contemporary regeneration of capitalism, it is not just the economy that is being re-shaped in ways that make it more abstract; so are consumers. They are being replaced with virtual consumers. These are creations of the administrative and economic models of powerful people in powerful institutions, like Sklair's members of the transnational capitalist class and Thrift's senior managers, though these people certainly would not apply the virtualism to themselves. The virtual consumer is gaining currency with the spread of auditing processes in all sorts of organisations. The audit, mandated from above, imposes goals on those who are audited, goals that are justified in terms of benefit to consumers, whether of soft drinks, health care or education. Miller's point is that the consumers who are supposed to benefit are not real consumers, but are defined by the managerial models that are imposed in the auditing process. These virtual consumers, then, reflect the institutional interests of managers, of the sort that Thrift describes. Moreover, the audits that are supposed to benefit those virtual consumers reduce the ability of the organisation to devote attention to real consumers, whose visibility to and power over the organisation is diminished. And just as Sklair's transnational capitalist class has its ideologues, so the spread of the virtual consumer of the audit is echoed, Miller notes, in academic life, with the spread of the postmodernist construction of the 'consumer society'. Like the auditor's consumer, this is decreasingly grounded in the study of actual consumption as a human practice, but is increasingly a creature of the academic imperatives and institutional positions of those who promulgate it.

Thus the old tale continues. A resurgent capitalism, transformed by the kinds of changes described by McMichael, Sklair and Thrift, seeks to free itself of the old constraints that Polanyi's great transformation imposed on it, and of the newer constraints of social democracy that were so noticeable after the Second World War. It also seeks to encompass, and so transform and turn to its own advantage, the public opposition through socialised consumption that capitalism itself had generated.

The different chapters in this collection pursue different aspects of a common theme, the way that social and political arrangements in much of the world increasingly are being shaped by economy. Neither the process nor the attention to it is new. Some time ago Louis Dumont (1977) argued that economy holds a central place in the ways that many of those in Western societies think of themselves, a point made more recently in a somewhat different way by Marshall Sahlins (1996). While Dumont and Sahlins doubtless are right, the concern of this collection is not with the importance simply of economy, but with the particular importance of a particular conception of economy, as it is embedded in institutions and policies, as it is enacted and supported in commercial organisation.

The tale told by these chapters is, however, an ambiguous one. The particular conception, neo-classical economics, is important in the discipline that thinks about economy, as it is important in the institutions that have the task of shaping economy. However, as the chapters in this collection indicate, this conception is flawed. As Fine and Nelson show, it springs from a misperception of how economists come to know about economy, as it misperceives the people who act in the economy. Similarly, as the chapters by McMichael and by Helgason and Pálsson show, attempts to implement the conception look not so much like realising a natural world waiting to spring forth, as they look like coercive impositions of an economic model that produces social and political resistance. Moreover, as Sklair and Thrift show, this conception certainly is not one that firms apply to their own senior management, who are not treated as economic actors trading to their own best advantage but are, instead, bound in and shaped by a set of institutional and social arrangements. Indeed, and as Polanyi observed of an earlier attempt at imposition, were that conception of economy to be applied rigorously, the result would be chaotic, as is evidenced by the debt crisis of the 1980s, the East Asian financial crisis of the 1990s, and the more numerous but less publicised social and political crises that so often follow structural adjustment.

With all this evidence against it, why does that conception of economy have the force it has? An answer that some put forward is that the evidence that appears to tell against the conception is only evidence that the conception has not been applied rigorously enough. The debt crises, the conflicts following structural adjustment, the East Asian financial crisis, all can be said to spring from a prior failure to conform to the model. While this answer is simple, it is also beside the point, for it simply presupposes the model.

It may be, instead, that the force of the model springs from the way that it appears to represent changes that are taking place in economy. The spread of transnational corporations and the growing power of international finance capital, the weakening of labour unions, tariff barriers and all the rest point to a world that looks increasingly like the level playing field of the neo-classical model. However, it seems to be the case that this convergence is misperceived by those who espouse that model. Where they see a virtual reality of autonomous economic actors in a featureless plain, the chapters by Sklair, Thrift and Miller see a world being shaped by the very institutional, social and political forces that the neo-classical model condemns, ignores or treats as merely epiphenomenal. Although their firms want to exploit international markets, the members of Sklair's transnational capitalist class and Thrift's managers make sure that their own lives and work are anything but anonymous and featureless. Although the model speaks of the greatest good for the greatest number of consumers, Miller's auditors make sure that real consumers are represented by virtual consumers, constructed to want what those auditors think that consumers ought to want. The economist's revealed preference is replaced by the auditor's defined preference.

If, then, the model's appeal springs in part from the way that it seems to predict the way the world is moving, that appeal may well be self-delusion. The forces that appear to be shaping the economic world are rather different from the autonomous actors who populate the model. The world they want and the world they bring about resemble the neo-classical model in only limited ways. But it is in that emerging world that the rest of us must live.

Acknowledgements

For their comments on various stages of this Introduction, I thank Simon Coleman, Ben Fine and Daniel Miller.

References

Agnew, Jean-Christophe 1986. *Worlds Apart: The Market and the Theater in Anglo-American Thought, 1550–1750*. New York: Cambridge University Press.
Becker, Gary S. 1996. Religions Thrive in a Free Market, Too. *Business Week* (15 January): 7.
Bloch, Maurice, and Jonathan Parry 1989. Introduction: Money and the Morality of Exchange. In J. Parry and M. Bloch (eds), *Money and the Morality of Exchange*, pp. 1–32. Cambridge: Cambridge University Press.
Borsay, Peter 1989. *The English Urban Renaissance: Culture and Society in the Provincial Town, 1660–1770*. Oxford: Clarendon Press.
Boyson, Rhodes 1970. *The Ashworth Cotton Enterprise: The Rise and Fall of a Family Firm, 1818–1880*. Oxford: Clarendon Press.
Brown, Jonathan 1986. *The English Market Town: A Social and Economic History, 1750–1914*. Marlborough, Wilts: Crowood Press.
Burke, Kenneth 1966. *Language as Symbolic Action*. Berkeley: University of California Press.
Carrier, James G. 1990. The Symbolism of Possession in Commodity Advertising. *Man* 25: 190–207.
—— 1992. Emerging Alienation in Production: A Maussian History. *Man* 27: 539–558.
—— 1997. Introduction. In J. Carrier (ed.), *Meanings of the Market: The Free Market in Western Culture*, pp. 1–67. Oxford: Berg.
Chapman, Malcolm, and Peter J. Buckley 1997. Markets, Transaction Costs, Economists and Social Anthropologists. In James G. Carrier (ed.), *Meanings of the Market: The Free Market in Western Culture*, pp. 225–250. Oxford: Berg.
Comaroff, John L., and Jean Comaroff 1987. The Madman and the Migrant: Work and Labor in the Historical Consciousness of a South African People. *American Ethnologist* 14: 191–209.
Commons, John 1934. *Institutional Economics: Its Place in Political Economy*. New York: Macmillan.
Dore, Ronald 1983. Goodwill and the Spirit of Market Capitalism. *British Journal of Sociology* 34: 459–482.

Dumont, Louis 1977. *From Mandeville to Marx: The Genesis and Triumph of Economic Ideology*. Chicago: University of Chicago Press.

Geertz, Clifford 1973. *The Interpretation of Cultures*. New York: Basic Books.

Granovetter, Mark 1985. Economic Action and Social Structure: The Problem of Embeddedness. *American Journal of Sociology* 91: 481–510.

Halle, David 1984. *America's Working Man: Work, Home, and Politics among Blue-Collar Property Owners*. Chicago: University of Chicago Press.

Harris, Olivia 1989. The Earth and the State: The Sources and Meanings of Money in Northern Potosí, Bolivia. In Jonathan Parry and Maurice Bloch (eds), *Money and the Morality of Exchange*, pp. 232–268. Cambridge: Cambridge University Press.

Harris, Rosemary 1987. *Power and Powerlessness in Industry: An Analysis of the Social Relations of Production*. London: Tavistock.

Heilbroner, Robert, and William Milberg 1995. *The Crisis of Vision in Modern Economic Thought*. New York: Cambridge University Press.

Hodgson, Geoffrey 1988. *Economics and Institutions: A Manifesto for a Modern Institutional Economics*. Cambridge: Polity Press.

Hollis, Martin, and Edward J. Nell 1975. *Rational Economic Man: A Philosophical Critique of Neo-Classical Economics*. London: Cambridge University Press.

Hutchison, Terence 1994. Jeremy Bentham as an Economist. In *The Uses and Abuses of Economics: Contentious Essays on History and Method*, pp. 27–49. London: Routledge.

Kahn, Joel S. 1997. Demons, Commodities and the History of Anthropology. In James G. Carrier (ed.), *Meanings of the Market: The Free Market in Western Culture*, pp. 69–98. Oxford: Berg.

Kanter, Rosabeth Moss 1977. *Men and Women of the Corporation*. New York: Basic Books.

Krugman, Paul R. 1994. *Peddling Prosperity: Economic Sense and Nonsense in the Age of Diminished Expectations*. New York: W. W. Norton and Co.

Kuhn, Thomas 1970. *The Structure of Scientific Revolutions*. Chicago: University of Chicago Press.

McCloskey, Donald N. 1986. *The Rhetoric of Economics*. Brighton: Wheatsheaf.

Mars, Gerald 1982. *Cheats at Work: An Anthropology of Workplace Crime*. London: George Allen & Unwin.

Marx, Karl, and Frederick Engels 1948 (1848). *Manifesto of the Communist Party*. New York: International Publishers.

Mitchell, S. I. 1981. Retailing in Eighteenth and Early Nineteenth Century Cheshire. *Transactions of the Historical Society of Lancashire and Cheshire* 130: 37–60.

Ong, Aihwa 1988. The Production of Possession: Spirits and the Multinational Corporation in Malaysia. *American Ethnologist* 15: 28–42.

Parry, Jonathan 1986. *The Gift*, the Indian Gift and the 'Indian Gift'. *Man* 21: 453–473.

Polanyi, Karl 1957a. Aristotle Discovers the Economy. In K. Polanyi, Conrad M. Arensberg and Harry W. Pearson (eds), *Trade and Market in the Early Empires: Economies in History and Theory*, pp. 64–94. Glencoe, Ill.: The Free Press.

—— 1957b. The Economy as Instituted Process. In K. Polanyi, Conrad M. Arensberg and Harry W. Pearson (eds), *Trade and Market in the Early Empires: Economies in History and Theory*, pp. 243–270. Glencoe, Ill.: The Free Press.

Sahlins, Marshall 1996. The Sadness of Sweetness: The Native Anthropology of Western Cosmology. *Current Anthropology* 37: 395–428.

Salaman, Graeme 1986. *Working*. London: Tavistock.

Schneider, David 1980. *American Kinship: A Cultural Account*. Second edition. Chicago: University of Chicago Press.

Smith, Adam 1976 (1776). *An Inquiry into the Nature and Causes of the Wealth of Nations*. Chicago: University of Chicago Press.

Veblen, Thorstein 1927. *The Theory of the Leisure Class*. New York: Vanguard Press.

Wade, Robert 1996. Japan, the World Bank, and the Art of Paradigm Maintenance: *The East Asian Miracle* in Political Perspective. *New Left Review* 217: 3–36.

Williamson, Oliver E. 1975. *Markets and Hierarchies: Analysis and Antitrust Implications*. New York: Macmillan.

–1–

Abstraction in Western Economic Practice
James G. Carrier

As virtualism is the attempt to make the world conform to an abstract model, so abstraction is virtualism's foundation. But it is important not to restrict attention only to systems of abstract thought like neo-classical economics. Such systems are important, but so is practical abstraction, abstraction in daily life and practice.

If abstraction can be taken as the removing of something from the social and practical contexts in which it previously existed, then one can talk about practical abstraction. That is, people can find that their practical activities have, for reasons beyond their control, been changed in a way that makes them more abstract: from the perspective of those who confront the changes, those practical activities have become more removed from the contexts in which they had existed. A simple example is when an organisation that had hitherto identified people by name decides to identify them by number. It is a good bet that, from the perspective of those who have them, names are more enmeshed in social life and activity than are the numbers that replace them. Those who deal with the organisation that stops using names and starts using numbers, then, confront practical abstraction, whether they will it or not: the practical activity of identifying themselves to the organisation has become more abstract than it was previously, more governed by the logic of the organisation (with its desire for numbers) than pre-existing social usage (with its names).

From the point of view of this collection, a particularly important sort of practical abstraction is that which takes place in the economic realm. It is this sort of practical abstraction that helps remove economic activity from the broader social contexts in which it had existed, and so helps it become a more distinct sphere, understood in its own peculiar terms and governed by its own peculiar logic, a sphere I call 'commerce' in this chapter. In saying this I do not mean that this distinct sphere is without social content or that it is divorced from practice. Economy is, after all, the land of practical social beings. However, from the perspective of those confronted with the sort of practical abstraction that concerns me in this chapter, the practice and social content are relatively alien.

It is this practical abstraction that encourages the sort of distinction between social and commercial life that David Schneider (1980) describes for the Americans he studied. Put in other words, one lesson to draw from the history of practical abstraction that I sketch here is that the separation that Schneider describes in *American Kinship* is not simply a feature of American culture – simply an aspect of how Americans see the world. Rather, that conceptual separation has a practical basis in the ways that people act, and are obliged to act, in different areas of their lives. Some time ago, Talcott Parsons (1959: 262), one of Schneider's teachers, pointed to this practical dimension, when he described important aspects of the distinction between the domestic and occupational realms in terms of the practical questions of rights, duties and obligations, of who is expected to do what.

In this chapter I present a brief sketch of practical abstraction in two important economic areas, production and circulation, especially in the period from the beginning of the eighteenth century to the middle of the twentieth. My focus is on production and circulation that are commercial, only a part of the whole but one that became increasingly important in people's lives during this period. As well, and partially to keep the task manageable, I restrict myself to Britain and the United States. This is partiality, but not, I think, debilitating: the trends that I describe were hardly unique to these two countries, which were the pre-eminent Western societies for the bulk of the period that concerns me. In spite of these restrictions, what I present is only a sketch, and one drawn with a broad brush rather than a fine pen. My purpose is not to provide a detailed description and analysis, but only to indicate general trends. And those trends are clear enough. During this period economic activities changed in important ways, becoming increasingly abstracted from the social contexts and relationships in which transactors existed. This is not to say that economic activities became stripped of social meaning or content. However, that content and meaning became purified, came increasingly to spring solely from the commercial organisation of the economic activity itself.

Production

I start with production, which I will describe relatively briefly, as the story I tell is likely to be familiar in its general outline. In the period that concerns me, there was an increasing divergence between the organisation and social relations that characterised production and those that characterised the rest of social life, particularly the household. The effect of this divergence on people's experience of economic life was magnified by the fact that, during this period, an increasing proportion of the population was entering paid productive work. One manifestation of this divergence is the growing distinction between the forms of relationships that characterised commercial activity and the household; another is the growing tendency for commercial and household activities to take place in distinct institutions and places.

I will approach this divergence by describing a sequence of four ideal types of production: cottage industry, putting out, early factory production, modern factory production. Although I describe these as a sequence, they are not a set of uniform stages through which all branches of production necessarily progressed uniformly. Equally, I do not take this sequence to reflect some inherent dynamic or search for objective efficiency (Sabel and Zeitlin 1985). However, these steps do identify the increasing abstraction of commercial production that people experienced over this period.

Cottage Industry

Cottage industry is production carried out and controlled by the household, of objects intended for sale. At the beginning of the eighteenth century, for almost all commercial production 'the basic unit of production remained the household' (Swanson 1989: 148), but textile production has been studied most, and I focus on it. This type of production was widespread and durable. It is the cottage-craftsman system that Esther Goody (1982: 12) describes in Yorkshire woollen manufacture in the eighteenth century, and it was still being used in France long after the bulk of textile production had been mechanised (see Tilly 1984).

This economic activity was enmeshed in broader social relationships. For instance, the needs of household members, rather than the demands and rhythms of the market, governed the pace and timing of production, though households certainly were aware of changes in the prices paid for cloth of different sorts. Partly this was because weaving families did not only weave. Commonly they had farm holdings as well, and produced cloth as one of a number of occupations, some for money and some not, that together provided for their subsistence (see Thirsk 1978; Thompson 1967). More notably, perhaps, production tended to be undertaken within the household by household members using household tools, equipment and raw materials. As Neil Smelser (1959: 54–55) describes it, 'the father wove and apprenticed his sons into weaving. The mother was responsible for preparatory processes; in general she spun, taught the daughters how to spin, and allocated the . . . [subsidiary tasks] among the children.'

In other words, production relations were household relations. The obligation to labour was a family obligation and the discipline used to coordinate and regulate production was family discipline. The son who helped his father weave was helping the man who had produced much of the food the child ate, who oversaw his up-bringing and who was training him in his craft, who would have a say in his marriage, who would bequeath property to the boy in his old age and who, in time, the boy would help bury.

Not all those who engaged in cottage industry were family members. Paid workers who lived with their employers were extremely important at this time. But even these were likely to be enmeshed in sociable and even household relations in their work. They were incorporated in the family, being housed, fed, and clothed, as well as paid wages, in return for their 'fidelity' and 'service'; and the developed Puritan (and Catholic) morality of the post-Reformation period required the householder to treat them as he would his children, and be responsible for their moral and spiritual, as well as material, welfare (James 1974: 23; see also Beier 1987: 24–25).

Here, Mervyn James is describing employees in middling farming families in County Durham in the sixteenth and seventeenth centuries; but the incorporation of paid workers into the family was common throughout Britain through the eighteenth century and into the nineteenth.

Putting Out

Putting out differs from cottage industry in that households produced at the direction of, and using materials supplied by, a merchant capitalist. In textiles, it emerged because cottage producers did not subordinate their work to the demand for cloth sufficiently to satisfy merchants, who sought to circumvent this by gaining greater control over production in order to assure a more regular and uniform supply of cloths. However, it had a longer history. It had appeared in the more crowded London guilds by the middle of the sixteenth century, as artisans with retail shops began to put work out to poorer artisans without shops (Davis 1966: 61; Earle 1989: 27), and it appeared sporadically even earlier, in crafts that involved intensive use of labour (Swanson 1989: 31). Equally, merchant capitalists were not alone in putting work out. Prosperous cottage weavers themselves put work out to other households, particularly carding and spinning (Smelser 1959: 55–56; for other industries see Rule 1987: 102–104). Also, like cottage industry, it was not simply a passing phase of production. It remains important, not just in the making of objects that carry an aura of craft production (see Ennew 1982), but also in many ordinary branches of industry (Benson 1989: 57–58; see generally Allen and Wolkowitz 1987; Boris and Daniels 1989; Pennington and Westover 1989), and some modern putting out retains a distinct family air (Beach 1989; Benson 1989: 60–63).

Responding to a commercial environment relatively alien to weaving households, the merchant who put work out brought about a degree of differentiation of production and control that helped remove production from the family context that was so important in cottage industry. Thus, the merchants gained control of the timing of production, one of the attractions that putting out had for them. Likewise, the merchant dictated the nature and quality of the cloth to be produced. Similarly, though not strictly relevant to the activity of production, the merchant disposed of the cloth without regard for the interests of the producer or the relationship between the producer and the eventual consumer. This contrasts with cottage industry, much of which was for local consumption, bought and sold in regulated local markets in a web of long-standing personal relationships.

Production under putting out was ordered by a logic and set of relations that were more removed from the broader social context of those doing the work than was the case with cottage industry. However, this abstraction was only partial. Even though raw materials belonged to the merchant, most producing households continued to own their tools and equipment. Even though obliged to produce within the time specified, producers were being paid to perform a task, and so were able to exercise some discretion about the pace of the work. And, of course, the immediate social relations of production remained household relations. The increase in abstraction, then, was gradual, and it continued in early factory production.

Early Factory Production

With factories, production moved out of the household to a separate place more directly under the supervision of the capitalist and hence more directly influenced by factors that did not spring from the social relationships that linked producers. However, the degree of control by the capitalist was restricted: in important ways, work was carried out by sets of people ordered by pre-existing social relationships. Commonly, capitalists employed contractors to produce a specified number of items by a certain date. These contractors then hired their own assistants, 'mostly – though not exclusively – family members or relatives' (Staples 1987: 68; see also Blauner 1964: 76–78; Hareven 1982: 113; Penn 1985: 65; Smelser 1959: 185). Typically, then, production occurred within the personal or familial relationship that linked contractor and assistant, though this itself existed within the context of the more purely commercial relationship between capitalist and contractor.

Early factories of this sort amounted to centralised workshops where workers carried out just about the same activities using the same equipment that they had under the putting-out system. However, centralisation facilitated the subordination of work to a commercial logic, as it allowed the owner to introduce new productive technology, especially powered machinery, more readily than could the merchant who put work out. This undercut the ability of workers to order production in terms of their social relationships, and so increased abstraction. Most notably, it tended to convert individual producers from workers shaping what they made by the exercise of their skill into routine operatives.

But even without mechanisation, the early factory brought other important changes in the relationships in which production took place. For instance, the factory-owning capitalist could oversee work more closely than the putting-out merchant (this is discussed in Marglin 1974). Indeed, the emergence of industrial capitalism was associated with a general concern with observation, supervision and control (see Thompson 1967; Foucault 1979). This oversight allowed the capitalist to see and try to undercut practices that may have been necessary for the social survival of the work group but that slowed production, such as the time contractors spent training their relative–assistants in their trades (cf. Grieco 1987: 11–14).

At the same time, the system of craft control of apprenticeship was being threatened by the growing advocates of the notion of free labour, a notion that was to lead to greater abstraction. This threat culminated in 1814 in the repeal of key sections of the Statute of Artificers of 1564, thereby allowing apprenticeships unregulated by craft associations (see Bauman 1982: 56–59). John Rule argues that the advocates of free labour were attacking the idea that skill and the use of it for gain was a possession of individual workers that was regulated by associations of workers. Critics denied that workers had rights in their skill, and saw attempts to exercise these rights as an unjust restriction on individual liberty. Rule (1987: 110) points to Thomas Paine, who argued that the old system denied people 'the freedom to make bargains over the "personal labour" which was "all the property they have"'.

While these craft communities were clearly linked to, and in a way sprang from, production, they also had a social aspect that went beyond production. Attacks on these communities, then, served to weaken the degree to which production was governed by pre-existing social relationships. To understand the nature of those relationships it is necessary to describe apprenticeship, which occasionally was through formal indenture but was more commonly a matter of being brought up in a trade by a parent or other relative (Rule 1987: 100–101).

Apprenticeship served important functions for the craft community. It provided training in the skills of the craft; it marked those who were to be admitted to the body of recognised artisans, those with the right to live by their trade; it regulated entry to the trade and so protected the property of skill of those who possessed it. However, while artisans' rights were exercised by individuals, they were maintained by the craft as a group, based on a common artisanal identity that was markedly social, cutting across the specific links between workers, their assistants and their employers.

Thus, property in a craft had aspects of a status identity, with the artisans collectively being the group embodiment of that identity. In part this is because, as Tim Ingold (1990: 11) argues, the production skills that apprentices acquired 'are particular sedimentations of experience and, as such, are active ingredients of personal and social identity'. Serving an apprenticeship, then, was not just the way to acquire a skill, it was the way that an individual acquired the appropriate social identity and the badges of that identity. These included special language, habits and clothing, the knowledge of artisanal custom and ritual, the obligations of artisans to each other, and a sense of the honour and dignity of the craft (Rule 1987: 108–110).

The successful attack on apprenticeship replaced the more social identity of craft members and their work with one that reflected more clearly the commercial logic of the employer. Where workers as a group had collectively possessed and been possessed by their productive skills, free labour substituted the individual worker negotiating the sale of Paine's 'personal labour', the ability to labour at the direction of the employer. As Zygmunt Bauman (1982: 8) notes, the repeal of the Statute changed 'beyond recognition' the 'very character of apprenticeship as an initiation into a totality of patterned existence of the closely-knit trade community: the craftsmen's resistance ... was a struggle for the restoration of such a community'.

Modern Factory Production

The increasing abstraction of production under the early factory system was a continuation and extension of the growing abstraction that I described first in the change from cottage industry to the putting-out system. The shift to modern factory production accelerated this process. Here, the capitalist controls production directly, subordinating the workplace more directly to the dictates of capitalist manufacture. As a consequence, abstraction in work increased as the older familial and craft-community relations among workers, along with much of the need for skilled work, faded.[1]

These changes accompanied mechanisation, but they do not spring directly from it. Rather, they spring from what Ingold (1990) calls the objectification of production, which can occur without mechanisation. This is illustrated by the changes in pottery production that Josiah Wedgwood introduced late in the eighteenth century (see Forty 1986: 30–34; McKendrick, Brewer and Plumb 1982: Chap. 3). Where a piece of pottery had been produced by a single potter, Wedgwood broke up the process into a series of steps, each the job of a single worker who, following a model, shaped, assembled or coloured the pottery. With this scheme, Wedgwood separated the skill of production from the potter, objectified it and re-ordered it to suit his own ends. This case also illustrates how commercial factors relatively alien to those who produce can affect people's work lives. Wedgwood instituted these changes because he marketed his pottery by displaying samples in showrooms, and in order to assure that the pieces the customer received matched those displayed, he had to prevent the inevitable lack of uniformity that the system

---

1 This subordination had a cultural dimension as well. Workers and owners were seen as different sorts of people who needed to be kept apart, just as in modern firms managers often think of labourers as a breed apart (Kanter 1977: Chap. 3; Ouroussoff 1993). Thus, around 1900, Home & Colonial Stores forbade workers buying company shares without permission, 'an offence the only adequate punishment of which is instant dismissal' (Mathias 1967: 143).

of craft production entailed. Hence, pre-existing familial and craft relations were subordinated to market logic.

Wedgwood's innovation was part of the transformation of the factory from a place where people made things to a purpose-built tool that embodied the interests of its owners and designers (see Braverman 1974). This is most apparent in manufacture using assembly lines, where the logic of production 'is embedded in the physical and technological aspects of production and is built into the design of machines and the industrial architecture of the plant' (Edwards 1979: 131). The classic example is the early Ford Motor Company plants on Bellevue Avenue in Detroit and, after 1910, at Highland Park. Henry Ford encouraged his engineers to modify the work environment, to turn the factory from a structure shaped in important ways by the organisation of craft skills and the broader social relations associated with them into a tool that Ford controlled and that reflected his interests.

Conventionally, factories had been laid out in terms of the different operations and skills used in production. There was an area for milling, an area for annealing and so on, and individual parts moved from area to area as appropriate. Because such factories were organised spatially around different sorts of operations, they were also organised around the different skills, tools and sets of workers used in them. This was not the strong social organisation of the craft community, but at the least it was an attenuated form of social organisation. Ford's innovation was to re-design the factory spatially in terms of the steps required in production. Walter Flanders, who was responsible for laying out the Bellevue Avenue plant, 'placed machine tools according to sequential operations on various parts . . . If hardening or softening or any such nonmachine operation needed to be carried out during the sequence, Flanders placed a furnace or whatever in the correct sequential location' (Hounshell 1984: 221). Thus, the spatial arrangement of the equipment used in production embodied as rigorously as possible, and furthered as much as possible, the production goals of Ford management. As a consequence, the work of production became much more abstracted from the social relations of those doing the work.

These changes meant the disappearance the older cooperation among workers as agents of production. It was replaced by their coordination as instruments, purchased by the company as commodities and applied to specific production operations (see Ingold 1988: 170–173), governed by management and mediated by the physical processes of production and the moving belt of the assembly line, intended to 'speed up the slow ones, restrain the quick' (Hounshell 1984: 248). The social interactions among workers that are necessary for cooperation disappeared; coordination required only that workers interact with the machines they tended or the parts they assembled. This facilitated the disappearance of social bonds between workers and the further abstraction of production (on the persistence of those bonds where workers must cooperate in automobile production, see Zetka 1992).

I have described briefly the process of abstraction in production over the past few centuries. With cottage industry, the organisation of production was another manifestation of the social organisation of the household and the craft community. As time progressed, however, the organisation of work came increasingly to reflect commercial interests, illustrated particularly clearly by the way that the needs of Wedgwood's marketing system led to changes in his pottery manufacture. The result was a system in which workers' social identities and relationships became decreasingly relevant to production. In extreme cases, as Theo Nichols and Huw Beynon (1977: 193) report of workers in an agricultural chemicals factory, 'the men . . . knew that they, as individuals, weren't really needed by ChemCo – that others could come in "off the street" and do their job. They were told this day after day' (but cf. Harris 1987: 73–84). This is just another way of saying that people have become increasingly likely to experience production in a realm abstracted from their lives and relationships elsewhere.

Circulation I: The Emergence of the Market

I turn now to retail trade, showing how the relationships in which circulation occurs have become increasingly abstracted from relations in other areas of life. Because work on retail trade is less well known than work on production, I will devote two sections to it. In this section I describe the emergence of the modern shop in the decades around 1800, primarily in London. In the next section I describe the development, beginning late in the nineteenth century, of mass retailing.

During the seventeenth century, shop trade, the precursor of modern retail trade, emerged slowly in urban areas of Britain (Chartres 1977: 49; Davis 1966: 60; Willan 1976: Chap. 3). These shops, however, were not retail establishments in the modern sense, but places where artisans sold their wares. Appropriately, the organisation of early shop trade typically sprang from and relied on social relations.

Like cottage industries, these shops were part of people's houses. Even in London, 'the commonest kind of retail shop occupied the ground floor of a house' (Davis 1966: 101). Similarly, shopkeepers did not see their shops as a corporation (see Gudeman and Rivera 1991), an autonomous business that the shopkeeper happened to own. Instead, shop and household were a single economic unit: 'The business and the household can be separated only for analytical purposes: in reality they were interwoven parts of a single function' (Alexander 1970: 189; see also Carruthers and Espeland 1991: 45; Clark 1979; Earle 1989: 112–113). Likewise, they were a single social unit, containing kin, both closer and more distant, and outsiders '"adopted" into the shop-household complex. . . . [T]he tradesman assumed responsibility for educating the apprentice in the trade and for promoting his moral and physical well being' (Alexander 1970: 189–190). In other words, like early producers, shopkeepers typically structured their economic lives in terms of the relationships and values that pervaded much of their social lives.

To a lesser but still noticeable extent, this was true also of their relationships with customers. Partly this was because shops served a small clientele, which facilitated personal, sociable interaction. Customer and tradesman were not, then, independent economic actors, but were linked in a relationship that was not just economic, but also personal and social, even if it was one that each struggled to control. Indeed, in the absence of such a relationship customers could find it difficult to buy reasonable goods at a reasonable price, for often traders mistrusted strangers (for example, Willan 1976: 123). Furthermore, as nothing was standardised or guaranteed, everything had to be thrashed out between shopper and trader. 'To shop successfully it was important to choose a reliable shopkeeper and come to terms with him. Not necessarily friendly terms; acrimonious terms would do just as well; but at least personal terms' (Davis 1966: 181).

Appropriately, traders appeared not to have thought of 'consumer demand' as an abstract aggregate. Instead, it was a set of people with ties to individual shopkeepers. Such an attitude helps explain why shopkeepers wanted to have an established body of customers and valued a regular patronage over an impersonal trade with higher volume – a concern felt by customers as well, who were reluctant to take their custom to a stranger (see, for example, Alexander 1970: 162). Established relations were as important among merchants as they were between merchants and customers. Running a respectable retail business required a range of dealings with different sorts of merchants, manufacturers, wholesalers and the like who could be trusted and who could trust the shopkeeper. Such a web of durable relationships emerged only slowly, often in years spent as an apprentice to an established merchant, and it was not lightly disrupted (see, for example, Mui and Mui 1989: 219).

I have described a system in which most retail trade was embedded in broader social relationships. However, from the start of the eighteenth century people increasingly espoused a newer, more impersonal view of commerce (see, for example, DeBolla 1989: Chap. 4.; Dumont 1977; Pocock 1975: Chap. 13, 1979; Thompson 1971). Both conceptually and practically, economic activity was becoming abstracted from social relationships. This was true particularly in London. Household and shop began to separate; mass marketing appeared; shopkeepers began to operate in terms of what we, though probably not they, would think of as 'the market'; customers increasingly purchased in impersonal economic transactions.

The growing differentiation of the shop from the household took a number of forms. The simplest was the emergence of a distinct appearance for shops late in the eighteenth century (Kalman 1972), when the classic bow-fronted Georgian shops appeared (Alexander 1970: 202). This differentiation was also marked by the appearance of the lock-up shop and the non-resident shopkeeper, particularly in London's West End, which was emerging as the main fashionable shopping area (Davis 1966: 196). By the middle of the nineteenth century, the shop in the West End and similar areas 'was much less a house from which its inhabitants traded than a commercial building', albeit one in which the shopkeeper still occasionally lived (Alexander 1970: 202). This was part of a general differentiation of residential and commercial areas in English towns in the eighteenth century (Borsay 1989: 107, 294).

Shopkeepers came increasingly to think in terms of an anonymous market, as is shown by their adoption of practices intended to attract the 'dropping trade', casual trade from passing strangers who dropped in to buy (Alexander 1970: 196–197). These practices included new forms of shop display, as shop windows got larger and retailers devoted more attention to producing an attractive display of their wares in areas of London where better-off customers made their purchases (Alexander 1970: 162–163; Davis 1966: 195). These stylish signs, these colourful and bright displays behind large glass panes, often illuminated to be visible in the long London evening, were very different from the old style of shop, oriented toward established customers, which had little glass and less need for it.

Orientation toward an impersonal public appears as well in three novel pricing practices. These are fixed pricing, open ticketing and single-pricing. Fixed pricing meant that the price of the object had been determined by the merchant in advance. This eliminated the possibility of haggling, and so made the buying transaction more mechanical, just as it reduced the discretion of sales staff and so made their work more impersonal. Single pricing (a policy of no 'abatement' or price reduction) presupposed fixed pricing together with a single price, which would not be abated (reduced) for different sorts of customers. Finally, open ticketing meant that the price was plainly visible to the customer considering a purchase. These pricing practices began to appear in the last quarter of the eighteenth century, though they were not always as straightforward as their names imply, and by the late 1780s London shops began regularly to announce that they had goods 'ready made, for ready money, and at a fixed price' (McKendrick, Brewer and Plumb 1982: 83; see also Mui and Mui 1989: 232, 234).

Taken together, these practices betoken the abstraction of the buying transaction from social relationships. It was becoming possible to buy without negotiating the reliability, or even the identity, of customer or shopkeeper: complete strangers could buy as easily as established customers. These changes meant the disappearance of the need for the 'stylized interplay [that] weaves the buyer and seller together socially' (Sennett 1976: 142). And they did not just mark the end of the need, they were the foundation of the end of the *practice*, for they made possible the appearance of the competitive pricing that was 'essential to the success of the "monster shops" and the "cutting shops" ' (Alexander 1970: 172) that relied on aggressive mass retailing.

Such shops began to appear in the last quarter of the eighteenth century. The stereotype was the London draper selling to the bottom part of the growing middling sort, aiming at high sales volume by attracting strangers who had never bought there before. Appeals were made by press advertisements, handbills pushed through letter boxes, window displays – all novel techniques used for touting cheap prices for ready money to an anonymous public (Davis 1966: 258; Mitchell 1981: 52). Mayhew (in Fraser 1981: 176) describes this late in the nineteenth century:

> Every article in the window is ticketed – the price is cut down *to the quick* – books of crude, bold verse are thrust in your hands, or thrown into your carriage window – the panels of every omnibus are plastered with show placards, telling you how Messrs —— defy competition.

The different changes I have mentioned all reflect the growing differentiation of the shop from the household, the growing reorientation of traders away from a distinct body of customers and toward 'the market' in the modern sense, the spread of the shop as a more purely commercial institution. These changes are intertwined. The large windows and artificial lights of the new-built Georgian shop both distinguished it from a residence and lured passers-by. Equally, the commuting shopkeeper was less able to rely on personal links with those who lived near the shop to secure trade, and so was obliged to attract strangers (Alexander 1970: 11). Linked to these in turn was the breaking down of the older notion of a relatively stable level of consumption. The moral economy of stable orders was being replaced by the political economy of aspiring individuals. In these changed circumstances, the older style of trade was no longer enough. Shopkeepers had to lure customers in.

Thus far I have described how the closing decades of the eighteenth century and the opening decades of the nineteenth show clear signs of a change to a form of retail trade that is abstracted from the social relationships in which it had been enmeshed previously. The signs of this change were largely restricted to London, but they mark the visible beginnings of a fundamental change, the emergence of the notion of the anonymous, mass market in retail trade, and with it the emergence of shops governed by a more purely commercial logic.

Circulation II: Institutionalising Abstraction

The more purely commercial retail firms emerged in more and more branches of retail trade, and these firms adopted institutional practices that increased the abstraction of buying. This was most pronounced in trade that drew on and reflected the growing working-class demand of the closing decades of the nineteenth century, demand that constituted the mass market in the statistical sense that complemented the mass market in the conceptual sense that I described in the preceding section. For England, this meant that the centre of change moved from the stylish West End shop to the industrial areas of the Midlands, the North and lowland Scotland, where large retail firms specialised in inexpensive common wares (Mathias 1967: 39–40).

The stores that catered to this growing working-class demand attracted customers by emphasising low prices. Their concern for commercial efficiency led them to sell a small range of mass-produced commodities. For example, in the United States A & P stores stocked only tea, coffee, sugar, spices, tinned milk and butter in the 1880s (Walsh 1986: 22–23). A more extreme case is Maypole Dairy, which became part of Allied Suppliers. In 1913 this firm had almost 800 shops, selling only eggs, condensed milk, tea, margarine and butter, and in 1914 they abandoned eggs (Mathias 1967: 172). In the way they traded large quantities and in the way they centralised and routinised their selling operations, these firms pursued the same commercial goals as the Ford Motor Company.

Different changes occurred at different times in different branches of trade, reflecting the peculiar economic, technical and organisational histories of different areas of production and distribution (for England, see especially Jefferys 1954). Here, however, I will restrict myself to four important changes that appeared in just about all branches: the growing scope of retail firms; the change in the nature of credit; changes in labour relations; and the appearance of manufacturers' brands and advertising. Some of these changes affected primarily the internal organisation of the shop, while some affected relationships between customer and shop. Each, however, was a response to commercial interest that affected the shop, and each contributed to the increasing abstraction of retail trade.

Scope of Stores

During this period many ordinary shopkeepers shifted their concern from dealing with established customers to attracting an ever-larger dropping trade, thereby increasing the scope of their stores. This took two main forms: stores got bigger and chain or multiple stores became more common. These changes, dictated by commercial logic, made it more difficult to establish even the weak social relationships with customers that were possible in the emerging modern shops that I described in the preceding section.

The classic retail shop was small. Often it was only 10–15 feet wide and 20–40 feet deep, into which had to fit shopkeeper and clerk, shelves and cabinets, counters and customers, not to mention the storage room at the back. This suggests that the shop served a relatively small body of customers. Staff and customers frequently knew each other and their interactions were noticeably social. However, in the last quarter of the nineteenth century shop size increased. For example, in 1879, the first year of operation, F. W. Woolworth's opened three stores, with an average size of 360 square feet. Nine years later, the company opened five stores, the smallest larger than any of the 1879 shops, with an average size of 1,350 square feet. These larger shops were busier shops. The gross annual sales per Woolworth's store were $6,012 in 1879, $20,565 in 1889 and $81,761 in 1899 (Woolworth 1954: 8, 17). More space, more customers and more transactions, dictated by commercial concerns, reduced the chance that relations with customers could have a social component: '[S]heer size does effectively destroy much of the opportunity for interaction . . . It is harder to remember faces if there are many of them' (McClelland 1962: 139).

Similarly, the spread of firms with multiple outlets made it more likely that the relationship of shopkeepers with their shops and the community would be governed by purely commercial concerns. Increasingly, these shopkeepers were managers, and many companies moved them about frequently in order to broaden their experience and to develop a body of loyal staff (see Darby 1928: 56, 113; Walsh 1986: 30–31). Frequent moves oriented managers to the owning company and their career in it rather than to the locality, clerks and customers. Further, managers' freedom of action was restricted by many corporate policies, which were concerned with the commercial goals of volume and profit. And branch managers were not the only shopkeepers affected by these policies. Even independent shopkeepers who valued durable relations with established customers were obliged to adopt more profit-oriented practices if they were to stay in business (Sofer 1965: 189).

The growing ascendancy of more purely commercial concerns over social ones was apparent to people at the time. Some American critics of large chains and mail-order companies charged them with 'destroying local independent businesses' and 'taking money out of the local communities' (Walsh 1986: 21), while others objected explicitly to the commercial orientation of these firms in terms that echo the older, moral economy. In the first decade of the twentieth century the American writer William Allen White complained: 'There is such a thing as "tainted" dry goods, "tainted" groceries and "tainted" furniture . . . All of such that are not bought at home, of men who befriended you, of men to whom you owe a living, are "tainted" because they come unfairly' (in Strasser 1989: 216). Equally, some managers objected to the constraint of corporate policy, which obliged them to act toward customers and competitors in ways that they found distasteful (Sofer 1965: 186).

Changing Credit

Just as the growing scope of the shop and shopkeeper tended to reduce the social aspects of trade, so too did the change in the nature of credit. During this period, especially in urban areas, credit became less and less common in many sorts of retail trade, as a growing number of shops sold for 'ready money' only, for cash. This was certainly the case by the middle of the nineteenth century with the high-volume drapers' shops in London, as it was with the corresponding dry-goods trade in New York (Hendrickson 1978: 28; Scull 1967: 79–82; but cf. Resseguie 1965: 312). The early chain and multiple firms were natural adopters of a cash-only policy. For Lipton's food stores in the 1870s, '[q]uick turnover, rapid returns, minimum book-keeping, and a maximum insurance against the risk of bad debts all implied cash sales' (Mathias 1967: 47; see also Alexander 1970: 184).

The near disappearance of store credit, ultimately to be replaced by the credit card, marks an important aspect of the growing abstraction of retail trade. The granting of credit by merchants through the early nineteenth century certainly involved a financial assessment of customers (Alexander 1970: 182–183). However, a credit relationship was as well a personal, reciprocal relationship of trust. The parties expected that each would support the other in good times as well as bad. Customers expected that the shopkeeper would carry them through bad times, through bouts of illness or injury, spells when there was no work, strikes and bad harvests, medical bills or funeral costs. In short, they expected the shopkeeper to trust them to repay when times got better. In turn, the shopkeeper was entitled to loyalty, buying there when times were good and purchases could be paid for in cash, even though the multiple shops might have the same goods for less. The importance of this mutual support helps explain why small shopkeepers had to extend credit if they were to get custom.

In such a relationship, buying a tin of milk was not the exchange of equivalents. Rather, and echoing an older pattern, it was the recreation of a durable relationship, harking back to previous transactions and anticipating future ones. This appears to have been marked by the common practice of never wholly paying off the debt; the small balance remaining marking the continuation of the relationship between shopkeeper and customer (Mars 1982: 173; Mui and Mui 1989: 215).

In abandoning credit, then, shopkeepers were signalling their decreasing willingness to engage in durable relations with established bodies of customers. Shopkeepers may have done so because they preferred to offer lower prices instead, feared a loss of customers to chain or multiple branches, or simply wanted to be up to date. But whatever the reason, the restriction of store credit restricted one of the social dimensions of shopping.

Labour Relations

Changing labour relations affected shopkeeper and assistants directly, rather than customers. I noted that the local shopkeeper was turning into a branch manager, a paid employee. The older, independent shopkeeper had been apprenticed in the trade, learning its craft mysteries and identifying with it like any other skilled worker. However, many retail corporations saw this bond between person and trade as a hindrance to commercially-motivated innovation, and often they were right (Sofer 1965). In the early part of the twentieth century A & P sought to avoid these problems by hiring 'young men with no retail experience' as store managers, for they had 'no built-in bad retail habits' to be overcome (Walsh 1986: 30). Like factory workers, these managers were allowed little discretion in their work. A & P dictated the layout, equipping and stocking of new stores (1986: 29, 30). Many managers were, doubtless, attached to their occupations and looked forward to a successful career within the firm. But that attachment was to a set of relationships and structures relatively abstracted from those of the shop itself and those who purchased there.

Changes were more pronounced among clerks – increasingly those with whom customers interacted when they shopped. Previously apprenticed to a master in the trade, clerks became wage labourers without skills, unlikely to learn any, employed by but not a part of the organisation that hired them (see, for example, MacLean 1899). As A. T. Stewart is supposed to have said of those who worked in his dry-goods store in New York City in the middle of the nineteenth century, '[n]ot one of them had his discretion. They are simply machines working in a system that determines all their actions' (in Resseguie 1965: 314; cf. Mars 1982: Chap. 3). The transformation of the clerk's job was marked in the same way as the transformation of the manager's. Firms preferred employees ignorant of retail trade, 'inexperienced people, on the grounds that they are more easily taught' (Darby 1928: 53).

Changes in selling practices facilitated this change in the position of clerks. Between the two world wars, variety stores like F. W. Woolworth's selected, organised and displayed their stock in a way that 'brought a revolutionary simplification of the selling function. The sales talk and the selling work are either eliminated or strongly reduced' (Pasdermadjian 1954: 50). Equally, department stores so standardised and routinised their organisation that it became 'possible to use for the lower positions [i.e., clerks] . . . less qualified personnel' (1954: 13–14; see also Benson 1979: 213–216), which likewise restricted the chances of promotion into management (Donovan 1929: 197–198). These changes, like those in Ford's Bellevue Avenue plant, reflected the commercial logic of the firm rather than pre-existing social relations.

As apprentice clerks became wage workers, the firm came to assess them on commercial criteria in a way that was alien to the older system. Thus at the beginning of the twentieth century the National Cash Register Company was touting its machines as a way of monitoring the efficiency and honesty of individual clerks (Strasser 1989: 236–237; Winstanley 1983: 66). That company was part of a growing chorus that was urging retailers to adopt 'sound business practice', which entailed thinking of the store as an independent commercial enterprise in the modern mode. The reluctance of the owners of small businesses to change their practices, which many reformers derided, suggests that many small retailers saw their shops in much more social terms (for example, Harvard University 1919: esp. 16–19).

Manufacturers' Brands and Advertising

Changes in labour relations reflected and furthered the growing influence of commercial logic on the internal organisation of the shop and thus, albeit indirectly, on the relationship between customer and shop. The spread of manufacturers' brands and advertising reflected commercial changes more distant from the shop than was the case with changing labour relations, though that emergence affected those labour relations, the position of the shopkeeper and the relationship between customer and shop.

The emergence of manufacturers' brands and advertising followed the development of mass production in the second half of the nineteenth century. In creating and advertising their brands, manufacturers sought to get customers to go to the shop and ask for a specific brand. Indeed, manufacturers encouraged customers to demand the brand, warning them against perfidious clerks who might try to sell them a substitute (Strasser 1989: 83–87). This reduced the clerk to a mere filler of orders and the shopkeeper to a mere stocker of brands. The shopkeeper's knowledge of the qualities of different products and of local tastes became pointless when the only work was unpacking cases of ready-to-sell and ready-to-use products (Bluestone, Hanna, Kuhn and Moore 1981: 18; Winstanley 1983: 33).

In fact, manufacturers' use of branding and advertising was one of the events governed by a rationality based outside retail trade itself that obliged retailers to treat their trade in more purely commercial terms. Retailers were put under pressure to stock brands that they may have thought unsuited to their customers' needs and tastes, inferior in quality to other brands, or more expensive than and indist-inguishable from other forms of the same commodity, as they often were. *The Grocers' Review* in 1904 complained about 'bare faced attempts to get between the grocer and his trade', and company salesmen routinely told reluctant retailers that they might as well buy the branded item now, as advertising would make local demand irresistible in the end (Schudson 1984: 167; Strasser 1989: 193–194). One commentator put it more decorously, when he said that with their own advertising the manufacturers assume some of the functions of distribution (Shaw 1912: 740–744). Shopkeepers' resentment continued into the 1950s. Cyril Sofer (1965: 185) said that the British food shopkeepers that he talked to 'felt that the manufacturers and their associated marketing companies determined demand by direct communication with the public . . . and left them to cope with the consequences of their actions'.

Brands allowed manufacturers to constrain retailers in other ways as well. By advertising their wares with prices listed, manufacturers could control both wholesale and retail prices. This allowed them to put pressure on retail profit margins. At the very least, shopkeepers were aware of this power, which pointed up the adversarial relationship between shopkeeper and manufacturer in a striking way (for example, Cherington 1913: 128–134). More subtly, the shopkeeper could be put under pressure to reorganise his shop in ways that reflected a more purely commercial logic, solely to reduce costs and stay in business (see Sofer 1965).

Conclusions

My purpose in this chapter has been a simple one: to show how abstraction can take a practical form in the economic realm. I have done this by describing changes in two important areas of economic life, production and circulation, attending especially to Britain and the United States from the eighteenth century to the middle of the twentieth. This is hardly an exhaustive treatment of Western economic practice, but it covers sufficient material on sufficiently central processes and regions to be indicative of more general trends.

Not only has my purpose in this chapter been a simple one; I have told the tale in a simple way. I have kept what I have said within manageable bounds by leaving out much detail and qualification, particularly in my treatment of production. In a more expansive treatment the nuances might have been more subtle; but the overall thrust of the tale I tell would not be changed. That is, in their practical activities in the realms of production and circulation, a growing number of people confronted institutions that decreasingly were ordered in terms of general social relationships like kinship, gender and craft identity. Instead, the ordering of those institutions was increasingly in terms of a distinctive logic that springs from the calculations of commercial institutions in a competitive environment. In David Schneider's terms, home and work, sociality and commerce, became increasingly separate realms.

Saying this does not mean that before 1700 the two were identical. Certainly they were not. There is enough published work available on markets before 1700 (for example, Agnew 1986) and in non-Western societies (for example, Parry and

Bloch 1989) to disabuse anyone of the idea of a golden age now irremediably lost. Thus, the thrust of my tale deals with changes in degree rather than kind. But the degree of change is significant, as the practices of economic life were governed more and more by distinctly commercial imperatives. That governance was, of course, never perfect, just as management within a firm is never absolute. As was noted in the Introduction to this collection, sociability is a weed that propagates on the most stony ground (see, for example, Carrier 1994: 56–58; Mars 1982). However, it is unwise to let this observation beguile one into thinking that the sort of changes I have described are subverted by sociality to the point that they are nullified. Instead, that subversion has been furtive and constrained, always threatened with the sack, and so possesses nothing like the legitimacy or influence in economic life that was possessed by institutions like craft communities or shopkeepers' households.

The changes I have described in this chapter are neither unique nor inconsequential. They are not unique, because they were surrounded by other waves of abstraction, both in practical and intellectual realms, mentioned by other chapters in this volume. At the very least, after all, this was the era both of the efflorescence of bureaucratic organisations and of Weber's analysis of them. Similarly, these changes were not inconsequential, because they shaped people's practical worlds in a way that made it more likely that abstraction in economic life would be taken for granted and seem self-evident. In doing so, they helped clear the way for the changes that followed.

References

Agnew, Jean-Christophe 1986. *Worlds Apart: The Market and the Theater in Anglo-American Thought, 1550–1750*. New York: Cambridge University Press.

Alexander, David. 1970. *Retailing in England during the Industrial Revolution*. London: Athlone Press.

Allen, Sheila, and Carol Wolkowitz 1987. *Homeworking: Myth and Realities*. London: Macmillan.

Bauman, Zygmunt 1982. *Memories of Class*. London: Routledge & Kegan Paul.

Beach, Betty A. 1989. The Family Context of Home Shoe Work. In Eileen Boris and Cynthia R. Daniels (eds), *Homework: Historical and Contemporary Perspectives on Paid Labor at Home*, pp. 130–146. Urbana: University of Illinois Press.

Beier, A. L. 1987. *Masterless Men: The Vagrancy Problem in England 1560–1640*. London: Routledge & Kegan Paul.

Benson, Susan Porter 1979. Palaces of Consumption and Machine for Selling: The American Department Store, 1880–1940. *Radical History Review* (Fall): 199–221.

—— 1989. Women, Work, and the Family Economy: Industrial Homework in Rhode Island in 1934. In Eileen Boris and Cynthia R. Daniels (eds), *Homework: Historical and Contemporary Perspectives on Paid Labor at Home*, pp. 53–74. Urbana: University of Illinois Press.

Blauner, Robert 1964. *Alienation and Freedom: The Factory Worker and His Industry*. Chicago: University of Chicago Press.

Bluestone, Barry, Patricia Hanna, Sarah Kuhn and Laura Moore 1981. *The Retail Revolution: Market Transformation, Investment, and Labor in the Modern Department Store*. Boston: Auburn House Publishing.

Boris, Eileen, and Cynthia R. Daniels (eds) 1989. *Homework: Historical and Contemporary Perspectives on Paid Labor at Home*. Urbana: University of Illinois Press.

Borsay, Peter 1989. *The English Urban Renaissance: Culture and Society in the Provincial Town, 1660–1770*. Oxford: Clarendon Press.

Braverman, Harry 1974. *Labor and Monopoly Capital: The Degradation of Work in the Twentieth Century*. New York: Monthly Review Press.

Carrier, James G. 1994. *Gifts and Commodities: Exchange and Western Capitalism since 1700*. London: Routledge.

Carruthers, Bruce G., and Wendy Nelson Espeland 1991. Accounting for Rationality: Double-Entry Bookkeeping and the Rhetoric of Economic Rationality. *American Journal of Sociology* 97: 31–69.

Chartres, J. A. 1977. *Internal Trade in England, 1500–1700*. London: Macmillan.

Cherington, Paul Terry (ed.) 1913. *Advertising as a Business Force: A Compilation of Experience Records*. Garden City, NY: Doubleday, Page, for Associated Advertising Clubs of America.

Clark, Christopher 1979. Household Economy, Market Exchange and the Rise of Capitalism in the Connecticut Valley. *Journal of Social History* 13: 169–190.

Darby, William D. 1928. *Story of the Chain Store*. New York: Dry Goods Economist.

Davis, Dorothy 1966. *A History of Shopping*. London: Routledge & Kegan Paul.

DeBolla, Peter 1989. *The Discourse of the Sublime: Readings in History, Aesthetics and the Subject*. Oxford: Basil Blackwell.

Donovan, Frances R. 1929. *The Saleslady*. Chicago: University of Chicago Press.

Dumont, Louis 1977. *From Mandeville to Marx: The Genesis and Triumph of Economic Ideology*. Chicago: University of Chicago Press.

Earle, Peter 1989. *The Making of the English Middle Class: Business, Society and Family Life in London, 1660–1730*. Los Angeles: University of California Press.

Edwards, Richard 1979. *Contested Terrain: The Transformation of the Workplace in the Twentieth Century*. New York: Basic Books.

Ennew, Judith 1982. Harris Tweed: Construction, Retention and Representation of a Cottage Industry. In Esther Goody (ed.), *From Craft to Industry: The*

Ethnography of Proto-Industrial Cloth Production, pp. 166–199. Cambridge: Cambridge University Press.

Forty, Adrian 1986. *Objects of Desire*. London: Thames and Hudson.

Foucault, Michel 1979. *Discipline and Punish: The Birth of the Prison*. New York: Random House.

Fraser, W. Hamish 1981. *The Coming of the Mass Market, 1850–1914*. London: Macmillan.

Goody, Esther 1982. Introduction. In E. Goody (ed.), *From Craft to Industry: The Ethnography of Proto-Industrial Cloth Production*, pp. 1–37. Cambridge: Cambridge University Press.

Grieco, Margaret 1987. *Keeping It in the Family: Social Networks and Employment Chance*. London: Tavistock.

Gudeman, Stephen, and Alberto Rivera 1991. *Conversations in Colombia: The Domestic Economy in Life and Text*. New York: Cambridge University Press.

Hareven, Tamara K. 1982. *Family Time and Industrial Time: The Relationship between the Family and Work in a New England Industrial Community*. New York: Cambridge University Press.

Harris, Rosemary 1987. *Power and Powerlessness in Industry: An Analysis of the Social Relations of Production*. London: Tavistock.

Harvard University Bureau of Business Research 1919. *Management Problems in Retail Grocery Stores*. Bulletin No. 13, Harvard University Bureau of Business Research. Cambridge, Mass.: Harvard University Press.

Hendrickson, Robert 1978. *The Grand Emporiums*. New York: Stein & Day.

Hounshell, David A. 1984. *From the American System to Mass Production, 1800–1932*. Baltimore: Johns Hopkins University Press.

Ingold, Tim 1988. Tools, Minds and Machines: An Excursion in the Philosophy of Technology. *Techniques et Culture* 12: 151–176.

—— 1990. Society, Nature and the Concept of Technology. *Archaeological Review from Cambridge* 9(1): 5–17.

James, Mervyn 1974. *Family, Lineage and Civil Society*. Oxford: Clarendon Press.

Jefferys, James B. 1954. *Retail Trading in Britain: 1850–1950*. Cambridge: Cambridge University Press.

Kalman, H. 1972. The Architecture of Mercantilism: Commercial Buildings by George Dance the Younger. In Paul Fritz and David Williams (eds) *The Triumph of Culture: 18th Century Perspectives*, pp. 69–96. Toronto: A. M. Hakkert, Ltd.

Kanter, Rosabeth Moss 1977. *Men and Women of the Corporation*. New York: Basic Books.

McClelland, W. G. 1962. The Supermarket and Society. *Sociological Review* 10: 133–144.

McKendrick, Neil, John Brewer and J. H. Plumb 1982. *The Birth of a Consumer Society*. Bloomington: Indiana University Press.

MacLean, Annie M. 1899. Two Weeks in Department Stores. *American Journal of Sociology* 4: 721–741.

Marglin, Stephen A. 1974. What Do Bosses Do? The Origins and Functions of Hierarchy in Capitalist Production. *Review of Radical Political Economics* 6: 33–60.

Mars, Gerald 1982. *Cheats at Work: An Anthropology of Workplace Crime*. London: George Allen & Unwin.

Mathias, Peter 1967. *Retailing Revolution: A History of Multiple Retailing in the Food Trades Based Upon the Allied Suppliers Group of Companies*. London: Longman.

Mitchell, S. I. 1981. Retailing in Eighteenth and Early Nineteenth Century Cheshire. *Transactions of the Historical Society of Lancashire and Cheshire* 130: 37–60.

Mui, Lorna, and Hoh–cheung Mui 1989. *Shops and Shopkeeping in Eighteenth Century England*. London: Routledge.

Nichols, Theo, and Huw Beynon 1977. *Living with Capitalism: Class Relations in the Modern Factory*. London: Routledge & Kegan Paul.

Ouroussoff, Alexandra 1993. Illusions of Rationality: False Premises of the Liberal Tradition. *Man* 28: 281–298.

Parry, Jonathan, and Maurice Bloch (eds) 1989. *Money and the Morality of Exchange*. Cambridge: Cambridge University Press.

Parsons, Talcott 1959. The Social Structure of the Family. In Ruth Nanda Anshen (ed.), *The Family*, pp. 241–274. New York: Harper and Row.

Pasdermadjian, Hrant 1954. *The Department Store: Its Origins, Evolution, and Economics*, London: Newman. (Reprint: New York: Arno Press, 1976.)

Penn, Roger 1985. *Skilled Workers in the Class Structure*. Cambridge: Cambridge University Press.

Pennington, Shelley, and Belinda Westover 1989. *A Hidden Workforce: Home-workers in England, 1850–1985*. Basingstoke: Macmillan.

Pocock, John G. A. 1975. *The Machiavellian Moment*. Princeton: Princeton University Press.

—— 1979. The Mobility of Property and the Rise of Eighteenth Century Sociology. In Anthony Parel and Thomas Flanagan (eds), *Theories of Property: Aristotle to the Present*, pp. 141–166. Waterloo, Ont.: Wilfred Laurier University Press.

Resseguie, Harry E. 1965. Alexander Turney Stewart and the Development of the Department Store, 1823–1876. *Business History Review* 39: 301–322.

Rule, John 1987. The Property of Skill in the Period of Manufacture. In Patrick Joyce (ed.), *The Historical Meanings of Work*, pp. 99–118. Cambridge: Cambridge University Press.

Sabel, Charles, and Jonathan Zeitlin 1985. Historical Alternatives to Mass Production: Politics, Markets and Technology in Nineteenth-Century Industrial-ization. *Past and Present* 108: 133–176.

Schneider, David 1980. *American Kinship: A Cultural Account.* Second edition. Chicago: University of Chicago Press.

Schudson, Michael 1984. *Advertising, The Uneasy Persuasion.* New York: Basic Books.

Scull, Penrose 1967. *From Peddlers to Merchant Princes: A History of Selling in America.* Chicago: Follett Publishing.

Sennett, Richard 1976. *The Fall of Public Man.* New York: Vintage Books.

Shaw, Arch W. 1912. Some Problems in Market Distribution. *Quarterly Journal of Economics* 26: 703–765.

Smelser, Neil 1959. *Social Change in the Industrial Revolution.* Chicago: University of Chicago Press.

Sofer, Cyril 1965. Buying and Selling: A Study in the Sociology of Distribution. *Sociological Review* 13: 183–209.

Staples, William G. 1987. Technology, Control, and the Social Organization of Work at a British Hardware Firm, 1791–1891. *American Journal of Sociology* 93: 62–88.

Strasser, Susan 1989. *Satisfaction Guaranteed: The Making of the American Mass Market.* New York: Pantheon.

Swanson, Heather 1989. *Medieval Artisans: An Urban Class in Late Medieval England.* Oxford: Basil Blackwell.

Thirsk, Joan 1978. *Economic Policy and Projects: The Development of a Consumer Society in Early Modern England.* Oxford: Clarendon Press.

Thompson, E. P. 1967. Time, Work Discipline and Industrial Capitalism. *Past and Present* 38: 56–98.

—— 1971. The Moral Economy of the English Crowd in the Eighteenth Century. *Past and Present* 50: 76–136.

Tilly, Louise A. 1984. Linen was their Life: Family Survival Strategies and Parent-Child Relations in Nineteenth-Century France. In Hans Medick and David Warren Sabean (eds), *Interest and Emotion: Essays on the Study of Family and Kinship*, pp. 300–316. Cambridge: Cambridge University Press.

Walsh, William I. 1986. *The Rise and Decline of the Great Atlantic & Pacific Tea Company.* Secaucus, NJ: Lyle Stuart, Inc.

Willan, T. S. 1976. *The Inland Trade.* Manchester: Manchester University Press.

Winstanley, Michael J. 1983. *The Shopkeeper's World, 1830–1914.* Manchester: Manchester University Press.

Woolworth, F. W. (Company) 1954. *Woolworth's First 75 Years.* New York: F. W. Woolworth Company.

Zetka, James R., Jr 1992. Work Organization and Wildcat Strikes in the U.S. Automobile Industry, 1946 to 1963. *American Sociological Review* 57: 214–226.

–2–

The Triumph of Economics; Or, 'Rationality' Can Be Dangerous to Your Reasoning

Ben Fine

The purpose of this chapter is to examine both closely and critically some of the work of a particular economist, Gary Becker. He is extremely prominent, having been awarded a Nobel prize in economics. He is also generally credited with being influential in some new developments within economics, most notably his founding contributions to human capital theory and, most recently, his equally important role in the new household economics. In both of these cases, and in his work more generally, the distinguishing feature is his treatment of non-market relations – the formation and use of education and skills and the economics of the family – as if they were pseudo-markets.

Of course, it could be argued that a focus on one economist is liable to misrepresent the discipline as a whole.[1] Indeed, Becker is judged to be too extreme by many of his fellow economists, for reasons that will become apparent in what follows. However, economists' reservations about Becker derive less from fundamental disagreement with him in principle than from disagreement with his analytical integrity. He takes the implications of mainstream, neo-classical economics to their logical extremes even though the results prove embarrassing to his less persistent colleagues, who prefer to overlook the inevitable *reductio ad absurdum*. In short, Becker represents in the sharpest form the way in which mainstream economics abstracts its analysis from its social context and constructs a virtual reality of so-called rational individuals. In other words, he is a distillation of what Heilbroner and Milberg (1995: 6) describe as the discipline's 'belief that economic analysis can exist as some kind of disembodied study'.

Contemporary economics is dominated by the neo-classical approach, and current innovation in the discipline focuses on the implications of imperfections and differences in knowledge across partners in making potential contracts. This is part of a revolution under way in or, more exactly, from economics (Fine 1997a), and it is appropriate to sketch this context before turning to Becker's work. Across

---

1. Similarly, Nobel prizes for economics are marked by their frequent idiosyncrasy, even if otherwise by their conservatism.

a broad front, it is invading the previously-ignored analytical terrain occupied exclusively by other social sciences. This process represents, in some respects, a reversal of the marginalist revolution of the 1870s, which set classical political economy aside and established the mainstream neo-classical orthodoxy that has persisted ever since.

Despite emphasis upon the reunification of economics with other social sciences, the abstractions and virtualism of the former have not been modified, abandoned or critically examined. Indeed, they have been strengthened and extended. This is notable in three key respects. First, as economics extends its scope to issues that were previously seen as non-economic, it has remained tied to the organising notion of equilibrium. At best, an equilibrium is taken as the abstraction from which the real world is understood as a deviation. The virtualism of mainstream economics includes the construction both of equilibrium as an organising concept and of the deviations from it as a way of understanding what are taken to be the real-world or empirical realities. Second, the economy is modelled mathematically, more or less reducing it to a physical mechanism, even if one subject to random variation. Any casual glance at standard economics journals or texts will reveal the extent to which abstract mathematical modelling has come to dominate the discipline. Third, and most important, economics is fundamentally based upon methodological indiv-idualism: there is no such thing as society other than as the aggregated outcome of individual behaviour.

Previously, the assumptions attached to this methodological individualism effectively sealed economics off from interaction with other social sciences.[2] First, for mainstream economic theory, consumer preferences (what people want, as revealed by what they do) are taken as given, as exogenous, without any attempt to explain how they might have been formed or how they might change or be changed. Consequently, individual preferences are presumed to be pre-formed, vitiating the need to explain how social factors might have influenced individuals, let alone created them as social beings. One corollary of this is that, in principle, preferences can be different for each individual, as there is no reason for patterns of preferences to be either uniform or heterogeneous (although, as will be seen, Becker sees preferences as ultimately determined biologically, albeit modified by personal experience). Taking preferences as given and heterogeneous across individuals, however, represents an affront to other social sciences, which are often concerned with, for example, the reasons for and consequences of social norms. Economics has either left such issues to other disciplines or summarily dismissed them as belonging to the realm of the irrational. As one standard text puts it: 'What most economists would classify as non-economic problems are precisely those problems

2. For a fuller account in the context of the treatment of consumption across the social sciences more generally, see Fine and Leopold (1993: Chap. 4).

which are incapable of being analyzed with the *marginalist* paradigm' (quoted in Heilbroner and Milberg 1995: 7). Significantly, economics uses 'tastes', 'preferences', 'satisfaction' and 'utility' interchangeably for the supposedly deterministic welfare that individuals can attain through consumption.

A second corollary of the dominant methodological individualism is that economics presumes that underlying individual preferences are translated into choices through what is deemed to be economic rationality, the maximum satisfaction of the level of preferences (or utility, in common parlance) subject to the constraints faced by the consumer in terms of the levels of prices and the amount of available income. This involves an unduly restrictive understanding of the motivations for choice as well as of the range of activities that surround consumption itself. Significantly, the theory of consumer choice within economics is identified with the theory of demand: how much is bought at certain prices, for example. As such, it is as if the consumer is a little entrepreneur, efficiently arranging for the maximum production of utility on the basis of available finance and the prices of inputs. Such casual treatment of both motivation and its translation into action stretches the imagination to disbelief when, as in Becker's pioneering work, it is extended to marriage, fertility decisions, the choice to become a drug addict and so on.

If pressed, most economists would reveal that these abstractions of individual behaviour have been attached to an informal and ill-defined limitation of the scope of their application. The given-ness of preferences and utility maximisation only apply to material goods available through well-defined markets and for periods short enough that preferences do not shift. Becker allows no such concessions, recognising no borders between where preferences are fixed and where they are not. Across all goods and activities, and even from one generation to another, individuals are simply making choices on how best to attain the highest utility.

Third, then, whatever is perceived to be its legitimate scope of application, not only is choice as an activity rendered simplistic and analogous to any other optimising activity, but the theory is also, as a corollary, neutral in its application across consumer goods. In other words, the theory is the same whether we are dealing with luxuries or necessities, or with inferior or superior goods. Indeed, these terms become technical labels for ways that patterns of demand shift with prices and income. The generality and simplicity of the theory of demand allows it to be extended to many, if not all, areas of activity, as long as they can be interpreted as providing utility at a cost. For Becker in particular, the same method is served up irrespective of the object of study, with all activity aiming at more utility as its ultimate goal. Not only are there no boundaries in this individualistic application of the economic approach to social life in general; there is also no analytical differentiation between economic and social activities except in so far as they are a more or less direct source of utility.

A fourth corollary of the discipline's methodological individualism, one that is a critical point of departure in the era of post-modernism, is that there is no attention to how the nature of choice is affected by the social meaning of objects. Essentially, even if only implicitly, consumption goods are treated as if they were merely the depository of physical properties, merely the physical inputs into a technical production process for the creation of the individual's maximum utility. Economists have never questioned the meaning of goods any more than they have examined why they should have the capacity to provide utility. When, as for Becker, the scope of what constitutes a good is extended indefinitely, there is an unsurprising abstraction from the social, from the being and meaning of both individuals and objects, as well as the ways in which they consort with one another. This represents a particularly profound and crude rejection of the social, with custom, tradition, culture and the rest all reduced to the more or less accidental coordination and mutual influence of individuals' satisfactions.

In short, economics is characterised by the reduction of choice and behaviour to demand for physical objects, because of the discipline's methodological individualism, and its assumption that preferences are given exogenously and that motivation is only utility maximisation. As an abstraction of the economic from the social, there is a corresponding abstraction of the individual, who is stripped of all but the most crude and ahistorical determinism. Moreover, as a discipline, economics has hardly been concerned at all with questioning these bizarre assumptions and their methodological implications. Rather, it has taken them as the basis from which to examine, and even to explain according to a naive empiricist methodology, how choice or demand shifts in response to shifts in income and prices. (For a critique of this in the context of the demand for food, see Fine *et al.* 1996: Chap. 7.) Such empirical preoccupations, in conjunction with the discipline's conceptual weaknesses, have had the added effect of insulating the economics of consumer choice from integration with other disciplines. Inevitably, what economics has assumed as exogenous, whether in motivating individual behaviour or in the social context in which it would be situated, has formed the subject matter for other disciplines. Consequently, two distinct but closely related barriers have previously separated economics from other social sciences. One was that rational economic behaviour was confined to the world of the economy, itself seen as scarcely embedded in a broader social context other than the market as a price system. The second was the inability of economics to explain the social, which it took as exogenous and the context within which individual optimisation is realised.

Corresponding to the breakdown of these barriers, the present revolution in economics has proceeded along two complementary colonising paths into the other social sciences. The first has been the extension of the optimising behaviour of individuals to all walks of life, not just the economy.[3] Such has been Becker's obsession. Significantly, however, this treating of non-economic relations as though they are akin to market trading still leaves open the unexplained presence of social relations. The second, more dramatic, path has appeared to square the circle, endogenising social relations on the basis of individual optimising behaviour, by reducing the social to individual attributes and their aggregate. New formal models, based in a variety of ways on the presence of imperfect and asymmetric information, have been able to demonstrate why individuals have an incentive to engage in social relations, to structure the economy and create institutions (for a critical assessment in the context of labour markets, see Fine 1998: Chaps 2, 4). This marks the ultimate abstraction of the individual from society, for it moves from a benign neglect of society to its aggressive reconstruction on the basis of its constituent individuals. In such a topsy-turvy virtual world, the social crystallises out of a collection, not a collective, of individuals, rather than vice versa.

Accounting for Becker

The concern in what follows is primarily with the first form in which neo-classical economics has burst its traditional boundaries, the simple extension of supply and demand to non-market relations. This timely exercise is assisted by the appearance of Becker's *Accounting for Tastes* (1996). He is the theorist, *par excellence*, of the extension of neo-classical economic abstraction to every walk of life. His new volume gathers together articles that have appeared over a twenty-year period, also adding a few new contributions, including an overview of analytical themes.[4] As the title of the book suggests, its primary concern is with the formation of tastes (or preferences and utility). Consequently, the work for which Becker is best known, on human capital and the new household economics, figures only in passing. However, in all these areas, Becker can be considered to have been in the vanguard of the revolution in economics. With human capital theory and the new household economics, for example, orthodox neo-classical reasoning has been well established in areas where it was previously absent, education and the family. Taken in general, Becker's work is remarkable for the extent to which it reveals the explicit goal of

---

3. As Xenos (1989: 71) perceptively puts it: 'There is an assumption about human nature and reason built into the foundations of neoclassical economics that at some deep level individuals experience the real world and react to it in the same way. In this manner, economics can be established universally as a discourse applicable to any society at any time, so long as a scarcity situation can be determined.'

4. Many of the contributions are jointly authored; but in what follows reference is generally made only to Becker.

forging the revolution in economic thought.[5] Consequently, a close consideration of Becker's book affords the opportunity not only to confirm the hypothesis of a revolution in economics itself but also to examine some of its consequences.

First, as revealed in his Nobel Prize acceptance speech of 1992, Becker is concerned to extend the traditional scope of economics as he conceives it, the deployment of 'the economic approach', by which he means fundamental analytical dependence upon the utility-maximising behaviour of individuals. 'My research uses the economic approach to analyze social issues that range beyond those usually conceived by economists' (1996: 139); or, as reported in Swedberg (1990: 39): '"Economic imperialism" is probably a good description of what I do.' Moreover, he welcomes the increasing attention that other economists are devoting to non-economic issues and suggests that other social scientists are being successfully drawn to the economic approach:

> I have been impressed by how many economists want to work on social issues rather than those forming the traditional core of economics. At the same time, specialists from fields that do consider social questions are often attracted to the economic way of modelling behavior because of the analytical power provided by the assumption of individual rationality. Thriving schools of rational choice theorists and empirical researchers are active in sociology, law, political science, and history, and to a lesser extent, in anthropology and psychology (1996: 156).

Remarkably, within the few pages of his introductory chapter, Becker is able to address a whole range of issues with no apparent sense of immodesty, ranging over smoking, addiction, going to church, playing tennis, child abuse, divorce, jogging, violence, lying, sexual abuse, psychotherapy, patriotism and government propaganda. Early notice is thereby served of the distant horizons encompassed by the economic approach.[6]

Further, Becker, and this might come as a surprise to some economists, even appears to regret that the marginalist revolution narrowed the range of social

5. I have considered various aspects of Becker's work elsewhere: household economics (Fine 1992); human capital (Agbodza and Fine 1996; Fine 1998: Chap. 3); addiction (Fine 1997*b*).

6. The economic approach does not appear to make much progress in encompassing death, as in suicide and wars. To some extent, this reflects a lack of comfort with conflict and violence, quite apart from the technical and conceptual issues involved in justifying a rational choice of what is presumably infinitely-negative utility. However, rational choices can be made over length versus quality of life (Ehrlich and Chuma 1987) and conflict can be accommodated by game theory (Hirshleifer 1987). Becker is prepared to accept that war and religion do pose problems for his approach (Swedberg 1990: 40). See Fine (1997*c*) for an account of how the advance of methodological individualism in Sen's entitlement approach to famine has been stalled by the reluctance to interpret mass starvation as the consequence of aggregated rational choice.

variables used to explain behaviour. He suggests that this is a consequence of the requirements of the formal modelling associated with analytical rigour: 'As greater rigor permeated the theory of consumer demand, variables like distinction, a good name, or benevolence were pushed further and further out of sight' (1996: 163). By bringing such variables back into sight, economics can shed light on the subject matter of the other social sciences:

> From a methodological viewpoint, the aim . . . is to show how [what] is considered important in the sociological and anthropological literature can be usefully analyzed when incorporated into the framework provided by economic theory. Probably the main explanation for the neglect of social interactions by economists is neither analytical intractability nor a preoccupation with more important concepts, but excessive attention to formal developments during the last 70 years. As a consequence, even concepts considered to be important by earlier economists, such as social interactions, have been shunted aside (1996: 194).

As will be suggested later, even when it is interpreted kindly, this reading of past economists and social scientists is highly selective.

Thus, Becker seeks to broaden the scope of explanation offered by the economic approach, by including more variables in the definition of utility: 'This book retains the assumption that individuals behave so as to maximize utility while extending the definition of individual preferences to include personal habits and addictions, peer pressure, parental influences on the tastes of children, advertising, love and sympathy, and other neglected behavior' (1996: 4). However, it is important to establish that the inclusion of social variables is not at the expense of excluding a continuing methodological individualism in which utility is maximised subject to prevailing prices and incomes: 'The economist continues to search for differences in prices or incomes to explain any differences or changes in behavior . . . one searches, often long and frustratingly, for the subtle form that prices and incomes take in explaining differences among men and periods' (1996: 25–26; see also 4, 25, 49).

This broader scope appears to pose a problem, however, for it encompasses situations and lengths of time in which people appear to change their minds. This is a problem because it seems to challenge the assumption that preferences are given and stable. By use of the extended utility function, however, Becker is able to explain why an individual's preferences appear to change over time, even rapidly, but do not, in fact, do so. For Becker, this use of the extended utility function rebuts what he takes to have been one of the most enduring criticisms of mainstream economics, its assumption that preferences are stable and endogenous. The analytical device involved is facile. Rather than utility depending upon a set of consumption goods, g_1, g_2, . . ., alone, it also depends upon a set of other factors,

$X_1, X_2, \ldots$[7] As a consequence, Becker can argue that utility is given by a stable function of the factors g and X. Further, he argues that any apparent instability in utility is an illusion, resulting from considering utility as only depending upon the factors g alone, or from not taking into account enough X factors. The apparent instability will be resolved once changes in sufficient X factors are incorporated.

Such formalism is only endowed with any substance beyond the existing propositions of mainstream economics once specific content is given to the factors $X_1, X_2, \ldots$ In keeping with his methodological individualism, Becker divides the variables into two sorts: those that, subject to constraints, are within the choice of the individual, and those that are determined by factors outside the control of individuals but that may be endogenous to the economic system as the aggregate outcome of their behaviour. These are termed personal, P, and social, S, capital, respectively. Added together, personal and social capitals make up total human capital, which becomes broader in content than its standard use as education, talent and experience.

As a term, 'human capital' is most familiar and common in the context of labour market theory, in which individual returns from employment are explained as fully as possible by differences in personal attributes such as education, skills, and work experience. Just as individuals can add to their personal human capital by choosing to study, so they can add to or subtract from their consumption capital, one of the components of P, by their past experiences of consumption. For example, the more experience one has of consuming a good, particularly one involving culture or aesthetics, the more enjoyment one can derive from its consumption in the future. On the other hand, in the case of addiction, present consumption can lead to a loss of consumption capital, as future utility is sacrificed, for given levels of consumption, in view of drug dependency, withdrawal symptoms and the like.

The idea of personal (consumption) capital allows Becker to explain why tastes (given by the subutility function u(g,X), taking no account of the stock of personal capital, P) change over time, even though the extended utility function does not change. Indeed, tastes must change over time, as successive bouts of current consumption build up experiences that shift the potential for future enjoyment. In principle, this is entirely unobjectionable. Most people will accept that habituation, for example, affects consumption and other patterns of behaviour. However, when wedded to the economic approach, shifting tastes are not construed only as an automatic consequence of past experiences, but also as the object of conscious choice, just as is education in the attempt to obtain more advantageous employment. Thus, we can choose our tastes by maximising our extended utility over time by a forward-looking choice of our accumulated total human capital. This is why we

---

7. Reference to g and X factors is purely formal in the narrow mathematical sense. It makes no difference to the theory what these factors are, even though they range over the full set of material goods and social influences.

are prepared to devote current resources of time and effort to learning to enjoy. Further, drug addictions, and a range of other phenomena such as eating disorders, are to be explained by rational choice over time. For addiction, as long as drugs (or smoking cigarettes) are not too expensive in the present, it will be optimal to take the pleasure now even at the expense of loss of utility in the future, whether this involves the pain of withdrawal or not (which can also be explained in terms of an optimal choice of whether to remain addicted or not).

So far the discussion has focused on personal capital, over which the individual has a degree of self-control or choice subject to external constraints. Significantly, the bulk of Part I of Becker's book, entitled 'Personal Capital', is primarily concerned with rational addiction, not least because addiction appears to violate the assumption of stable and unchanging preferences. 'Social Capital' is the title given to the second part of the book. It is distinct from personal capital in that it is heavily determined by factors outside the control of the individual: 'Men and women want respect, recognition, prestige, acceptance, and power from their family friends, peers, and others . . . the effects of the social milieu, an individual's stock of social capital depends not primarily on his own choices, but on the choices of peers in the relevant network of interactions' (1996: 12).

Some social capital is entirely outside the control of the individual, not least when a child is building up experiences that are imposed rather than chosen. More generally, social capital is only indirectly or marginally affected by the personal choices of individuals, and Becker draws an analogy with externalities (1996: 12). An individual reduction in polluting behaviour, for example, does little to address overall pollution levels. Similarly, participation in, and benefit from, social networks depends upon their prior existence and evolution, the latter itself depending upon how and how many individuals participate. This can give rise to multiple equilibria, in which all are subject to peer pressure, for example, to submit either to a culture of drinking or to a culture of abstinence. Thus: 'The interaction between habits and social forces can produce explosive changes in drug use that lead either to heavy addiction or drug-free behavior' (1996: 16).

More important from the methodological point of view is the fact that the social has been incorporated into the model despite the analytical dependence upon individualism. Reference is made to social forces, interactions and networks. In their use, two features are crucial, at least in principle (although the practice is slightly different, as will be discussed below). The first is that the social is simply an argument or variable in the definition of the individual's extended utility function. It adds to or subtracts from social capital. Second, the social does not exist independently of the individuals who compose it, but evolves over time in the light of the aggregated choices that individuals make. These points are tellingly illustrated by two different examples Becker uses to distinguish himself from other theorists, although each example is motivated by the axiomatic denial that shifts in extended utility are permissible.

The first example is in response to the notion associated with John Kenneth Galbraith, that advertising might manipulate preferences. Becker (1996: 37) argues that this is not so. What advertising does is to change the stock of consumption capital. Whether it does so favourably or not depends upon the sort of knowledge imparted. In addition, the extra knowledge attached to advertised and branded goods, regardless of the veracity of product claims, allows the household to produce more utility in its use and consumption of these goods. The important point is that advertising does not have to work by changing underlying preferences. Irrespective of the validity of Galbraith's treatment of the effects and intents of advertising, which itself depends upon a questionable distinction between true and false wants, Becker's approach is a remarkable example of a virtual creation. In place of the empirical realities with which our daily lives make us all too familiar, and which are proudly professed by the advertising profession, we are offered an intellectual abstraction that is based on deeply-buried and fixed underlying preferences.

That the latter are sacrosanct is also a feature of the second example, Becker's critique of Sen (1977) for the suggestion that individuals may hold to a set of meta-preferences based on moral judgements, as opposed to preferences for personal welfare alone. Becker's judgement is that there is no case that

> [h]igher-order rankings are either necessary or useful in understanding behavior since ethics and culture affect behavior in the same general way as do other determinants of utility and preferences. In particular, considerations of price and cost influence ethical and moral choices – such as whether to act honestly – just as they influence choices of personal goods (1996: 18).

Accordingly, Becker denies the moral dilemma of a gap between the preferences we do have and those that our ethical considerations might make us like to have. Rather, the divorce between actual and desired preferences is reinterpreted as dissatisfaction with inherited personal and social capital, just as, for example, we do not necessarily have different preferences over consumption goods because we choose differently both quantitatively and qualitatively when we enjoy different levels of income or wealth. Once again, the abstraction proffered by Becker is a virtual creation contrary to our common experience of, or reflection upon, daily life. This is because Becker's model logically precludes the possibility that people might hold to a moral system of beliefs that are inconsistent with pursuit of their own personal welfare.

This is indicative of the crudest reification of social relations and individual being. All personal and social factors are reduced to various stocks of capital that contribute directly or indirectly to the satisfaction of the extended utility function. The implications of such reification are apparent in treating physical objects as lacking any socially-constructed meaning that defines the nature of what we do consume, such as has been a major component of postmodernist discourse. The naive extension of such a physicalist approach to all areas of social intercourse is truly astonishing. It is even formalised explicitly with the way the stocks of personal and social capital are treated in exactly the same way as physical capital, being added to by current behaviour (corresponding to investments) and being subtracted from by depreciation!

Complementing the treatment of the social as thing is its incorporation within the extended utility function. Significantly, whilst Becker admits the use of 'meta-preference', he differentiates himself from Sen by treating meta-preferences as simply a way of referring to the extended utility function. Morals, ethics or whatever are chosen and form part of the inherited total human capital. This is a particular example of the analytical procedure Becker adopts. Whatever explanatory factor is deployed by others, whether to account for a shift in preferences or not, it can be reinterpreted as a variable to be incorporated within the extended utility function as personal or social capital.

Becker's analytical strategy can now be laid out explicitly, together with its correspondence to the revolution in economics. It starts from the standard neo-classical model of economic behaviour, firmly rooted in the maximisation of a stable and given utility function. This is extended to all walks of life, most notably human capital and the household. Where old or new applications do not work empirically, implying that tastes have shifted, the utility function is extended to include varieties of personal capital, so that past experiences affect choice, which is also forward-looking and able to embrace addiction and habit. Finally, once again in deference to empirical anomalies, social factors are also incorporated into the extended utility function so that individuals can choose the networks in which they participate, collectively causing those networks to evolve over time to one or other equilibrium.[8]

An important, but not logically necessary, feature of Becker's work and of this analytical strategy is that as much as possible should be explained by as little as possible, which means departing as little as possible from the original core of the economic approach and its reliance upon optimisation in markets in response to available prices and incomes. Equally, the core model is not questioned; it is only extended by way of the extended utility function as empirical anomalies emerge for explanation. A corresponding analytical movement occurs as the boundaries shift between what is taken as exogenous and as endogenous. In broad terms, the

---

8. The explanation of social institutions like networks is the weakest part of Becker's contribution and is scarcely broached at all except as the unwitting or game-theoretical outcome of individual behaviour. As discussed above, the more radical path taken by the revolution in economics is the one that addresses the question of why individuals might set up institutions on the basis of self-interested optimisation.

original model takes personal and social capital as fixed; then personal capital becomes endogenous and, finally, social capital is endogenised.

Yet a core of exogenous or unexplained factors remains. It tends to be overlooked because the analytical movement is always to further uncritical and unreflective endogenising. It is the merit of Becker's discussion that he reveals in a scattered way exactly what is taken as exogenous and that, sporadically, he attempts to justify it. The answer is far from surprising, for, just as tastes are given in the core economic model, so the extended utility function is taken as given. Moreover, with the major exception of the differences between the genders, the logic of parsimonious use of factors in explanation leads to the assumption that all humans have the same biologically-given extended utility function. The idea is that apparent differences in individuals can be explained entirely by different external circumstances and hence choices of, and outcomes for, personal and social capital. Consider the treatment of the extended utility function.

First, it is invariant across individuals and across time: 'The establishment of the proposition that one may usefully treat tastes as stable over time and similar among people is the central task' (1996: 25); and again: 'The utility function itself is independent of time, so that it is a stable function over time of the goods consumed and also of the (personal and social) capital goods . . . the extended utility function . . . is stable only because it includes measures of past experience and social forces' (1996: 5). Second, as was previously indicated, apparent differences in individuals' tastes may be the consequence of identical underlying extended utility functions in conjunction with differences in experiences and opportunities across a whole range of circumstances: 'The influence of childhood and other experiences on choice can explain why rich and poor, whites and blacks, less and more educated persons, or persons who live in countries with totally different traditions have subutility functions that are radically different' (1996: 6). Third, with minor qualification, there is an appeal to biological determinism, at least as a starting-point: 'Each person is born perhaps not as a *tabula rasa* – an empty slate – but with limited experiences that get filled in by childhood and later experiences' (1996: 126). Finally, with a breathtaking and unjustified leap of faith, we are informed that the economic approach extends not only to the other social sciences but also to the natural sciences: 'I believe the main reason habitual behavior permeates most aspects of life is that habits have an advantage in the biological evolution of human traits. For as long as habits are not too powerful they have social as well as personal advantages' (1996: 9).

Social Science Viewed from the Economic Ivory Tower

His cavalier attitude to social order and issues is revealed more extensively in Becker's scattered references to other social sciences. So limited is his discussion and yet so wide-ranging are the conclusions he draws that one can only speculate about Becker's thought on these topics. However, I suggest that his thought is characterised by a mixture of arrogance, contempt, ignorance and plunder.[9]

Regarding arrogance and contempt,[10] there is no evidence that Becker has made any attempt to understand other social sciences on their own terms. Rather, if works in those disciplines are read at all, they are simply read through the prism of the economic approach, as indicated already in Becker's discussion of the loss of the social from classical political economy with the marginalist revolution. Bluntly, anything that does not conform to the economic approach is dismissed. Thus:

> We were impressed by how little has been achieved by the many discussions in economics, sociology, history, and other fields that postulate almost arbitrary variations in preferences and values when confronted by puzzling behavior . . . personal and social capital are crucial not only for understanding addictions . . . but also for most other behavior in the modern world, and probably in the distant past as well (1996: 6).

Not surprisingly, only the economic approach can deliver the goods: 'We assert that this traditional approach of the economist offers guidance in tackling these problems – and that no other approach of remotely comparable generality and power is available' (1996: 25). The assumption, common in the other social sciences, of differences in underlying preferences is simply arbitrary and weak, and nothing is to be expected from those social sciences in explaining them: 'No significant behavior has been illuminated by assumption of differences in tastes . . . [which] along with assumptions of unstable tastes, have been a convenient crutch to lean on . . . ad hoc arguments that disguise analytical failures' (1996: 49).[11]

The case for Becker's ignorance of other social sciences is primarily guilt by lack of association. There is no evidence that he has read or understood much at all: 'After reading Parsons, I decided sociology was just too difficult for me'

9. Heilbroner and Milberg (1995: 6) suggest that the economic approach's lack of a vision of an order beyond the individual marks 'an extraordinary combination of arrogance and innocence'.

10. Becker is arrogant about the people in his discipline, claiming that 'economists are cleverer but sociologists have wider scope' (Swedberg 1990: 38). There is also a personal arrogance, as when he compares the exhaustion he felt on completing his *Treatise on the Family* with that of Bertrand Russell on completing *Principia Mathematica* (Swedberg 1990: 148). Becker also basks in the glory of his colleagues, as when he endows his collaborator, Kevin Murphy, with 'the ability to see problems quickly and to devise solutions [that] shows genuine brilliance' (Swedberg 1990: vii).

11. Not surprisingly, Becker (1996: 12, 22) harshly dismisses psychology for its reliance upon multiple personalities and cognitive imperfections. In a similar vein, Gray (1987: 35) advises that optimisation on the basis of fixed objects '[s]hould not be taken as reason against fashioning better theories of belief formation which deploy the Becker scheme. In fact, the application of the economic approach to questions of cognitive psychology would seem to be one of its most promising research prospects.' This does not seem to have been borne out in practice.

(Swedberg 1990: 29). Interestingly, if not tellingly, many of Becker's references to other works have come with an acknowledgement that others have brought them to his attention, and often those works are treated as relics from past classics that, if torn from their context, might anticipate the economic approach. When he does give an explicit account of someone who stands outside the economic approach, he demonstrates profound ignorance and prejudice, as in his dismissal of Herbert Gintis's 1974 article on endogenous preferences, as work that is pioneering but 'marred by an excessive ideological slant' (1996: 18). Not surprisingly, his treatment of Marxism is facile, as in his statement: 'Marxists claim that the upper classes in effect "brainwash" lower classes to internalize behavior that benefits the upper classes, but how the brainwashing is accomplished has not been made clear' (1996: 225).[12]

Finally, in an instance of theory copying reality, there is the plunder that accompanies the arrogance, contempt and ignorance, as economics colonises the other social sciences. This is apparent when one considers the question of the intellectual origins of Becker's social factors.[13] Variables such as networks, interactions, peer pressure, the family, prestige, habituation, the desire for distinction, guilt and anger are all core elements of other social sciences. In addressing a colonised topic, the economics approach involves identifying an empirical anomaly, as far as the assumption of fixed tastes is concerned, and corresponding social factors with which to address it – factors considered by other disciplines. The factors are then stripped of all social content other than that allowed by the maximisation of the extended utility function. The demands this technique makes upon intellectual ingenuity can be considerable; but, necessarily, they are so only within a methodology and a range of variables that are breathtakingly thin. Thus, for example, Becker sees social norms not as socially defined group properties, but as simply the values that individuals choose to share in common, determined as the aggregated behaviour across individuals: 'Norms are those common values of a group which influence an individual's behavior through being internalized as preferences' (1996: 225). In short, there appears to be a tension in Becker's work in so far as the presence of concepts such as social capital signifies

---

12. Similarly, he claims that, 'unlike Marxian analysis, the economic approach . . . does not assume that individuals are motivated solely by selfishness or material gain' (1996: 139). Note how, here and in the brainwashing passage, he approaches Marxist analysis through the prism of methodological individualism.

13. Whilst the emphasis in this chapter has been upon economics colonising the other social sciences, there are some who argue otherwise. Thus, whilst Swedberg (1990: 57) discusses with Coleman whether sociology serves as a scout for economics, he also discusses with Akerlof (Swedberg 1990: 73) and Schelling (Swedberg 1990: 194) whether the attempt is being made to bring sociology to economics rather than vice versa.

that social, and not just individual, factors play a role. However, appearance deceives, as the significance of the social is purely fleeting, at least in principle, for 'the social' is a temporary and convenient assumption of exogeneity or historical inheritance (on which see below), which must ultimately be dissolved in a finer analysis by reference to the individuals who have made the social what it is.

In general, this dissolution is an impossible task – one that gives rise to an unwitting plunder of other social sciences, as well as being associated with a divorce between principle and practice in much of his analysis. I have suggested that, at least in principle, a fully specified, biologically determined, extended utility function ought to be the starting-point from which the evolution of all social phenomena follows. In practice, however, the shifting boundary between exogenous and endogenous, and hence between economics and other social sciences, usually depends upon taking some social factors as exogenously given, although this sets up the potential for a further encroachment on the other social sciences, as what is exogenous is then translated into economic terms and made endogenous. As a simple example, we are asked why Jews are not farmers (1996: 25). The answer is that, historically, they have been persecuted and required to flee so that it made more sense for them to have accumulated human capital in the form of personal, mobile capital such as business and other skills.[14] But this solution then raises the question of why they chose to be Jews in the first place, and so defines the next exogenous factor that needs to be made endogenous.

Becker treats more thoroughly the assumption that different socioeconomic groups can have different preferences. For example, he says that the incidence of addiction is dependent upon the value of the individual's discount rate, the premium that is given to present over future consumption. As drugs are presumed to give pleasure in the present and pain in the future, a higher discount rate is more likely to induce addictive behaviour. But why should some individuals have different discount rates than others? This difference is explained as a consequence of optimisation, within the framework of the extended utility function. Thus, the young, for example, appear to have high rates of discount because their lives are in part a voyage of discovery, the building up of personal and social capital in which learning about what gives pleasure has high returns in the early years of life.[15] Thus there is a building up of what is termed 'imagination' capital: 'People change the weight they attach to future utilities by spending more time, effort, and goods in creating personal capital that helps them to better imagine the future' (1996: 10–11).

14. Although, in this context, the question is not raised of why they are persecuted.

15. A more sophisticated account, one referred to by Becker, is offered by Rogers. His conclusions about the evolution of the rate of time preference occasionally rest on curious grounds, such as, at the close of the text, 'the fact that offspring are imperfect genetic replicas of their parents' (Rogers 1994: 478).

This differential building up of personal and social capital would, however, appear to be unable to explain the different life experiences and choices of those who are otherwise more or less identical in every relevant respect. Why do some become criminals and others become members of a religious community? For Becker, this can only be explained by random circumstances. For him, small differences in (mis)fortune can lead to radically divergent optimisation strategies. As will be seen, this is most apparent in the differences in outcomes between men and women, with biological differences sufficing as the basis on which gendered outcomes cumulatively diverge.

With the extension of the scope of the economic approach, the boundary between the exogenous and the endogenous is shifted in favour of the latter. The tension between the exogenous and endogenous is common and long-standing within economics, as in the co-existence of partial and general equilibrium analysis (looking at one and all markets, respectively). Traditionally, that co-existence has been associated with taking the social or non-economic as exogenous, in order to be able to focus on supply and demand as simple artefacts of the market. Similarly, the explanation of the non-economic, which includes the genesis of fixed tastes and the initial endowments of resources, is left to other disciplines, such as psychology and history.

With the extension of the economic approach, such hand-waving deference to other social sciences is no longer permissible. Nonetheless, that extension still leaves unresolved, other than through biological determinism, the question of how the exogenous is determined. The answer is inevitably left to history and the distant past. Never mind where these initial conditions originated, they are the here and now from which analysis must proceed. In itself, this is unobjectionable. However, when it is wedded to the methodological individualism of the economic approach, fundamental methodological issues are sidestepped, even though they have long been of central concern to social science.

In particular, how do we know what are the initial conditions until we have a social science with which to address them? How can we define them other than as social and not as a temporary moment in an aggregate set of individual optimising strategies for extended utility? It can not be emphasised too strongly that methodological individualism is incapable of addressing the social except through infinite regress, either to biological determinism or to some historical moment. For this reason, the social sciences beyond economics have not assumed the validity of methodological individualism, but have debated the nature of the social and social theory and their relationship to the individual. Further, such debate has also been forced to range over most other methodological issues, such as the nature and role of empirical evidence. Only by a combination of arrogance, contempt, ignorance and plunder has the revolution in economic theory been able to proceed, so often oblivious of the intellectual traditions and results that have preceded it.[16]

From Colonist to Colonised

For the virtualism constructed by Becker to gain any influence other than amongst fellow economists playing at social science, it must in some form be received by and prove acceptable to those in other disciplines. This is an appropriate point at which to shift perspectives and address how other social sciences are receiving the assault from economics. Limitations of space and expertise preclude much more than the posing of a few generalities, made difficult by the fact that the reception and extent of penetration of the economic approach is highly uneven across the social sciences and across the topics that lie within them or straddle their boundaries. The revolution is moving forward at different paces and in different forms.

The economics expansion does not always confront a hostile reception, as the economic approach may have emerged spontaneously from within other disciplines, without external stimulus. This is, for example, notable in the case of the political theory of collective action associated with Mancur Olson, whose marriage with neo-classical economics gives rise to the new political economy based on a calculus of economic and political interests. Similarly, the Sraffian version of political economy has readily promoted rational choice or analytical Marxism, especially in the context of theories of justice and their focus on individualistically-inclined moral principles.

If the full implications and analytical content of the economic approach as outlined in previous sections were understood, it would be rejected out of hand by most other social scientists, both because of general methodological weaknesses (not least the effective denial of the social itself) and because of the lack of acceptability of specific assumptions in any specific application. Consequently, the colonisation of other social sciences by economics does not proceed through the critical study and absorption of economics' formal mathematical models and

16. Ingham (1996: 262) offers a similar, but more general, assessment: 'It is difficult not to share this irritation when confronted, for example, with ... "agency theory" which quite simply tries to reduce the complexity of social and economic organisation to the individual propensities of the amoral maximiser ... The issue is not merely that this form of theorising can easily be made the subject of cogent theoretical and empirical critiques ... but that the authors were so structurally insulated by the social organisation of intellectual specialisation that they were able to disregard the huge non-economic literature on the very problems that they had posed for themselves.' Note that Ingham suggests that colonisation by economics will meet considerable resistance. This is, in part, the consequence of his confining his attention to the new institutional economics and, in part, the consequence of his treating as problematic and contentious the analytical compromises that will need to be, and are being, made.

their statistical counterparts. Rather, the process is much more insidious, with the concepts that have been deployed in the economic approach becoming absorbed, amalgamated and utilised in non-economic applications with little or no regard for their underlying weaknesses. This is so much so that even critical commentary on the concepts often leads only to their modification, not their rejection.

The new household economics, for example, is now fairly widely deployed across the social sciences even by those who would declare themselves violently opposed to its methodological individualism (see, for example, the debate between Fine 1995 and Kotz 1994, 1995). Further, the neo-classical framework tends to set the terms of debate and progress, with the basic model modified by considerations of patriarchy, power, and intra-household conflict over distribution, none of which necessarily challenges the underlying analytical framework or even addresses the extent to which the concepts ultimately rest on biological determinism.

The terrain upon which the revolution has made most progress, however, is almost certainly that defined by the application of the concept of human capital, not least because it is relatively old. Becker himself (1996: 145) provides a telling summary of the difficulties that had to be confronted and overcome:

> Human capital is so uncontroversial nowadays that it may be difficult to appreciate the hostility in the 1950s and 1960s towards the approach that went with that term. The very concept of *human capital* was alleged to be demeaning because it treated peoples as machines. To approach schooling as an investment rather than a cultural experience was considered unfeeling and extremely narrow. As a result, I hesitated a long time before deciding to call my book *Human Capital* . . . and hedged the risk by using a title that I no longer remember.

Once again, use of the term has become widespread across an enormous range of applications with little or no attention to the validity and implications of the concept and its analytical origins. This is despite the very contradiction within the two words through which the concept is itself constituted, which goes far beyond the tension, noted by Becker, caused by treating people as analytically synonymous with machines (ultimately for generating extended utility). Often, the notion of human capital is transplanted into an entirely inconsistent analytical context in order to be able to take account of differences in educational or other attainment, for example, even though the primary concern is with social groups or interactions understood without reference to individualism.

One reason for the ready acceptance of concepts such as human capital is the lack of close attention to, possibly even the intimidation by, the formal mathematical models and statistical techniques that are the counterpart in modern mainstream economics of its continuing conceptual weaknesses. Axiomatic formalism and the running of regressions on data accepted naively serve to cover a multitude of analytical sins. The result is also to confer a false respectability on the concepts deployed – what mainstream economists are wont to dub 'rigour'. Consequently, the concepts or results of the economic approach enter other social sciences with a false reputation for having been endowed with analytical respectability from within economics.

The economic concepts are, however, necessarily transformed in the process of absorption into other disciplines, often to be endowed with a rigour of a different type, so that they can sit more comfortably within their new home. Such a process does require fluidity, if not eclecticism, among those who adopt those concepts. In short, it is not enough to say that economics takes on a revolutionary, colonising role relative to the other social sciences. That colonisation has been able to proceed because the analytical environment in the other social sciences is too weak to resist economic encroachment or, more likely, is sufficiently flexible to be able to accommodate it. Such an environment certainly has been provided by post-modernism. Paradoxically, the analytical climate becomes even more favourable to a colonising economics as the influence of postmodernism comes to be replaced by a wish to return to a more soundly-based realism, one in which there is more of a material and, by implication, economic content. In short, those who flee from postmodernism run the risk of being driven into the analytical embrace of a poorly-understood, even if distorted, neo-classical economics. Becker's extreme, abstracted vision can prosper in such an environment, as its apparently hard-headed realism and rigour are paraded within unfamiliar surroundings, the study of the household, fertility, addiction and the like.

Shifting Theory and Ideology

It is presumably no accident that the ideological environment in which the revolution from economics has been taking place is one that signifies the triumph of the market. With the collapse of communist regimes, the rise of neo-liberalism and the Washington consensus, globalisation, Thatcherism and so forth, the free market has been constructed as the abstraction, virtual reality and virtualism of the recent period. If free-market economics should prevail in the market-place, why should it not be extended to the theory of other areas of social activity? And from here it is easy for the virtual reality of such theories to become the virtualism of policy, a transformation that follows from treating a theoretical assumption that society can be treated as equivalent to a market as justification for the proposition that as much social activity as possible should be governed by the market or pseudo-markets. The apparent triumph of the market has induced analysis as if society were market-like, even amongst those who oppose the market, and paved the way for this transformation.

Not surprisingly, this gives rise to profound consequences for the political and ideological, as well as for the academic, climate. This is because the rational choice approach, especially in the hands of those such as Becker, tends to be profoundly reactionary in two ways. The first is that methodological individualism and a universal and fixed underlying extended utility function almost inevitably lead to the conclusion that the rational is the desirable and efficient choice, other than in the case of (extended) market failure. This is, however, no longer economic *laissez-faire* writ small, but economic imperialism, as the scope of application is extended almost infinitely. The second way, particularly pronounced in Becker's work, is the concern to be parsimonious, to resist the incorporation of any explanatory concepts that do not accord with the basic neo-classical model and its associated focus on optimising individuals.

It is worth running over the consequences of such analytical predilections in Becker's own work. In many instances, a sentence or two is all he needs to pass judgement on issues that have commanded considerably greater, if less narrowly focused, effort and attention from others. Thus, for instance, he explains why communism can not succeed:

> The evidence on communism provides an obvious counter-example to the claims about the tyranny of culture over behavior . . . every communist regime, regardless of culture, failed to achieve any lasting reorientation. Since pay was not sensitive to how hard people worked, they invariably chose to work little, no matter what the culture. And since such behavior became habitual, many persons in the former communist nations have not yet acquired good work habits (1996: 17).

Further, he applies such simplistic nostrums as readily to what he sees as work-shy and irresponsible minorities in capitalist countries as he does to a considerable proportion of the world's (formerly) communist populations: 'Government entitlement programs and other government policies sometimes have sizable effects on preferences. Welfare discourages the independence and self-reliance of recipients, while social security weakens the ties that bind together older parents and their children' (1996: 19).[17]

His treatment of discrimination is equally simplistic. He says (1996: 141) that racial or other discrimination in the market-place depends upon the combined effect

17. Indeed: 'Many persons appear to recognize that participating in public programs may greatly change their preferences. A sizable fraction of those eligible for welfare and other transfer programs do not enroll . . . perhaps because they anticipate that receiving these benefits would actually lower their utility through the development of dependency and other bad habits' (1996: 21). Note here the telling stripping of any volition from the individual, despite the extreme heights of rational choice in other contexts: even though we are able to recognise that reliance upon welfare is a form of temporary dependence, we are unable to prevent ourselves from becoming addicted to it!

arising from 'employers, workers, consumers, schools, and governments'. The incidence of discrimination across these agents is either magnified or eroded according to the relative weights of the majorities and minorities. Ultimately, then, in view of their consumer sovereignty in choosing work mates and lower cost over prejudice in what they buy, '[o]f greater significance empirically is the long-run discrimination by employees and customers, who are far more important sources of market discrimination than employers' (1996: 142). This approach allows him to explain easily the democratic transition in South Africa: 'Blacks are some five times as numerous as whites. Discrimination against blacks has also significantly hurt whites, although some white groups have benefited . . . Its sizable cost to whites suggests why Apartheid and other blatant forms of Afrikaner discrimination eventually broke down' (1996: 142).

Turning to crime and criminal justice, Becker says that the economics of crime involves balancing the costs and benefits to the criminal (who is not deviant, merely optimising) against those of the state and those it seeks to protect. It follows that a cut in expenditures on catching criminals could be offset by a sufficient rise in the punishment of those convicted. Given the uncertainties involved, the judicial system should punish according to level of probability of guilt, suitably weighted by the deterrent effect on others as measured by net social benefit, rather than relying on the principle of innocent until proven guilty. Or: 'The State should also consider the likelihood of punishing innocent persons' (1996: 144).[18]

Finally, turning to gender, Becker uses the new household economics to explain very large differences in the material outcomes for men and women by the slightest biological differences:

The economic approach to the gender division of labor . . . does not try to weight the relative importance of biology and discrimination. Its main contribution is to show how sensitive the division of labor is to *small* differences in either. Since the return from investing in a skill is greater when more time is spent utilizing the skill, a married couple could gain much from a sharp division of labor because the husband would specialize in some types of human capital and the wife in others. Given such a large gain from specialization within a marriage, only a *little* discrimination against women or *small* biological differences in child-rearing skills would cause the division of labor between

---

18. For a more sophisticated analysis, see Polinsky and Shavell (1984), who treat fines and imprisonment as alternative ways of screening the population and providing for an efficient outcome. Note that there is a parallel between this sort of analysis and that of unemployment and the use of income benefits and work requirements as sorting devices to maintain a given level of income for all. To achieve the latter at the lowest cost, it may be necessary to provide income support to some that raises them above the minimum (otherwise they will prefer to pretend to be unemployable). See Besley and Coate (1995) and Fine (1998: Chap. 4) for a discussion.

household and market tasks to be strongly and systematically related to gender (1996: 151).[19]

Just as the sorts of equilibrium solutions offered by Becker provide an organising principle by which the economy can be understood by way of deviation from his restrictive assumptions, so less extreme stances can be adopted on the broader political issues just covered. As Akerlof puts it: 'The economic model . . . always gives you a null hypothesis . . . some kind of base, and then you can figure out how all kinds of deviations would modify that' (in Swedberg 1990: 70). However, unlike those innocents who might be justifiably punished by the state for the common good, the free market as null hypothesis is innocent (perfect) until proven guilty (or imperfect).

More generally, the decline of Keynesian welfare models with the end of the post-war boom provided fertile ground for the revival of *laissez-faire* ideology. Recently, however, there has been a discernible shift in the balance of debate over the relative merits of the state and the market back towards a more positive attitude towards the state. The result, however, is not a simple shift back towards the models of the post-war boom. Rather, the new Keynesianism, as is made clear by Akerlof, is based on the market imperfections that arise out of the optimising behaviour of individuals. It is the perfection of, not a break with, methodological individualism (see Fine 1998: Chap. 2).[20] Becker's virtualism need not imply a virtual reality in which the market always works best, especially when deployed by those who are more inclined to acknowledge the pervasive presence of market imperfections, even if suitably tempered by government imperfections. Nonetheless, any such newly-constructed virtualism construes the market and the non-market realms as equally individualistic in content. The state ceases to be the source of social provision on a non-individualistic basis in anything other than name, and becomes an alternative, possibly more equitable and efficient, form of private provision. Indeed, quite apart from the commercialisation of state activities itself, even the language of social provision has come to parody that of the private sector: so, for example, those to be housed and healed become clients and customers.

19. I could go on. Becker treats advertising as a positive complement to consumer goods; he treats the notion of social norms, such as church-going, as a way in which the wealthy minority can bribe the poorer majority to accumulate conciliatory social capital; in the context of personal capital alone (i.e. no demonstration effects in preference formation), he thinks that legalising drugs will make them cheaper and hence more used.

20. Heilbroner and Milberg (1995: 87) note: 'From this viewpoint, "micro" and "macro" merge, in that microbehaviour cannot be understood without taking cognizance of its social origins, and social forces remain empty abstractions unless they enter into the motivational concreteness of one or more individuals.'

Nor are such concerns confined to theory for the advanced capitalist economies (see the application of the notion of social capital to the developing world in Evans 1996). Equally, there is a shift in development thinking as the market versus state agenda of the World Bank and of the IMF, with their heavy bias in favour of the market, is giving way under a number of pressures. As Wade (1996) has observed, the rise of Japan as a source of international aid and of foreign investment, with its own specific economic interests and experiences, is increasingly undermining the dogmatic verities of the Washington consensus, not least because of the extent of the policy failures attached to structural adjustment and stabilisation and the growing weight of academic studies demonstrating these failures (see Fine and Stoneman 1996; and Fine 1997d). If a new period of interventionism is in prospect, its practical, academic and ideological contours have yet to be fully settled. It would be tragic if economics' colonisation of the social sciences leads to a pale revisitation of the Keynesian welfare model that preceded the rise of monetarism and the market. The alternative is for social science genuinely to embrace political economy in a way that allows the category of capital to be fully and properly understood, not least in its relationship to class, state and social relations more generally.

In summary, a close analysis of the work of Becker reveals that the abstractions, virtualism and virtual realities peddled by mainstream economics are absurd. The logical thrust is that anything incompatible with a particular version of methodological individualism is filtered out as non-existent. We are offered a sort of alchemy in which, even with social concepts and realities as our raw materials, our gold is the goal of explanation of and by individual behaviour, and our concoctions are guaranteed success. Nonetheless, the very formalism, generality and simplicity (nay, crudity) of the analysis opens up the logical possibility of the extension of this economic to the non-economic world. In the process of its colonisation of social theory and ideology, economics has served as a Trojan horse, with its analytical core concealed and tempered by the contexts and traditions within it has been received. In the current climate of retreat from both postmodernism and neoliberalism, the economic approach is highly seductive because of its capacity to broach the social and to point to market imperfections even if on the basis of methodological individualism. But social science should beware of economists bearing analytical gifts.

Acknowledgement

My thanks to James G. Carrier for comments on an earlier draft.

References

Agbodza, Christian and Ben Fine 1996. The Genealogy of Human Capital Theory: One Step Forward, Two Steps Back. MS.

Becker, Gary S. 1996. *Accounting for Tastes*. Cambridge, Mass.: Harvard University Press.

Besley, Timothy, and Stephen Coate 1995. The Design of Income Maintenance Programmes. *Review of Economic Studies* 62: 187–221.

Ehrlich, Isaac, and Hiroyuki Chuma 1987. The Demand for Life: Theory and Application. In Gerard Radnitzky and Peter Bernholz (eds), *Economic Imperialism: The Economic Method Applied Outside the Field of Economics*, pp. 243–270. New York: Paragon House Publishers.

Evans, Peter 1996. Introduction: Development Strategies across the Public–Private Divide. *World Development* 24: 1033–1037.

Fine, Ben 1992. *Women's Employment and the Capitalist Family*. London: Routledge.

—— 1995. Reconsidering 'Household Labor, Wage Labor, and the Transformation of the Family'. *Review of Radical Economics* 27(2): 106–116.

—— 1997a. The New Revolution in Economics. *Capital & Class* 61 (Spring): 143–148.

—— 1997b. Playing the Consumption Game. *Consumption, Markets, Culture* 1: 7–29.

—— 1997c. Entitlement Failure? *Development and Change* 28(4): 617–647.

—— 1997d. Apologists and Academia: A Critical Review of 'Bureaucrats in Business'. MS.

—— 1998. *Labour Market Theory: A Constructive Reassessment*. London: Routledge. (Forthcoming.)

Fine, Ben, and Ellen Leopold 1993. *The World of Consumption*. London: Routledge.

Fine, Ben, and Colin Stoneman 1996. Introduction: State and Development. *Journal of Southern African Studies* 22: 5–26.

Fine, Ben, Michael Heasman and Judith Wright 1996. *Consumption in the Age of Affluence: The World of Food*. London: Routledge.

Gray, John 1987. The Economic Approach to Human Behavior: Its Prospects and Limitations. In Gerard Radnitzky and Peter Bernholz (eds), *Economic Imperialism: The Economic Method Applied Outside the Field of Economics*, pp. 35–50. New York: Paragon House Publishers.

Heilbroner, Robert, and William Milberg 1995. *The Crisis of Vision in Modern Economic Thought*. Cambridge: Cambridge University Press.

Hirshleifer, Jack 1987. The Economic Approach to Conflict. In Gerard Radnitzky and Peter Bernholz (eds), *Economic Imperialism: The Economic Method*

Applied Outside the Field of Economics, pp. 335–364. New York: Paragon House Publishers.

Ingham, Geoffrey 1996. Some Recent Changes in the Relationship between Economics and Sociology. *Cambridge Journal of Economics* 20: 243–275.

Kotz, David 1994. Household Labor, Wage Labor, and the Transformation of the Family. *Review of Radical Political Economics* 26(2): 24–56.

—— 1995. Analyzing the Transformation of the Family. *Review of Radical Economics* 27(2): 116–123.

Polinsky, A. Mitchell, and Steven Shavell 1984. The Optimal Use of Fines and Imprisonment. *Journal of Public Economics* 24: 89–99.

Rogers, Alan 1994. Evolution of Time Preference by Natural Selection. *American Economic Review* 84: 460–481.

Sen, Amartya 1977. Rational Fools: A Critique of the Behavioral Foundations of Economic Theory. *Philosophy and Public Affairs* 6: 317–344.

Swedberg, Richard 1990. *Economics and Sociology, Redefining Their Boundaries: Conversations with Economists and Sociologists*. Princeton, NJ: Princeton University Press.

Wade, Robert 1996. Japan, the World Bank, and the Art of Paradigm Maintenance: *The East Asian Miracle* in Political Perspective. *New Left Review* 217: 3–36.

Xenos, Nicholas 1989. *Scarcity and Modernity*. London: Routledge.

−3−

Abstraction, Reality and the Gender
of 'Economic Man'

Julie A. Nelson

The abstract concept of 'economic man', that is, the idea of the individual human being as a rational, self-interested maximiser of utility, is at the base of all neo-classical economic theorising, which in turn influences the formation of numerous government and business-sector policies. The strength of this abstraction within the economics discipline can be seen as an outstanding illustration of the power of particular abstractions to create virtual realities within which scholars function.

More open to debate is the question of to what extent such a virtual reality can become a virtualism, to what extent can people bring the world into conformity with it. Both empirical work and social-science and feminist theorising suggest that such virtualism may not be an automatic, or even a possible, next step. An inquiry into the assumption of social and natural disembeddedness personified in 'economic man', from a perspective informed by both empirical study and feminist theory, reveals both the truly mythological nature of this image and the underlying emotional rationale for its appeal. The realities of human life must, at least to some degree, limit the extent to which this virtual reality can become a virtualism.

An examination of the gender-based and emotional appeal of the tendency to rely on such abstractions, however, has important implications for the explanation of the social power of contemporary neo-classical economics, and for formulating ways of escaping some of its less benign consequences.

The Historical Roots of Economic Man

It was John Stuart Mill who first argued that political economy should adopt 'an arbitrary definition of man, as a being who inevitably does that by which he may obtain the greatest amount of necessaries, conveniences, and luxuries, with the smallest quantity of labour and physical self-denial with which they can be obtained in the existing state of knowledge' (quoted in Oakley 1994: 155), or 'who desires to possess wealth, and who is capable of judging the comparative efficacy of means for obtaining that end' (quoted in Persky 1995: 223). A more modern understanding of economic man, the agent of the prototypical economic model, retains the assumptions of self-interest and rationality, but replaces the notion of maximisation of wealth with the notion of maximisation of utility.

Economic man has been a frequent target of criticism, from both inside and outside the economics profession, for the lack of realism implied by his rather one-dimensional psychology (for example, Leibenstein 1976; Meeks 1991). Implicit in the assumptions underlying economic man are the dualisms of self-interest vs. other interest, rationality vs. emotion and separation from others vs. connection to others, with economic man unabashedly taking from only the first term of each pair. Sometimes the critics of economic man focus on the aspect of selfishness, in the light of their observation of types of human behaviour that do not appear to be self-interested. At other times, they review the assumption that economic man knows what is best for himself and pursues this logically, in the face of contrary evidence about human cognition from the disciplines of psychology and philosophy. Such critiques are fairly well known (Lewin 1996).

Yet other critics focus on economic man's social isolation: 'What remained missing in . . . economic man, was any recognition that "human thought, feeling, and action" are all profoundly functions of intersubjective relations with others' (Oakley 1994: 178). On this last point, consider that in this conception of human nature individuals are radically separate from others and from nature; the emphasis is on separation, distance, demarcation, autonomy, independence of self. As Hobbes put it: 'Let us consider men . . . as if but even now sprung out of the earth, and suddenly, like mushrooms, come to full maturity, without all kind of engagement to each other' (quoted in Benhabib 1987: 161). Sometimes critics express their reservations about this isolation by drawing a sharp dualism between economic actors and commodity exchange on the one hand, and on the other social actors and gift exchange (for example, Carruthers and Espeland 1997; problematised by Carrier 1995).

So far, however, attempts to include broader aspects of human behaviour such as cooperation within economic analysis tend to expand upon, rather than replace, the same core assumptions, as Ben Fine makes clear in his chapter in this volume. The modelling of cooperation as a game-theoretical outcome based on a model of rational, self-interested agents, for example, or as an evolutionary, socio-biological outcome of self-interested genes, is an up-and-coming field (Ben-Ner and Putterman 1996).

Economic Man's Role in Epistemology and Methodology

It would be a mistake, however, to evaluate the model of economic man solely on the basis of its actual content. The idea that human actors could be characterised by such a parsimonious psychology and an absence of social and natural ties also played a major role in the methodological development of both classical and neo-classical economics. While it is apparent that Mill recognised a much richer actual human nature, it was methodological principles that caused Mill to argue for the use of this abstraction. The method of science, Mill believed, was axiomatic-deductive. Therefore, the science of political economy must start with simplified 'laws of human nature' and from there deduce the laws of social functioning related to the production of wealth (Oakley 1994: 150–151).

A neo-classical economist will, then, tend to reply to criticism of the substantive assumptions contained in the idea of economic man with the argument that the idea is not meant to be realistic, and so criticisms of his adequacy as a model of human selfhood are beside the point. Such an argument has been recently advanced, for example, by economist Joseph Persky (1995: 230), who claims that any suggested alternative set of assumptions 'must be parsimonious', including only a 'manageable' set of human motivations, lest the ability of the model to yield 'tightly reasoned generalizations' be lost. Whether economic man is right or wrong, he is necessary for 'science'.

The assumptions of economic man and the form the analysis takes have been closely linked in economics ever since the adoption into economics of concepts from eighteenth-century physics (Mirowski 1988). W. Stanley Jevons described economics, by 1924, as the study of 'the mechanics of utility and self-interest' (quoted in Georgescu-Roegen 1971: 40). When economics is assumed to be centred around mathematical models of individual choice, assumptions about the behaviour of humans take on the status of axioms (Becker 1976), while nature becomes a mathematical 'commodity space' (Debreu 1991). The study of actual markets tends to give way to the study of ideal, abstract markets or hypothetical games. In fact, the less research has to do with actual economies, the higher the status within the discipline.

Moreover, the assumptions of rationality envisioned as calculation, and of humans as detached from outside influences, are not only assumptions about the objects of economic study, but are also assumptions about the nature of the economist as knower. The model of the knower as the detached calculator is deeply rooted in Cartesian philosophy and is reflected in economists' affinity to theorem, proof and closed, elegant systems. Purely abstract models are commonly referred to as being 'highbrow', 'capital "T"' or 'pure' economic theory, while models that bring in some institutional detail are only 'middlebrow', 'small "t"' or 'merely applied' economic theory. Attempts to explain phenomena that do not include a mathematical model of individual choice are not seen as economic theory at all. The 'acid test' of articles in economic theory, said Nobel laureate Gerard Debreu in his 1990 presidential address to the American Economic Association, comes in 'removing all their economic interpretations and letting their mathematical infrastructure stand on its own' (Debreu 1991: 3). Thus the Cartesian voice echoes down through the centuries.

Actual economies hence tend to be of less concern to academic economists than are the theoretical axioms and the process of deduction; allowing one's research to be influenced by anything other than logical progression may be considered, in fact, a sign of undesirable impurity. The questions of application are left to the politician, entrepreneur or bureaucrat. Some may argue that this detachment from practical concerns, combined with the use of methods that guarantee objectivity, makes science value-free. Such a science is considered, then, to be above the realm of purely humanistic concerns. The only moral imperative it recognises is that of correctly following the implications of logic. From a larger perspective, it is clear, however, that such a view of science is implicitly built on another very important ethical judgement, the valuation of detachment over connection. The contradictory nature of this position is revealed in its attachment of great value to detachment; in its passion for dispassionate analysis.

Virtualism and Economic Man

Many economists (most notably economic theorists, but since they are at the core of graduate economics education, most of the profession) are, quite clearly to any informed observers, obviously living in their own academic virtual reality. D. McCloskey (1991: 11, 14–15) has noted how economic theorists (of any formal sort, not just the highly mathematical) draw conclusions only about toy economies on blackboards.

> [Economists] have retreated from the library and laboratory to the blackboard. The research in many fields of economics does not cumulate. It circles . . . [The emphasis on formalization] has resulted in graduate students who believe . . . that economics is about certain mathematical objects called 'economies'. The students have no incentive to learn about the economy.

When Arjo Klamer and David Colander asked graduate students whether having a thorough knowledge of the economy was very important for academic success in economics, only 3.4 per cent said it was (McCloskey 1991: 15). McCloskey argues that economics needs more empirical, quantitative study as opposed to abstract proofs. In an interesting study of economic rhetoric, linguists Meriel and Thomas Bloor (1993: 164) concluded that 'economists do not find [substantive] claims to be central to the game they are playing'. It was claims about models and methodology, not about actual economies, that were carefully hedged in the published articles that the Bloors analysed, and therefore marked as of central concern.

But the degree to which neo-classical models of the world, including the axioms regarding economic man, could displace the real world must be studied carefully. While it has institutional power, not least through economists' intimidation of other social scientists and policy-makers through the use of marginally-intelligible mathematics, the neo-classical world-view is one that must be disputed, for it is not a foregone conclusion that neo-classical virtualism will succeed in re-shaping the world. As James G. Carrier points out in the Introduction to this volume, people tend to 'socialise and complicate their economic relationships when they can'.

The extent to which studying the model of self-interested agents interacting in anonymous markets might actually lead, empirically, to more self-interested, socially detached, behaviour has been a topic of recent debate among economists. Reviewing Margaret Radin's book *Contested Commodities* (1996), in which she argues that the hegemony of market rhetoric may have real and negative consequences for personal integrity, economic theorist and Nobel laureate Kenneth Arrow (1997: 762), asserts that '[t]he effect of discourse on action is first of all an empirical question'. 'It is hard to believe that standard modes of expression and discourse do not have some influence on thought and action', he writes, '[b]ut the extent of the influence is certainly hard to determine'. Note here how a noted theorist is on McCloskey's side in calling for empirical evidence and quantitative measures. An abstract assertion about abstraction will not suffice! The mere existence of a logical argument as to how such effects could exist is not proof that they actually do exist, much less that they are large.

Writing in the *Journal of Economic Perspectives*, Robert Frank, Thomas Gilovich and Dennis T. Regan (1993) follow up the logical argument that learning that people are motivated by self-interest would lead to more self-interested behaviour with a survey of and a contribution to empirical literature on the subject. They cite results of experimental and survey research consistent with the hypothesis that those who have studied economics are less likely to act cooperatively in at least some situations than those who have not, and that this lessened cooperation may be due in part to the training itself. For example, one of the studies they describe surveyed university students in introductory economics and astronomy courses, once at the beginning and once at the end of the semester. Students were asked whether they would return a lost envelope containing $100 to its owner. Those in the economics class tended to increase in dishonesty over the course of the semester, compared to the students in the astronomy class. However, in a subsequent study, Anthony Yezer, Robert Goldfarb and Paul Poppen (1996) disputed the idea that such survey evidence translates into real-world behaviour. They found, in a small 'lost letter' experiment, that the economics students were actually considerably more honest. Robert Frank, Thomas Gilovich and Dennis T. Regan (1996: 191) reply that their claim was 'not that economics training transforms people into serial killers, but that it makes them marginally less likely to cooperate in social dilemmas', and that the evidence supports their view:

> In our survey of faculty members in different disciplines, for example, we found that economists were as likely as others to say they voted in presidential elections; and that, although they reported giving less to charity than others with similar incomes, the shortfall was less than 10 percent; and that, although they were more than twice as likely as members of any other group to report giving no money at all to private charity, fewer than 10 percent of economists fell in this category.

They say that while the differences between economists and others are small, even a small reduction in cooperation should be a matter of concern.

Further evidence undermining the (abstract, logical) argument that learning about the world in terms of market rhetoric will necessarily lead to the commoditisation of social life comes from sociological evidence about people's actual economic behaviour. Viviana Zelizer, in *The Social Meaning of Money* (1995), turns the frequent sociological argument that money is an objectifier and commoditiser that destroys personal relationships and undermines non-pecuniary values on its head, arguing that *social life* also invades and changes money. People differentiate and particularise money, considering, for example, a tip to be different from a wage or a gift, and even create special currencies (gift certificates, coupons) in order to imbue money with the appropriate social meanings. Similarly, Eric Helleiner (1997) writes about the role of national currencies in creating national identities. He gives evidence that, in contrast to economic-man assumptions, people tend to imbue even this prototypical economic substance, money, with personal meaning. These examples do not deny that a commoditising discourse can have effects that are detrimental socially, but they do indicate that personal integrity and social life may be somewhat resilient, and that the road from market and money to personal meaning and social interaction runs both ways.[1]

Yet a stronger point can be made. While changes in human behaviour at the margin, due to cultural understandings of human nature, are certainly possible and even likely, economic man is not, and can never be, a good description of actual human behaviour on a large scale. The reason for this is that implicit in the envisioning of selves as autonomous, rational and independent lie important assumptions about the existence of *other* selves who, while denigrated and ignored, are assumed to embody the opposite of these characteristics. This brings us to the question of the *gendered* nature of the assumptions about rationality and detachment regarding the object of study and in the theory of the knower.

---

1. Thomas Carlyle argued for this resiliency in 1847: 'Never, on this Earth, was the relation of man to man long carried on by Cash-Payment alone. If, at any time, a philosophy of Laissez-faire, Competition and Supply-and-demand, start up as the exponent of human relations, expect that it will end soon' (quoted in Arrow 1997: 757).

Gender Links

Hobbes's ideas about 'mushroom men' to the contrary, humans do not simply spring out of the earth. Humans are born of women, nurtured and cared for as children, socialised into family and community groups and perpetually dependent on nourishment and shelter. The neglect of these aspects of human life is often justified in philosophical and other scholarly work by the argument that they are unimportant or intellectually uninteresting or merely 'natural'. It is not just coincidence that they are also the areas of life thought of as 'women's work'. If we grant that connection to one another and to nature is indispensable for human existence, then *homo oeconomicus* appears in a new light. Far from being the rugged individualist whose status as a modelling tool is dictated by rationality and realism, he might well be the projection or dream of a boy who, scared of the powers that might fail to protect his fragile hold on life, denies to himself his own dependence. 'Economic man' in pure form can exist only in the mind of the economist, who feels compelled to believe in him.

Feminist scholars like Susan Bordo (1986) consider acceptance of the Cartesian model of objectivity, based on dispassion and detachment, to be an outgrowth of anxiety created by the loss of the medieval feeling of connection to nature. If science has been considered masculine, one may wonder where the feminine fits into the picture. The counterpoint to rational, detached 'man' is

> woman [who] provides his connection with nature; she is the mediating force between man and nature, a reminder of his childhood, a reminder of the body, and a reminder of sexuality, passion, and human connectedness. She is the repository of emotional life and of all the nonrational elements of human experience (Fee 1983: 12).

In the Cartesian view, the abstract, general, separated, detached, emotionless, 'masculine' approach taken to represent scientific thinking is radically removed from, and clearly seen as superior to, the concrete, particular, connected, embodied, passionate, 'feminine' reality of material life.[2] Such associations were sometimes explicit in the language used by the early scientists to define their endeavour. Henry Oldenburg, an early Secretary of the Royal Society, stated that the intent of the Society was to 'raise a masculine Philosophy . . . whereby the Mind of Man may be ennobled with the knowledge of Solid Truths' (E. Keller 1985: 52).

Feminist scholarship has highlighted the gendered nature of the dualism of separation and connection. The relation of gender to the privileging of separation and independence over connection and dependence (or interdependence) has also

---

2. The historical and contemporary links between thinking about science and thinking about gender have been further explored by writers like Sandra Harding (1986) and Evelyn Fox Keller (1985).

been traced through psychological development, through personal ethical development and through myth and religion. The work that attracted the most popular attention was Carol Gilligan's (1982) *In a Different Voice: Psychological Theory and Women's Development*. Gilligan, in turn, related differences in orientation to separation and connection to the formation of gender identity early in life, drawing on the influential work of Nancy Chodorow (1978: 169), who argued: 'Boys come to define themselves as more separate and distinct, with a greater sense of rigid ego boundaries and differentiation. The basic feminine sense of self is connected to the world, the basic masculine sense of self is separate.'

While these views have been influential in subsequent feminist scholarship, the assertion of a sex link has been questioned by other feminist scholars. Some have suggested, for example, that it is not so much distinction between boys and girls as distinction between privileged and less-privileged groups (defined by race or class as well as sex), that forces some groups into the lesser-valued, identification-by-connection role (Harding 1987). It is more helpful, I believe, to focus on how separation and connection have been *culturally and metaphorically* linked with notions of masculinity and femininity, and with power and domination.

The projection of autonomy on to masculinity and connection to nature and society on to femininity is 'embarrassingly empirical', to borrow a phrase from Catherine Keller (1986: 201). Abstract philosophy connects with gendered experience in everyday distinctions between who does the thinking vs. who does the dishes; who writes the journal articles vs. who writes the Christmas cards; the man who envisages 'man' as individual and autonomous vs. the woman who changes her name to 'Mrs Jones' when she marries. What could be a recognition of physical embodiment and social connectedness, as well as individuality, within each person becomes a negative complementarity. The male's transcendence of nature and society is made possible only through the subjection of the female to full-time maintenance of the social and physical connections that are, after all, indispensable for human existence (Fee 1983; C. Keller 1986).

The autonomous, rational, detached, masculine projection and the dependent, emotional, connected, feminine one are equally mythical and distorting. Men's traditional façade of autonomy has always been propped up by the background work of mothers and wives; to believe that women are passive requires turning a blind eye to the activity of women's lives. Economic man, then, is not a reasonable image of general human behaviour, but is rather a construct that is coherent only within distinctly masculine-biased world-views. A virtualism based on this model, a changing of human behaviour to make it conform to the abstraction, is fundamentally impossible because of the necessity of the suppressed opposites.

The virtualism-like relationship that has historically existed between cultural abstractions about masculinity and femininity and the actual behaviour of men and women, however, is more obvious. Until cross-cultural, historical and especially feminist studies proved the contrary, it was widely believed that, for instance, women were less intelligent, that men were more active, and that behaviour to the contrary reflected a deviation from essential 'natures'. While metaphorical associations of gender with traits and concepts may continue to be part of our thinking as a result of cognitive habits and linguistic constructs (Nelson 1996), the feminist criticism of essentialism, of the tendency to mistake socially-constructed gender patterns as sex-based natures, is a project of making the virtual reality based on these abstractions less real.

Alternatives

Simple recognition that the basic assumptions of the concept of economic man and its link to preferred methods have particularly masculine associations does not, however, suggest a unique response for scholars concerned with the quality of economic practice. One response might be to endorse these associations so that economists can go on doing as they have always done. If this is masculine economics, so be it. The only alternative to masculine economics, our usual way of thinking about gender tells us, would be emasculated, impotent economics.

Another response might be to turn the tables and seek to replace abstract, hard, objective, active, androcentric economics with detailed, soft, subjective, passive gynocentric economics. One might, for example, assume that all agents are other-interested instead of self-interested, and eschew all logical proof in favour of qualitative research. While this might be appealing to those who consider modern economics to be responsible for many of the ills in the world, such a response merely trades one set of biases for another.

A third response, particularly associated with the intellectual currents of postmodernism, might be to deconstruct the dualisms on which modern definitions of economics depend. That is, in deconstructionist theory all human projects are simply texts or discourses to which techniques of literary criticism can be applied. In this view, neither the distinction between science and non-science nor that between masculine and feminine reflects any non-linguistic reality. This approach, however, yields little guidance about how to judge the quality of economic practice.

A fourth approach is adopted here (and in Nelson 1996). It does not require endorsing one side or the other of the masculine–feminine dualism, nor does it require forgoing evaluation. The key to this approach lies in a separation of our judgements about value, about what is more or less meritorious in economic practice, from our perceptions of gender.

The notion that masculine assumptions create a good economics depends on a general cultural, metaphorical association of masculinity with superiority and femininity with inferiority; or, in other words, a mental linking of value (superior

Julie A. Nelson

vs. inferior) and gender (masculine vs. feminine) dualisms. Any reader who might question the asymmetry of this linking, perhaps preferring to think of gender differences in terms of a more benign complementarity, should ponder some of the more obvious manifestations of asymmetry in the social domain. Rough 'tomboy' girls are socially acceptable and even praised, but woe to the gentle-natured boy who is labelled a 'sissy'; a woman may wear trousers or pants, but a man may not wear a skirt. The sexist association of femininity with lesser worth implicit in such judgements, it should be noted, is not a matter of isolated personal beliefs but rather a matter of cultural and even cognitive habit.

Research on human cognition suggests that dualisms such as superior vs. inferior and masculine vs. feminine play an essential role in structuring our understanding (Lakoff and Johnson 1980; Nelson 1996: Chap. 1). Human cognition is not limited to such simple two-way associations, however. Consider the different interpretations we can make if we think of gender and value, instead of being parallel to each other, as being *orthogonal*, producing something I call a gender–value compass:

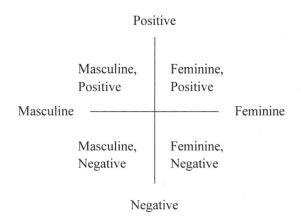

Then we can think of there being both valuable and harmful aspects to qualities culturally associated with masculinity, as well as both valuable and harmful aspects to qualities associated with femininity.

Consider, for example, the idea that a 'hard' economics is clearly preferable to a 'soft' economics. This judgment relies on an association of hardness with valuable, masculine-associated *strength*, and softness with inferior, feminine associated *weakness*. However, hardness may also mean *rigidity*, just as softness may also imply *flexibility*. A pursuit of masculine hardness that spurns all association with femininity (and hence with flexibility) can lead to rigidity, just as surely as a pursuit of feminine softness (without corresponding strength) leads to weakness:

M+	F+
strong-hard	flexible-soft
M–	F–
rigid-hard	weak-soft

There is no benefit in gendered extremism: neither rigidity nor weakness, the two extremes of hardness and softness, are desirable. There is benefit, however, in exploiting complementarity. Strength tempered with flexibility would yield a balanced and resilient economics. This is just one abstract example of how new thinking about gender could change how we think about the discipline; more concrete examples follow.

Alternatives to Economic Man

Individuality has been stressed for men, while women have been associated with connection, as:

M+	F+
individuated	connected
M–	F–
isolated	engulfed

However, the conventional idea of identity stresses gender valuations that lie along the northwest–southeast diagonal, M+ to F–. With this idea, any lack of individuality or differentiation, any move away from M+, implies a move toward F–, the dissolving or engulfing of the individual into the larger whole of nature or society. The gender connotations are masculine for the positively-valued individuality and feminine for the engulfed state. But differentiation can go too far, into radical separation or isolation. And the message of the feminist scholarship discussed above is that connection and relation do not necessarily imply the dissolving of individual identity. The positive complementarity of the upper two terms in the diagram refers to the recognition of selfhood as including both individuality and connectedness or relatedness. Or, in Alfred North Whitehead's (1925: 206) words, we are 'organisms' who require 'an environment of friends'. The boundaries between oneself and others and between oneself and nature are not strict, but neither does this imply that one is therefore swallowed up. The separation of the gender and value dimensions creates a way of seeing that individuality is not definitive of the human condition.

To take a slightly different perspective, one may note, in this context, that the relaxation of social bonds associated with the expansion of a more market-oriented, individualistic world-view can sometimes be liberating rather than flattening. The acquisition by women of the ability to act in their own interests and make their own market contracts, rather than being defined by their status relationships to their husbands or fathers, is not particularly a movement to be mourned.

The dualism of separation and connection also has important ties to cultural interpretations of the relation between reason and emotion; reason, of course, being associated with masculinity and emotion with femininity. The philosopher Martha Nussbaum has outlined how, in much of the Western philosophical tradition and in some Eastern traditions, rational judgement has been associated with an ideal of self-containment and impermeability. This is the idea of the wise person as one who is complete, invulnerable and impervious to fortune because of complete self-sufficiency. Emotions, in these traditions, are opposed to rationality, since to be affected by something not under the control of one's rational will is taken as a sign of weakness and vulnerability. Emotions are 'holes, so to speak, in the walls of the self' (Nussbaum 1993: 11). Nussbaum reinterprets emotions as playing an important part in truly rational judgement: in a world in which human life is in fact vulnerable to mortality, illness and want of all kinds, emotional acknowledgment of need is, though sometimes painful, a prerequisite for good judgement. With notions of reason being highly associated with notions of objectivity and adequacy in current scientific (and economic) study, this reinterpretation of the role of emotion is important for re-evaluating economic science.

Alternative Methodology

The association of economics with formal, logical reasoning can be addressed in the framework of the gender–value compass. In the simple, dualistic view, reason is identical with formal logic and masculinity; any exposition not explicitly conforming to the laws of logic is identified as being illogical and, by implication, inferior.

A more sophisticated idea of what it means to reason and to know, suggested in many works on metaphor and cognition, identifies reason instead with a complementarity of logic on the one hand, and on the other reasoning by other means, such as analogy or pattern recognition. For example, Howard Margolis (1982) sees cognition as a combination of 'reasoning why', or step-by-step critical analysis, with 'seeing that', which involves a no less important perception of the bigger pattern. Nicholas Georgescu-Roegen's (1971) distinction between 'arithmo-morphic' and 'dialectical' concepts is helpful in suggesting terms for the missing feminine–positive, masculine–negative diagonal in the gender–value compass. He calls 'arithmomorphic' those concepts that can be manipulated by formal logic. He argues, however, that most of our thoughts are concerned with forms and qualities and concepts that overlap with their opposites, and dealing with these requires dialectical thought. Georgescu-Roegen's (1971: 45) examples of dialectical concepts include 'good', 'justice', 'likelihood' and 'want'. Another example of the contrast between logical and dialectical thinking is given by Howard Margolis's (1987: 94) discussion of the meanings of the word 'or'. In formal logic, 'or' means 'either or both, and not neither'. But in common usage its possible meanings are various and mutually contradictory: in 'Cream or sugar?' it means 'either, both or neither'; in a judicial decision of '$100 or 10 days' it means 'either, but not neither and not both'; in a waiter's question of 'Soup or salad?' it means 'either or neither, but not both'. Yet, in context, these are all meaningful and reasonable formulations. It is hard to imagine any discussion of economic issues that would not rely heavily on such understanding of context.

The 'position that dialectical concepts should be barred from science because they would infest it with muddled thinking' Georgescu-Roegen (1971: 52) labels 'arithmomania'. Logical reasoning can deal only with the abstract; attentiveness to context and substance requires dialectical reasoning. Such a richer understanding of the nature of rationality can be summarised in a gender–value diagram as

M+ logical reasoning	F+ dialectical reasoning
M– arithmomania	F– illogic

The extensive verbal explanations economists often call 'intuition' are examples of dialectical reasoning, not merely cases of degraded or diluted logic. The identification of reasoning with logical reasoning alone ends up, in Georgescu-Roegen's (1971: 80) words, 'giving us mental cramps'. The usefulness of two-dimensional over one-dimensional thinking about gender and value comes from the exposition of relationships that are hidden by the usual linking of reason with masculine with superior and intuitive with feminine with inferior. These simple linkings can be seen to involve the too-easy collapsing of reason into logic and the false identification of other valid forms of reasoning with illogic.

The emphasis on mathematics as the key to rigorous understanding in economics, and the down-playing of language as having any importance in the business of knowledge-seeking, can be understood using the diagram:

M+	F+
precise	rich
M–	F–
thin	vague

The left side highlights aspects of mathematical language and the right side aspects of common language. The advantage of mathematics is the precision it supplies, as opposed to the vagueness or ambiguity that may be associated with words in all their diverse meanings. On the other hand, pure mathematics is precisely content-free; the application of mathematics to the usually rather messy and complex problems of human behaviour can come only through treating mathematical formulae as metaphors for some real phenomenon, a process that involves the use of words. In the process, meanings beyond those immediately present in the mathematical metaphor will also be suggested. Mathematics can certainly be helpful in overcoming the failings of imprecise words; but if attention is concentrated on maintaining the gender boundary rather than on recognising the value boundary, the inadequacies of thin, empty mathematics may sneak in unobserved. Precision is a virtue in economics; this analysis suggests we also consider richness to be good, and furthermore that we recognise the pursuit of precision alone, without richness, as a vice.

To put it bluntly, I argue that much of the power of the neo-classical virtual world is subtly tied to the sting of the insult, 'sissy'. No one wants to be thought 'soft' in one's work, since (perhaps subconsciously) by implication this is to be thought feminine. None of the gender associations needs to exist at a conscious level, of course. In fact, once such biases are established, institutional inertia may be sufficient to keep the discipline moving down the masculine path, even if the majority of practitioners were no longer to associate masculinity with value in other areas of their lives.

The approved position of the scientist relative to the object or phenomenon to be investigated is often described as one of detachment or distance, facilitated, it is often believed, by a mathematical and logical approach. An investigator who, instead, is involved in, influences, is influenced by or has an emotional connection to the object of study is often considered to have insufficient objectivity. Acknowledgment of the socially-influenced nature of knowledge does not, however, leave only radical relativism as an alternative. The philosopher Sandra Harding (1993) calls the usual, detachment-based notion of objectivity 'weak objectivity', because it excuses the social community of science from the domain of criticism. The quest for reliable knowledge is enhanced, not damaged, by reflection on and critical examination of cultural influences. The alternative advocated is not relativism or subjectivism, but a *strong* form of objectivity, which takes the location of the knower into account. The philosopher and economist Amartya Sen (1992: 1) uses the term 'positional objectivity' to describe 'an objective inquiry in which the observational position is specified (rather than being treated as an unspecified intrusion – a scientific nuisance)'. He argues that any attempt at position-independent objectivity must *build on* positional views (that is, be 'trans-positional'), rather than ignore the dependence of view on position.

Or, as it is put by the feminist philosopher Helen Longino:

> The *objectivity* of individuals . . . consists in their participation in the collective give-and-take of critical discussion and not in some special relation (of detachment, hardheadedness) they may bear to their observations. Thus understood, objectivity is dependent upon the depth and scope of the transformative interrogation that occurs in any given scientific community. This community-wide process ensures (or can ensure) that the hypotheses ultimately accepted as supported by some set of data do not reflect a single individual's idiosyncratic assumptions about the natural world. To say that a theory or hypothesis was accepted on the basis of objective methods does not entitle us to say it is true but rather that it reflects the critically achieved consensus of the scientific community. In the absence of some form of privileged access to transempirical (unobservable) phenomena it's not clear we should hope for anything better (Longino 1990: 79, emphasis added).

This does not imply that it is acceptable for any group of people to choose to believe any desired theory. There is a real world, and a scientific approach requires that we seek evidence from the world to support or disprove our hypotheses. However, decisions about which hypotheses deserve investigation and about what constitutes acceptable and convincing evidence are made by scientific communities. The process of understanding is cooperative work. Isolated scientists are as mythological as isolated agents. Rigid methods only give a veneer of objectivity (weak objectivity or 'objectivism'), and can do so only after the ground rules have been set by a restricted community, influenced by its own position and interests.

Alternative Definition of Economics

Does highlighting the connections as well as the distinctions between humans, and between humans and nature, require that a wider, encompassing economics has to be about 'life, the universe, and everything?' (Adams 1983). I do not think so. The relationship of economics with other social sciences could be closer and more cooperative, of course, and based on shared understanding of the multiple dimensions of human experience (rather than imperialistic, based on the imposition of a model of radical separativeness of the sort described by Ben Fine in this volume). But economics need not be undifferentiated. As a practical matter, I suggest that the discipline *take as its organisational centre the down-to-earth subject matter of how humans try to meet their needs for goods and services*. Economics should be about how we arrange provision for our sustenance (Nelson 1993). This core corresponds better to the common-sense use of the term 'economics' (and to its etymological roots in the Greek words meaning 'household management') than does the present central concept of the idealised market. This core grounds the discipline both socially and materially. Economic provisioning and the sustenance of life becomes the centre of study, whether it be through market, household or government action, and whether it be by symmetric exchange, coercion or gift. This definition dethrones choice, scarcity and rationality as central concepts, and relegates them to the status of potentially useful tools. It brings previously taboo or fringe subjects like power and poverty into the core.

Why the Alternatives are Important

An extreme story of virtualism might portray the concept of economic man as a sort of dangerous cancer that threatens to erase the humane and connected aspects of human experience, perhaps by fomenting the spread of impersonal markets and justifying the taking of individualistic and self-interested views.

The position taken here, while not denying the possibility of such effects, presents humans and human society as more resilient. Economic man, neo-classical economics and impersonal markets are not all-powerful. They can not be, because they reflect only one side of human experience. Instead of a metaphor of a malignant cancer, the relevant metaphor would be more of a discipline and a society that is off-balance, leaning too much to one side, trying to hop along with only one strong leg, the other withered and neglected.

The distinction is important, since while the first metaphor would tend to see expansion of markets and self-interest as intrinsically bad, the second would only caution that they should not be taken too far. Consider, for example, current discussion surrounding marketed child care. There is something repulsive to many humanistic thinkers, including feminists and many on the left, about paying someone to provide care to one's children, about exchanging money for a substitute for parental love and concern. The parent–child relation is emblematic of deep human connection; yet the market is an icon of impersonality and anonymity. It would seem that extending the market and the profit motive into child care would corrupt and depersonalise caring relationships. What is more, the placement of children into paid care is sometimes perceived as a self-interested move by mothers. (Informal surveys of the sort carried out by advice columnists indicate that it is much more acceptable for a woman to work and put her children into alternative care 'because she has to' financially, than it is if she prefers her life this way.)

But is it always true that the market corrupts and that self-interest is bad? Only if we have already accepted the notion that real markets behave like the caricature of idealised, abstract, impersonal markets does the cancer metaphor apply. In actuality, the market for child care can be quite rich in personal relationships. Rarely do the payer or payee subjectively experience the contract as 'paying for love', much less as supplanting the parent–child relation. It is more likely that the parents find people who, they believe, will form the type of relationship they want with the child, and then pay the care-giver for his or her *time*. 'Spending money on' need not necessarily be synonymous with 'commoditising'.

Another case would be that of reparations payments to, for example, women forced into prostitution by Japan during the Second World War. To think of such a payment simply as a quid pro quo, of course, only exacerbates the prostituting nature of the relationship (payment for sexual services). To think of it as carrying symbolic meaning, of apology and a seeking to set things right, however, puts it in opposition to commoditisation, even though it is a payment of money.

Neither is self-regard unambiguously bad and other-interest always good. While the overcoming of self-interest in order to serve the interests of others has long been a major theme of both religious and ethical discussions, it is not free of gender bias. While most theologians and ethicists have seen the primary manifestation of sin for traditional males as over-blown selfishness, some have argued that the primary manifestation of sin for traditional females is over-blown self-abnegation (see Hampton 1993; C. Keller 1986: esp. 12). Males tend to fail by becoming too separate from others; females are more likely to fail by not developing individual selfhood at all. Does not the idea of a lack of self-regard describe for some the ideal traditional wife and mother, who has no identity of her own apart from her husband and children? Yet such a person has usually not been seen as particularly virtuous, either because (as for women) such devotion is thought to be 'only natural' or because it is recognised that a lack of individual identity also means, in an ethical or spiritual sense, a corresponding erasure of individual responsibility. Feminist research reminds us that guard must be kept against a too-thorough eradication of the self, that a true person has both an individual identity and a sense of solidarity with others.

These points can be seen in terms of the gender–value compass:

M+	F+
loves self	loves others
M–	F–
loves self only	loves others only

Instead of a fear of self-interest as a malignant force, this diagram suggests the virtues of a balance of self-interest and other-interest.

The substantive and methodological strength of the 'economic man' metaphor as a virtual reality within economics can not be ignored. However, this does not mean that it will become a virtualism. The extent to which real persons can be made to conform to the assumptions of individual, rational, self-interested maximisation is a topic of debate, both empirical and theoretical. The image of the economic man is based on a gendered bifurcation of human experience, and the methodological justification for its use is based on a gendered understanding of the nature of knowledge. Rather than working within binary dualisms like self-interest vs. other-interest and commodity vs. gift, the alternative to the image of economic man suggested here draws on an understanding of the use of metaphor in human cognition, and on a richer model of both human nature and scientific methodology.

References

Adams, Douglas 1983. *Life, the Universe, and Everything*. New York: Pocket Books.

Arrow, Kenneth J. 1997. Invaluable Goods. *Journal of Economic Literature* 35: 757–765.

Becker, Gary S. 1976. *The Economic Approach to Human Behavior*. Chicago: University of Chicago Press.

Benhabib, Seyla 1987. The Generalized and the Concrete Other: The Kohlberg–Gilligan Controversy and Moral Theory. In Diana Meyers and Eva Feder Kittay (eds), *Women and Moral Theory*, pp. 154–177. Totowa NJ: Rowman and Littlefield.

Ben-Ner, Avner, and Louis Putterman 1996. Economics, Values, and Organization. Presented at the Conference on Economics, Values, and Organization, 19–21 April, Yale University.

Bloor, Meriel, and Thomas Bloor 1993. How Economists Modify Propositions. In Willie Henderson, Tony Dudley-Evans and Roger Backhouse (eds), *Economics and Language*, pp. 153–169. London: Routledge.

Bordo, Susan 1986. The Cartesian Masculinization of Thought. *Signs* 11: 439–456.

Carrier, James G. 1995. Maussian Occidentalism: Gift and Commodity Systems. In J. G. Carrier (ed.), *Occidentalism: Images of the West*, pp. 85–108. Oxford: Oxford University Press.

Carruthers, Bruce G., and Wendy Nelson Espeland 1997. The Price is Right: On Money and Morality. Presented at the American Sociological Association annual meeting, 9 August, Toronto.

Chodorow, Nancy Julia 1978. *The Reproduction of Mothering: Psychoanalysis and the Sociology of Gender*. Berkeley: University of California Press.

Debreu, Gerard 1991. The Mathematization of Economic Theory. *American Economic Review* 81: 1–7.

Fee, Elizabeth 1983. Women's Nature and Scientific Objectivity. In Marian Lowe and Ruth Hubbard (eds), *Women's Nature: Rationalizations of Inequality*, pp. 9–27. New York: Pergamon Press.

Frank, Robert H., Thomas Gilovich and Dennis T. Regan 1993. Does Studying Economics Inhibit Cooperation? *Journal of Economic Perspectives* 7: 159–171.

—— 1996. Do Economists Make Bad Citizens? *Journal of Economic Perspectives* 10: 187–192.

Georgescu-Roegen, Nicholas 1971. *The Entropy Law and the Economic Process*. Cambridge, Mass.: Harvard University Press.

Gilligan, Carol 1982. *In A Difference Voice: Psychological Theory and Women's Development*. Cambridge, Mass.: Harvard University Press.

Hampton, Jean 1993. Selflessness and the Loss of Self. *Social Philosophy and Policy* 10: 135–165.

Harding, Sandra 1986. *The Science Question in Feminism*. Ithaca, NY: Cornell University Press.

—— 1987. The Curious Coincidence of Feminine and African Moralities: Challenges for Feminist Theory. In Diana Meyers and Eva Feder Kittay (eds), *Women and Moral Theory*, pp. 296–315. Totowa NJ.: Rowman and Littlefield.

—— 1993. Rethinking Standpoints Epistemology: 'What is Strong Objectivity'? In Linda Alcoff and Elizabeth Potter (eds), *Feminist Epistemologies*, pp. 49–82. New York: Routledge.

Helleiner, Eric 1997. National Currencies and National Identities. Presented at the American Sociological Association annual meeting, 9 August, Toronto.

Keller, Catherine 1986. *From A Broken Web: Separation, Sexism, and Self*. Boston: Beacon Press.

Keller, Evelyn Fox 1985. *Reflection on Gender and Science*. New Haven: Yale University Press.

Lakoff, George, and Mark Johnson 1980. *Metaphors We Live By*. Chicago: University of Chicago Press.

Leibenstein, Harvey 1976. *Beyond Economic Man: A New Foundation for Microeconomics*. Cambridge, Mass.: Harvard University Press.

Lewin, Shira B. 1996. Economics and Psychology: Lessons for Our Own Day from the Early Twentieth Century. *Journal of Economic Literature* 34: 1293–1323.

Longino, Helen 1990. *Science as Social Knowledge: Values and Objectivity in Scientific Inquiry*. Princeton, NJ: Princeton University Press.

McCloskey, D. N. 1991. Economic Science: A Search Through the Hyperspace of Assumptions? *Methodus* 3(1): 6–16.

Margolis, Howard 1982. *Selfishness, Altruism and Rationality: A Theory of Social Choice*. Chicago: University of Chicago Press.

Meeks, Gay 1991. *Thoughtful Economic Man: Essays on Rationality, Moral Rules and Benevolence*. Cambridge: Cambridge University Press.

Mirowski, Philip 1988. *Against Mechanism: Protecting Economics from Science*. Totowa NJ: Rowman and Littlefield.

Nelson, Julie A. 1993. The Study of Choice or the Study of Provisioning? Gender and the Definition of Economics. In Marianne A. Ferber and J. A. Nelson (eds), *Beyond Economic Man: Feminist Theory and Economics*, pp. 23–36. Chicago: University of Chicago Press.

—— 1996. *Feminism, Objectivity and Economics*. London: Routledge.

Nussbaum, Martha C. 1993. Emotions and Women's Capabilities. In M. C. Nussbaum and Jonathan Glover (eds), *Women, Culture, and Development*, pp. 360–395. Oxford: Oxford University Press.

Oakley, Allen 1994. *Classical Economic Man: Human Agency and Methodology in the Political Economy of Adam Smith and J. S. Mill*. Brookfield, Vermont: Edward Elgar.

Persky, Joseph 1995. The Ethology of Homo Economicus. *Journal of Economic Perspectives* 9: 221–231.

Radin, Margaret J. 1996. *Contested Commodities*. Cambridge, Mass.: Harvard University Press.

Sen, Amartya 1992. Objectivity and Position. The Lindley Lecture, University of Kansas, 5 March.

Whitehead, Alfred North 1925. *Science and the Modern World*. New York: The Macmillan Company.

Yezer, Anthony M., Robert S. Goldfarb and Paul J. Poppen 1996. Does Studying Economics Discourage Cooperation? Watch What We Do, Not What We Say or How We Play. *Journal of Economic Perspectives* 10: 177–186.

Zelizer, Viviana A. 1995. *The Social Meaning of Money*. New York: Basic Books.

−4−

Development and Structural Adjustment
Philip McMichael

At the turn of the twenty-first century a new spectre haunts the world: the spectre of globalisation. It is a project promoted by those who expect to gain from the global circulation of money, capital and goods, and it is justified in the name of the market. Since the 1980s the world has experienced a cumulative process of restructuring of economic, social and political landscapes. The rhetoric of restructuring centres on the market's role in fostering efficiency, comparative advantage and wealth creation. This rhetoric has been deployed in stages, beginning with the management of the debt crisis in the 1980s via structural adjustment programmes. Financial discipline was the stated objective, but it depended on extensive political and social restructuring to open Third World states and economies to global investors and markets. In retrospect, the debt management regime was a dress rehearsal for a more universal approach to restructuring, now broadcast under the slogan of free trade and institutionalised in the World Trade Organization.

In undermining 'developmentalism', Third World solidarity and the stability of Second World regimes, the debt crisis and its management set the stage for capitalist triumphalism in the 1990s. With the collapse of the Cold War and its tripartite sub-division of the world, the virtual reality of First World market culture became the unqualified standard. Firms, finance ministers and political elites, multilateral institutions and global bankers, all spoke the same language, the rhetoric of the market. The rhetoric had currency in part because it was implemented as a virtualism, notably in the form of structural adjustment programmes, which reconfigured power relations both within and between states. The pursuit of financial discipline empowered those ministries in indebted states that favoured global market relations. And once the political and ideological sub-division within the state system collapsed, global markets and the virtual reality that justified them were in a position to subject all states, firms and producers to their competitive force. Thus restructuring moved from being an individually-instituted condition, via multilateral decree, to being a universal condition of the market. In this movement, governance has been redefined, and has become evaluated according to how effectively states adopt market-oriented economic policies.

Many commentators referred to the 1980s as 'the lost decade', as if the South simply lost ground. For our purposes, the 1980s ushered in an era in which states also lost horizon, or historical purpose. We are perhaps witnessing the extension of this process to Asia in the late 1990s, as currency crises threaten to transform national projects on the Asia–Pacific rim. When states submit to structural adjustment policies they adopt new priorities with a double edge. In the first instance they adopt market, rather than social, priorities – a shift in governing values that typically discounts specific developmental coalitions forged across time through national struggle and debate. Second, these new market priorities, a virtual reality expressed in abstract and universal principles, have specific political and economic import. In promising a new golden age of the global market-place, they strengthen global corporate and financial power as the counterpart to the erosion of national development capacity. In sum, a reversal of thinking is under way, where the present is no longer the logical development of the past (as in the modernity project); rather, it is increasingly the hostage of the future (in the double sense of the spectre of riches and of deterioration accompanying the globalisation project). The measure of this may well be the greater vulnerability of a more integrated global economy to speculative financial crises, as a consequence of the structural adjustment policies forged in the 1980s.

The Self-regulating Market Revisited

The spectre of globalisation is a virtualism that echoes an earlier attempt to install a self-regulating market. That first attempt, documented by Karl Polanyi in *The Great Transformation*, occurred during the century following the 1830s, culminating in financial and economic collapse as a result of the protection movement, which took a national form. In the present era, the move to free global markets in money, labour and land differs significantly from the original attempt. The difference is that the current virtualism begins with markets already instituted nationally, stemming from the protectionist outcomes of the original Polanyian 'cycle'. Market freedom today represents a frontal assault on the institutions of the nation-state (or citizen-state). It is not that states are being eliminated; rather, they are the object of powerful restructuring forces that would turn nation-states into 'global' states, that is, institutions that conform to the virtual reality that drives globalisation, geared to securing global circuits of money and commodities and governed by consumer-citizens.

In order to accomplish this transformation, national and international globalising elites invoke the rules of a virtual 'market rationality', which abstract from the populations to which they are applied. These rules seek to remove uncertainties in circuits of capital, rather than express democratic input. The logic of market rule is the subordination of constitutional rule to alternative institutional forms. The virtual reality of neo-classical economic theory, based in the model of the self-regulating market, posits a borderless global economy. But, as Polanyi noted, a self-regulating market in fact requires institutionalisation, which I would term global regulation (as historic counterpart to national regulation). Global regulation combines the supranational facility of multilateral financial and governance institutions like the International Monetary Fund (IMF) and the World Trade Organization with a reconstructed system of states adhering to market rule – whether through neo-conservative coalitions or through free-trade agreements that secure such rule by overriding national economic powers.

Global forms of regulation reproduce capitalism on a global scale via the relaxation of national controls. Since monetary relations are governed by the hypermobility of finance capital, global regulation ultimately means avoiding financial collapse by underwriting and rescheduling debt on a decidedly *ad hoc* basis. This much was clear in the financial bail-out of beleaguered Southeast Asian banking systems in October 1997 by IMF packages supplemented with Northern financial assistance. The IMF's role is to exact financial adjustment in the assisted states to sustain global capital flows. It was argued at the time that until Southeast Asian states accepted IMF disciplines, firms and speculators would put pressure on their national currencies (see Glain and Stein 1997).

The effect of this kind of global regulation is to impose market criteria on states, reducing their freedom to pursue national redistributive and macroeconomic policies. Such 'state shrinking' has eroded public welfare and national protections, including full employment and an adequate wage. The subversion of the national regulation that was part of developmentalism emerged as a corporate project in the 1970s, as is indicated by the discussion of the spread of transnational corporations in Sklair (this volume). It blossomed in the 1980s under the debt regime that targeted the Third and Second Worlds, but had recursive effects on the First World via wage reduction and economic stagnation. It is now, in the 1990s, a full-blown project on a global scale, contributing to a growing crisis of governance. This crisis expresses the hold of virtualism, where neo-classical abstractions shape public discourse and policy-making in such a way that social ends and means yield to selective private solutions.

Policy Virtualism

The rhetoric of restructuring pervades economic policy-making and the new discourse of development that conditions it. Its most basic assumption is that material well-being depends on the freedom of the market, understood as an independent and rational force. This assumption coincides with the elaboration of a global money market, based in the micro-electronics revolution and the financial deregulation that marks the fourth quarter of the twentieth century. Financial globalisation has resulted in a profound elision, where the market sheds its social foundation in the nation-state and becomes a medium for the reproduction of money. In other words, the premium on financial viability subverts the social goal of development or, as one commentator has put it: 'Driven by the imperative to replicate money, the system treats people as a source of inefficiency and is rapidly shedding them at all system levels' (Korten 1996: 13).

Under late twentieth-century conditions of 'financialisation' (Arrighi 1994), the virtual reality of the monetarist premiss now drives development discourse. Because monetarism's measures are purely quantitative economic indicators, and because restructuring reforms release or accelerate these economic indicators, they may behave as self-fulfilling prophecies. But they misrepresent the underlying social and historical context. Such consistent misrepresentation is a form of economistic virtual reality, whereby recent development models embody economic abstractions as premiss, prescription and practice. Let me offer two recent examples.

On 15 July 1997 the Argentinian government agreed to a deal with the IMF whereby that institution would provide a line of credit that depended on evidence of 'good governance'. This included shifting public spending priorities toward improving the health and education of the workforce, 'overhauling the tax system, improving court practices, strengthening private property rights and opening Government ledgers' (Lewis 1997: D1). This deal illustrates the growing power of global institutions to reshape national government according to the doctrine of 'reducing state intervention in the economy'. The IMF's managing-director, Michel Camdessus, terms this operation 'the second generation of structural reform in Latin America'. Also, the deal models development behaviour, as the IMF's seal of approval paves the way for private investors who, at the present time, can not themselves reform governance. Because this arrangement improves Argentina's ability to attract lower loan rates in private credit markets, it is being touted as a 'model for developing countries in Latin America and possibly other areas, giving private business and investment a bigger share of the role that the monetary fund has played' (Lewis 1997: D1). In effect, financial aid not only discounts government sovereignty in the name of the market (managed by the IMF), but also it reformulates 'governance' to mean the reproduction of global monetary circuits.

The second instance is of a different kind. It concerns the justification of the global 'sweatshop' by influential US national and international economic advisers such as Jeffrey Sachs of Harvard and Paul Krugman of MIT. In an article in the *New York Times* in June 1997, Sachs and Krugman were quoted as offering a 'principled rationale' for sweatshops, as 'an essential first step toward modern prosperity in developing countries' (Myerson 1997: 5). While each economist opposes the morality of exploitative sweatshop conditions, Krugman said that 'It's always sweatshops' that constitute the first stage of development, and Sachs argued that 'Those are precisely the jobs that were the stepping stone for Singapore and

Hong Kong, and those are the jobs that have to come to Africa to get them out of their backbreaking rural poverty' (quoted in Myerson 1997: 5).

Such comparison with previous models or instances of economic development is fallacious, because it abstracts the sweatshop from the historical phase in which it exists, recasting it in term of economistic virtual reality. In short, it ignores the ways that the conditions under which sweatshops operate today differ from those in the nineteenth century or even in the 1960s, when the East Asian tigers deployed the sweatshop to export their way into middle-income status in the hierarchy of 'development'. As we shall see below, that was a time when national develop-mentalism was still intact and when the Pacific Rim geopolitical strategy of the US privileged the East Asian perimeter as a showcase in the Cold War (see, for example, Grosfoguel 1996). The possibilities for replication of this model have evaporated as geopolitical relations have changed and as global commodity chains, growth triangles and free trade zones, rather than nations, have become the new sites of development (see, for example, Bonacich *et al*. 1994; Ohmae 1995; Palat 1997). In this new historical phase, sweatshops are not stepping-stones to national development but stepping-stones for corporate sub-contractors scouring the global economy for flexible and low-wage production platforms. They are no longer simply sweatshops, but 'global sweatshops', even though they employ local women and children, temporarily. And finally, sweatshops are the product of structural reforms that remove barriers to state protection of wage levels, working conditions and trade and investment flows.

Both of these instances provide a glimpse of the longer-term consequences of a series of structural adjustment programmes instituted in the 1980s, primarily in Southern states. The restructuring of governance, and of the spatial relations of commodity production and circulation, constitute broad structural changes. These changes express, and intensify, the institutionalisation of economic models devoid of social and historical dimensions. In embracing structural reforms, national political elites subscribe to the higher authority of global markets and price efficiency. This higher authority subordinates political and social history to highly selective and quite disembedded economic forces, undermining the integrity of national political economy. To make sense of how this has come about, we need to situate the episode of structural adjustment in the collapse of the 'development project' that flourished after the Second World War. At the same time, we need to understand how and why the 'global economy' has emerged as a virtualism, a material and a discursive construct with the power to dictate development policy.

The Development Project and Globalisation

Global exchanges of goods, people and cultural artefacts pre-date the capitalist era and framed the rise and geopolitical organisation of capitalism. Global economic integration is, however, not the only reality, even today. At present, about 80 per cent of the world's population of more than five billion exist outside or on the fringes of global consumer networks (Barnet and Cavanagh 1994: 383).

For centuries there has been a layered set of economies, on global and local scales, where global trade has existed alongside, and sometimes linked to, local markets and populations. The difference today, in the postcolonial era, is that much of the world's population is under the jurisdiction of a completed state system, in which states have sought to incorporate or subordinate local populations in national development. That is, postcolonial societies inherited a world order in which the only legitimate form of political organisation was the nation-state. With the nation-state form came nation-building, modelled on the European experience and episteme and centred on the notion of development (Cowen and Shenton 1996). In the post-war context, this modelling took a particular form, which I have termed the 'development project' (McMichael 1996). Its rise and fall is the context for the current global restructuring.

The development project was a vehicle for the institutional stabilisation under US hegemony of the world capitalist economy after the Second World War. Just as early capitalism emerged within distinct political frameworks – pre-nineteenth-century mercantilism: trade organised to enlarge national wealth; nineteenth-century liberalism: free-trade imperialism to enlarge capitalist markets – so capitalism in the middle of the twentieth century was organised within the framework of the (now universal) nation-state system. The stabilisation of post-war capitalism was managed on global and national scales, via a regime of 'embedded liberalism' (Ruggie 1982). This regime, known as the Bretton Woods agreement, combined the principles of mercantilist and liberal organisation, subordinating international trade to national economic management, anchored in strategic economic sectors like steel and farming. The centrepiece of this strategy was the management of national economic growth via macroeconomic policy. It depended on the regulation of international capital movements and on fixed exchange rates, pegged to the American dollar and coordinated by the US Federal Reserve. International and national institutions jointly regulated monetary and wage relations to stabilise national capitalisms within this liberal trade regime, constituting the Free World.

For our purposes it is important to note that 'embedded liberalism' privileged social and political relations over economic relations. In fact, the rise of the nation-state was premised on the formation of national industrial classes, constitutional rule and the establishment of national currency regulation via central banking (Hobsbawm 1990; Polanyi 1957). These institutions and policies conditioned the rise of the social-democratic movement, resulting in the 'citizen state' as the model modern state (Hobsbawm 1996). Social democracy, while never complete in the Third World (see, for example, Migdal 1986), gained substantial political influence in the First World through the maturation of industrial capitalism and the institutional facility of the Bretton Woods system of fixed currency exchanges and capital controls (see Teeple 1995). Here, the economy was embedded in the nation-state, thereby completing what Karl Polanyi called 'the great transformation'.

As former colonies achieved independence, they adopted, or were forced to adopt, the nation-state as their form of political organisation. While this provided continuity to the political organisation of the world's subject populations, it was by no means an equal state system. Further, the state system embodied a set of regulatory institutions that imposed a particular view of social organisation privileging European political economy materially and ideologically. In this schema, non-European cultures were viewed as undeveloped in cultural and economic terms (Escobar 1995; Sachs 1992). This shaped the extension of the 'development project' to the so-called 'Third World' as decolonisation unfolded, generating the paradigm of developmentalism.

Under the development project, states were responsible for managing national economic growth, with trade as a stimulus. While there was rich national variation, the universal macroeconomic goal was to consolidate national welfare in the context of stable monetary relations. Prescriptions by the Economic Commission for Latin America for 'import-substitution industrialization' pursued the North American model of 'inner-directed' economic growth that defined the goals of the development project in this period (Lehman 1990: 5–6). This national developmental path later dovetailed with the green revolution (concerned with the local production of basic foodstuffs for growing industrial classes) to shape Third World national economic growth.

Embedded in this multilateral arrangement were Cold War geopolitical realities. The United States, in particular, deployed Marshall aid to redistribute dollars to capital-poor regions of the world – from Europe, through East Asia to Africa. This established the dollar as the international reserve currency and promoted freedom of enterprise, which became the litmus test of the Free World (Arrighi 1982). Export credits, extended to Marshall Plan recipients, facilitated the transfer of American technology. In turn, the World Bank and other multilateral institutions disbursed long-term loans to encourage the development habit (Rich 1994). The target, and instrument, of this developmentalist movement was the nation-state. It is important to understand this historic connection, because today developmentalism evaporates with the metamorphosis of the nation-state into the global state.

The Nation-State: The First Obstacle to Virtualism

For Polanyi, the social disembedding of the commodity market was an institutional act engineered by British capitalists to facilitate machine production and its need to expand inputs and market outlets. Classical political economy articulated economic laws, modelled on natural laws, to legitimate this institutional initiative.

In these terms, unlimited commoditisation required the dominance of the price-form, extending to land and labour. And, given the international setting, the self-regulating market needed a universal commodity equivalent, gold, to facilitate global exchanges. In an early reference to virtualism, Polanyi described land, labour and money as fictitious commodities, since land and labour are not produced for sale and the production of gold could never match the changing money-commodity needs of the business cycle. In other words, the concept of the self-regulating market was an abstraction, and worse, when this virtual reality became a virtualism, it threatened to destroy the social fabric by fetishising human and natural relations as market relations.

Polanyi's historical presentation of the rise and regulation of markets is fundamentally a critique of economic liberalism *qua* virtualism. As such, it also treats the formation of the nation-state as the re-embedding of the market in social relations. This is arguably a normative, as well as a historical, characterisation of the nation-state. In his powerful exposé of economic liberalism, Polanyi demonstrates that the process of institutionalisation of the self-regulating market constituted the organisational substance of the nation-state. For example, the gold standard (as the self-regulating mechanism for money markets on an international scale) required currency management to preserve stable national environments for accumulation. Central banks, with their credit policies, became essential national institutions in mediating the national balance of trade through adjustment of monetary and fiscal policy. Adjustment was quite political, and this in turn encouraged constitutional government as a vehicle of political input for different social interests: farmers, workers, manufacturers, professional classes and so forth.

In the English case, the 1834 Poor Law Act and the Bank Act of 1844 institutionalised the labour market and central banking system, stabilising the accumulation of English capital. The 1846 repeal of the Corn Laws encouraged imports of cheap grain from the New World to reduce the cost of staple foods for wage labourers. In combination, these measures instituted the markets in labour, currency and land that underpinned Britain's global commercial hegemony. In this way, the establishment of the self-regulating market generated the infrastructure of informal imperialism.

The infrastructure of the self-regulating market simultaneously secured British hegemony and stimulated rival national mobilisations. Through the global market, British commerce generated a protective cycle of market regulation across the world of constitutional states, leading eventually to the fragmentation of the British-centred world economy early in the twentieth century. Various national forms of regulation evolved: land markets and agricultural trade generating agricultural tariffs and notions of national food security; labour markets generating union and labour-party movements resulting in labour legislation and industrial tariffs; money markets generating currency management to stabilise national economies. In these ways, the consolidation of national administrations and national economic protections not only challenged British hegemony but also challenged the virtualism of Britain's free-trade posture. In the aftermath of the collapse of the nineteenth-century world economy, reconstruction centred on national controls over circuits of money and goods, becoming synonymous with twentieth-century notions of development.

The Contradictions of Developmentalism

Developmentalism, as an attempt to universalise the nation-state form, inevitably failed. This was so for three reasons. In the first place, the nation-state was essentially a West European institution (see, for example, Davidson 1992). As such, it was not necessarily suited either to Eastern Europe (witness the collapse of Yugoslavia) or to the postcolonial world (witness the series of implosions of various African states and the current fragility of the Colombian state). In addition, as Polanyi and Marx both demonstrate, the Western nation-state rested on the colonial pedestal. The legacy of this historical fact is played out in the current erosion of social-democratic politics associated with the migration of ex-colonials to the West, generating a decidedly uncivil politics of ethnic conflict. In short, the universalisation of the nation-state form has been quite problematic.

The second reason developmentalism failed was that it was not simply an attempt to initiate a process of national replication of First-World modernity. As has already been suggested, it involved an attempt by the United States to reconstruct the world in its own image. Polanyi's conception of the world market underestimates the hegemonic dimension of the British free-trade regime, where the 'workshop of the world' posture was in fact an attempt to impose a colonial system writ large, around a British metropolis (McMichael 1985). Through protective-response mechanisms such as industrial protectionism and formal imperialism, rival states eventually undercut the unity of the British-centred world economy. Similarly, the United States' hegemonic strategy of instituting a regime of embedded liberalism imposed the construct of New Dealism by projecting the American version of the welfare state into the Cold War state system (see, for example, Wallerstein 1995). Here, foreign aid came with strings attached, notably adherence to the principle of freedom of enterprise (Arrighi 1982). The context for the implementation of developmentalism was one in which the US controlled 70 per cent of world gold reserves, monopolised Free World military power and dominated international development institutions and their discourse (see Escobar 1995). In fact, the restructuring of world political economy embodied contradictory geopolitical dynamics whereby the showcase states of the Cold War (for example, Taiwan, South Korea, Chile) served to confirm the development project while most of their erstwhile Third World partners never did replicate the First World development path.

The third reason developmentalism failed was that the institutional structure of the development project promoted transnational economic integration through bilateral and multilateral aid programmes and foreign investment. Freedom of enterprise not only encouraged transnational corporate activity, but also generated an offshore dollar market that ballooned in the 1970s with the recycling of petro-dollars: growing from $3 billion in 1960, to $75 billion in 1970 and to over $1 trillion in 1984 (Strange 1994: 107). A global money market arose and, with rapid developments in information and communication technology, global banks gained prominence.

Each of these movements undid the original conditions upon which the development project was elaborated. Alongside the commodity chains that defined the international division of labour (notably tropical products processed in the First World), a series of links among subsidiaries and sub-contractors producing components as inputs defined transnational industrial and agro-food complexes geared to world, rather than national, products (Friedmann and McMichael 1989; Harris 1987). But this compromise of the possibility of national economic coherence (especially for 'developing countries') paled under the compromise visited upon all states as a consequence of the role of the offshore dollar market in compelling the abandonment of capital controls and an international financial order premised on currency stability.

The 1960s growth of offshore dollars, beyond the regulatory controls of the Bretton Woods regime, eventually put such pressure on the dollar that the American government, mired in the Vietnam War, separated it from gold in 1971. Within three years the US had removed capital controls and effectively sabotaged the Bretton Woods regime. This was part of a unilateral initiative to institute a liberal financial regime in the global economy, and so to protect the autonomy of American policy by separating it from financial claims in the offshore markets. US officials correctly perceived that the removal of exchange controls would allow the US to shift the adjustment burden associated with its large current-account deficit on to other states, via their own speculative purchases of the dollar or revaluation of their own currencies (Helleiner 1996: 112).

The 'dollar weapon' expressed and preserved US financial hegemony, encouraging financial liberalisation across the First World through the 1980s, but not without establishing an era of speculative instability and an epochal decoupling of financial capital from productive capital (Arrighi 1994). As a result, the global economy has entered a period of intense restructuring under the dictates of financial capital, as evidenced in the structural adjustments associated with the 1980s debt crisis. The debt management policies involved a far-reaching assault on, to put it in Polanyi's (1957: 203) words, 'the constitutive importance of the currency in establishing the nation as the decisive economic and political unit'. As Colin Leys (1996: 7) remarks:

By the mid-1980s the real world on which 'development theory' had been premissed had ... disappeared. Above all, national and international controls over capital movements had been removed, drastically curtailing the power of any state wishing to promote national development, while the international 'development' community threw itself into the task of strengthening 'market forces' (i.e., capital) at the expense of states everywhere, but especially in the Third World.

The two salient observations here concern the diminished power to manage national economic development by states, and the movement toward what I term the 'globalisation project': privileging the management of the global economy (see McMichael 1996). The management of global economic relations is equivalent to Polanyi's 'instituted market', although this time it is a transnational entity, aspects of which are described by Leslie Sklair (this volume). The debt regime presaged the institutionalisation of the global market.

Situating the Debt Regime

The debt regime, which continues today in a different guise, was instituted early in the 1980s when Third World debt became a liability rather than a vehicle of development, as it had been in the 1970s. The regime had four pertinent character-istics. First, it was an attempt to preserve the financial capital that had over-reached itself in the rush to recycle offshore dollars through financing Third World development initiatives. Second, in preserving financial capital, the burden of adjustment was placed squarely on the shoulders of Third World states, effectively puncturing the 'development illusion' (Arrighi 1990). Third, the debt regime functioned to restructure states from within and to appropriate state power from without through its administering agencies, the IMF and the World Bank (Bienefeld 1989, 1992). And fourth, the debt regime instituted a model of adjustment con-forming to the requirements of the concept of a 'self-regulating market' on a world scale. As such, this regime has imposed a form of virtualism by insisting that all nations are better off competing in the global economy. The privileging of the global market over national markets involves a double fiction: it dissolves historically-specific political cultures, and it replaces them with an economic abstraction.

The global market is an abstraction because it is not an independent force. It is an instituted complex privileging money managers and the US as the most powerful nation-state. The rhetoric of globalisation justifies this global order. The idea of subjecting producers to a supposedly self-regulating global market dissociates economic activity from political citizenship, subjecting all participants to an ethic of efficiency without regard for social justice. This is a form of commodity fetishism, whereby market relations assume in thought a false autonomy from their social origins. So, for instance, global market prices may appear to signal a rational allocation of resources in terms of relational efficiencies (comparative advantages), but in fact they are shaped by relational power in the market. This power can take various forms, such as historical advantages (for example, the natural and political–economic infrastructure subsidising American corn producers outstrips Mexican corn producers through the NAFTA), or class income power (for example, where affluent consumers, through their ability to purchase higher-value foods, support the production of feed-grain for livestock at the expense of grain production for people). So, to unleash global market forces is to privilege well-placed global producers and consumers. This real outcome contradicts the rhetorical, rationalist outcome predicted in the neo-classical paradigm that fetishises market efficiencies.

The fallacy in globalisation rhetoric is twofold, then. It is not just that the idea of the self-regulating market is a fiction, markets being historically and socially embedded. It is also that instituting the global market involves state and multilateral management, not the unleashing of a natural form of transaction. But the adjustment package intended to bring about the unleashing of the global market is a formula that abstracts each state from the specificities of its social and political history and organisation, seeing it only in terms of the virtual reality of neo-classical economics (see Gibbon 1996). In addition, structural adjustment commits the fallacy of composition by pushing states to export their way out of debt in export markets that are increasingly saturated. Downward pressures on commodity prices are one consequence. Another, characteristic of the debt crisis of the 1990s, is the further de-industrialisation of the North as firms capitalise on lowered wage costs in the restructured Mexican and Asian states. The resulting loss of global purchasing power is likely to condemn the world to continuing currency crises and competitive devaluations, as further evidence of virtualism in action.

The social consequences of the debt regime involved privileging banks and lowering living standards across the Second and Third Worlds, where market efficiency meant austerity. When the Federal Reserve Board reduced the money supply in 1980 to protect the dollar from escalating offshore claims as states borrowed their way to development, bank lending slowed and shortened. Monetarism reversed financial flows and undermined debt-financed development strategies. By 1986, Third World debt totalled $1 trillion, with some Southern states devoting new loans entirely to servicing previous loans. Northern, and especially US, power was consolidated with the centralisation of global economic management and the politicisation of financial power, symbolised in the IMF's assumption of the role of *de facto* global banker. Bank debt was to be managed on behalf of Northern creditors via a regime of structural adjustment loans assembled by the IMF with World Bank support.

Structural Adjustment

Structural adjustment loans implemented monetarist principles of privileging markets. Monetarism had gained legitimacy in the 1970s as a tool to restructure the balance of power within First World states, putting labour and social programmes on the defensive. Its rise as a conservative political philosophy, targeting the institutions of social democracy, coincided with the collapse of Bretton Woods capital controls and the growing global power of the financiers. From a conservative national political programme originating in the Anglo-American North, monetarism found its real venue in the political management of the global economy. The opportunity for a dress rehearsal came with the debt regime of the 1980s.

The centrepiece of the globalisation project is the management of monetary relations in the interest of reproducing commodity money. The debt regime was initially implemented to preserve money on a global scale. Following a loan binge of the 1970s, when private banks recycled offshore dollars into huge unsecured loans available to Third World states (especially the Newly Industrialising Countries), monetarism sought to re-establish discipline. But, as Polanyi reminds us, financial discipline comes at a social price. The price of monetarism during the 1970s was an assault on high-priced labour and social programmes. The associated corporate restructuring and relocation of investment off shore helped to reverse the historical project of socialisation of capital as a partner in the Keynesian welfare state (McMichael and Myhre 1991).

On the global scale, monetarism reversed the development project, especially within the South (Arrighi 1990). The fact that the combined Southern debt of $1 trillion was only half the US national debt did not matter; the 'debt crisis' was managed as a liquidity problem of debtors rather than as a systemic problem (Corbridge 1993). While Southern and Eastern-European states devoted new loans entirely to servicing previous loans, the US continued the fiction of a paper-dollar standard. New loans were conditional upon restructuring developmental initiatives, and included privatisation of public assets, severely reduced social expenditures, wage reduction, currency devaluation, liberalisation of trade and investment laws and export enhancement. With the assistance of the World Bank, the IMF established a regime based on these conditions: from 1978 to 1992, more than 70 countries of the South undertook 566 stabilisation and structural adjustment programmes (SAPs) imposed by the multilateral financial institutions (Bello, Cunningham and Rau 1994). Across the state system, these loan conditions were designed to underwrite and sustain the viability of the global financial system.

The IMF and the World Bank, while known as multilaterals, reflect the policies of the dominant Group of Seven states, and in particular those of the United States (Pauly 1997). From the Southern perspective, the policies and practices of the institutions of debt management were those of the Northern states. Indeed, the South Commission declared, in 1990:

> What is abundantly clear is that the North has used the plight of developing countries to strengthen its dominance and its influence over the development paths of the South . . . While adjustment is pressed on them, countries in the North with massive payments imbalances are immune from any pressure to adjust, and free to follow policies that deepen the South's difficulties. The most powerful countries in the North have become a *de facto* board of management for the world economy, protecting their interests and imposing their will on the South. The governments of the South are then left to face the wrath, even the violence, of their own people, whose standards of living are being depressed for the sake of preserving the present patterns of operation of the world economy (South Centre 1993: 13).

This observation, while certainly exonerating Southern elites from responsibility for accepting structural adjustment, captures the deeper truth that the debt regime secured a global power relation.

Analogous to Polanyi's description of the nineteenth-century use of gunboat diplomacy against the non-European world by European powers in the service of debt repayment, IMF conditions disciplined Southern and Eastern-European states and populations similarly. But the difference is that the discipline was through political, rather than military, relations. The institutions responsible for managing global monetary relations enlisted the service of finance ministries within debtor states, thereby restructuring power relations within those states as they turned on their own social ministries in the push to re-establish creditworthiness.

In Mexico, for example, against a background of falling real wages and rising unemployment during the 1980s, the health budget fell from 4.7 to 2.7 per cent of public spending, the rate of infant deaths due to nutritional deficiencies almost tripled and overall public spending on education declined almost 21 per cent. Meanwhile, public enterprises declined from 1,155 to fewer than 50 between 1982 and 1994 (Heredia and Purcell 1996: 277–278). In Jamaica, the proportion of the national budget that went to ministries responsible for public infrastructure, agriculture and youth and community development declined by more than 50 per cent between 1970 and 1990, and the portion going to education and health declined by about 20 per cent, while the portion going to national security and finance ministries rose – finance taking over half the total by the early 1990s (Pacific Asia Resource Center 1993). This pattern was repeated across the states subjected to structural adjustment programmes.

Structural adjustment measures were adopted generally, whether imposed or voluntary, with the latest, 1990s, round affecting Southeast Asia and Europe, although with some resistance (particularly from the French unions). Those states that did not formally undergo structural adjustment have done so informally in order to compete in the global economy, justifying the measures in the name of market conditions. Indicating the force of this justification, the Bank of International Settlements stated in its 1992 annual report that 'in many countries, explaining monetary policy decisions in terms of external constraints has been helpful in securing public acceptance' (quoted in Drainville 1994: 110). The point is that 'external constraints' is the rhetoric of efficiency, which abstracts from the social organisation of the world market. While typically accepted at face value, in fact this rhetoric masks the reality of a historically-uneven global economic system, in which transnational firms and investors plot their short-term strategies of financial gain. It is the reality, or threat, of capital mobility across widely-varying wage and skill structures that imposes the discipline on producers and workers, not some abstract and universal market logic.

Structural adjustment programmes allowed the multilateral institutions, in alliance with state managers and financial classes, to redefine development by reformulating the role of the state. The reformulation is enabled by the new-found legitimacy of neo-liberalism, which stresses something that commonly has been ignored by critics of the Western establishment, the fact that Third World state administrations often have channelled loans into conspicuous consumption projects rather than development initiatives (see Toye 1993: 143). Under structural adjustment programmes, states were pressured to pursue creditworthiness and competitiveness in the global economy, at the expense of purely national priorities, especially welfare enhancement and the sustaining of political constituencies supportive of national economic integration. Export production, and attracting foreign investment, became the new priority, alongside an extraordinary decrease in public investment in the South, as privatisation increased tenfold during the 1980s (Crook 1993: 16), enriching both national elites and foreign investors as beneficiaries in the globalisation project.

This shrinking of the state reduces its capacity as a national institution at the same time that it shifts power from social to economic ministries. This means that state agencies that support and regulate economic and social sectors affecting the lives of the majority of the citizenry, especially the poorer classes, lose resources. The debt regime, in structurally adjusting countries on a case-by-case basis but with a standard package of adjustments, transformed the discourse of development in two distinct ways. First, the conditions imposed on debtors for renewal of credit enabled the debt managers to reframe the national project to bring it into line with the virtual reality of neo-classical economics. Second, austerity measures, privatisation and export expansion renewed the global economy (or the global financial system) rather than individual national economies. Austerity measures lowered wages to encourage foreign investment; privatisation ensured renewal of the principle of the global freedom of enterprise; export expansion sustained the flow of products to the wealthier zones of the global economy.

Each measure potentially undermined the coherence and viability of pre-existing national economies. Lowered wages reduced local purchasing power, which meant that the market for goods produced locally contracted. Privatisation of public enterprises reduced the capacity of states to enter into joint ventures with private firms and the capacity to use these ventures to set production priorities. Reduction in public expenditure generally reduced states' capacity to coordinate national economic and social programmes. As a consequence, living standards declined for substantial portions of the South. Average per capita income in Latin America fell 15 per cent during the 1980s, which meant that 50 million more Latin Americans were living in poverty. This was overshadowed by a decline in per capita income of 30 per cent in Africa (Bello 1996: 292; Singh 1992: 138–139).

State expenditure on rural development infrastructure, extension services and agricultural credit declined as shrinking public resources were concentrated in the external financial sector (Canak 1989). Fiscal restraints have concentrated resources in the most profitable portions of the food sector, those aimed at export, and large-scale firms have often prospered owing to their monopolisation of available credit and their access to substantial private investments. At the same time, producers of basic foodstuffs have experienced decapitalisation (McMichael and Raynolds 1994). By the end of the 1980s, the percentage of Mexican *campesinos* with access to official credit fell from 50 to less than 20 per cent, stimulating the rise of alternative, *campesino* credit organisations (Myhre 1994). In Central America, as elsewhere, the intensification of export agriculture for debt servicing and short-term profits wrought widespread social and environmental harm (Murray and Hoppin 1992).

Certainly export expansion to earn foreign currency to service debts appears to be a logical strategy for individual debtor nations to pursue. However, when all debtor nations try to export their way out of debt the fallacy of the structural adjustment blueprint becomes clear. When countries submitted to SAPs in the 1980s, a glut of exports resulted in the lowest commodity prices on the world market since the 1930s. For example, cocoa producers in West Africa expanded exports by 25 per cent between 1986 and 1989, only to suffer a 33 per cent price fall in world cocoa prices. The non-governmental organisation Oxfam termed this syndrome the 'export-led collapse' (Rich 1994: 188).

In these various ways, and more, the outcome of structural adjustment has been to subordinate social and political goals to the market, on the pretext that sound finance depends on market signals. This pretext, which informed the prescription of liberalisation and public impoverishment, also subordinated Southern and Eastern-European national projects to the First World project of rescuing over-extended banks. As Louis Pauly (1997: 121) writes, the 'debt strategy of the early 1980s successfully shielded the economies of net creditors by giving their banks time to buy an insurance policy in the form of increased reserves'. In other words, the strategy of avoiding a financial collapse similar to that of 1929 involved a vastly more extensive programme of restructuring that entailed a reversal of social history on a global scale in the name of the market.

By the 'reversal of social history' I mean the manner in which the debt regime punctured the illusion of developmentalism (Arrighi 1990), in which states and their citizens understood development to be a national project. While development historically proved to be more selective than its rhetoric implied, and while states incorporated citizens into market and surveillance systems via its rhetoric, development remained a universal ideal that mobilised political constituencies and nascent civil societies in the Third (and eventually Second) worlds around a national debate. This social process extended Polanyi's protectionist counter-movement into these regions, even though markets were by no means as extensive. Development discourse was central to the rhetoric of nation-building in the era of decolonisation (Escobar 1995).

The debt regime effectively ended the rhetoric and expectations of development. In the process, it dismantled development constituencies and undermined the capacity to reduce the deprivations arising from the (now global) commoditisation of money, labour and land. As I have argued here and elsewhere (McMichael 1995, 1996), the development project is yielding to the globalisation project, geared to political management of the global economy in the interests of the powerful Northern banks, firms and states and their Southern class allies. It replaces the universalist rhetoric of development with the selective rhetoric of comparative advantage and market efficiency. Whereas the development project reified processes of capitalist accumulation as evolutionary benefits vested in the rights of national citizenship, the globalisation project reifies not only the accumulation process, but also its individual recipients (consumers), whose loyalty is now to an abstract market devoid of community and, apparently, of authority.

Conclusions

Polanyi argued that instituting a money market in the nineteenth century encouraged constitutionalism, but today the same process generally erodes it. State power is increasingly centralised in the hands of the adjusters, who slight social initiatives in the name of the market. Citizenship, once embedded in the idea of the social contract, is disembedded in the idea of market voluntarism, emptying it of its historical and institutional meaning. This is evident in the SAP-initiated attempts to engineer Eastern European transitions, to substitute market rule for central planning overnight. For instance, the World Bank characterised Romania's 1993 privatisation plan as a model for the creation of responsible 'nations of share-holders', the citizens of the new world order (Drainville 1994: 63). Similarly, in Africa the Bank encourages a 'voluntary development initiative' as a counterweight to the 'patrimonial state', but in contexts where the social resources necessary for such initiatives are already severely depleted (Gibbon 1996: 770).

The shortcomings of such attempts by the development establishment to replace state initiatives by community institutions are rooted in the fetish of individualism. Neo-classical voluntary individualism, as the seed-bed of the new 'social capital' paradigm, forgets that individuals need social resources to support community initiative. SAPs dismantled many of the institutions and programmes sustaining social resources; globalisation intensifies the process by eroding the tax base and privileging productive activities linked to global circuits. The Bank's new interest in 'state effectiveness', apparently a belated recognition of this, is part of a broad strategy of stabilising unstable social conditions. However, it is a recognition rooted in a continuing faith in the organising myth of globalisation as the path to economic well-being. This strategy is implicit in the following passage from the *World Development Report 1997*:

> The cost of not opening up will be a widening gap in living standards between those countries that have integrated and those that remain outside. For lagging countries the route to higher incomes will lie in pursuing sound domestic policies and building the capability of the state. Integration gives powerful support to such policies – and increases the benefits from them – but it cannot substitute for them. *In that sense, globalization begins at home. But multilateral institutions such as the World Trade Organization have an important role to play in providing countries with the incentive to make the leap* (World Bank 1997: 12, emphasis added).

The Bank's stance highlights the inextricable connection between global integration and the reformulation of governance. This reformulation is patent in the way that the World Trade Organization embodies the mature version of what Stephen Gill (1992) has called the 'new constitutionalism', whereby the political and bureaucratic elites responsible for managing global economic flows do so with growing insulation from popular scrutiny. The World Trade Organization has the potential authority to challenge national and local laws behind closed doors. Its rules, concerning freedom in investment and trade as well as intellectual property protection, are binding on all members, and any member can file a complaint regarding restraint on flows of money and commodities by any other member state. This neo-constitutional movement is expressed perhaps more concretely in the regional rule-making by Free Trade Agreement (FTA), in which a global property regime is secured through legislative action in states that join FTAs (see Panitch 1996). In this movement, states surrender power to bureaucratic institutions and yield to the authority of abstract market rules. But as the recent Asian currency crises have revealed, abstract market rules are in fact quite anarchic, and require regular political management to restore their authority.

To conclude, the reformulation of governance in terms of market abstractions and their bureaucratic instruments stems directly from the virtualism of the debt regime. In this regime SAPs impose a standard formula across a range of nation-states, elevating market logic over historical and cultural specificities. However, current global institutions such as the World Trade Organization target the state system at large, and in effect reformulate the meaning and site of governance. Whereas SAPs focus on policy on a case-by-case basis, a global property regime works on the premiss of universal adherence to market rules. And these rules are administered by multilateral and national agencies quite immune to political input from the political constituencies of their member states. When the IMF talks about 'getting prices right' and the Bank says 'globalisation begins at home', the message is that development assistance will depend on the evaluation of local governance on the criterion of market-friendliness. As we have seen recently, however, market-friendliness breeds contagious financial speculation. The combination of substituting the consumer state for the citizen state, and exposing populations to heightened speculative instabilities, marks the highest stage of virtualism, and embodies clearly the spectre of globalisation.

References

Arrighi, Giovanni 1982. A Crisis of Hegemony. In Samir Amin, Giovanni Arrighi, Andre Gunder Frank and Immanuel Wallerstein (eds), *Dynamics of Global Crisis*, pp. 55–109. New York: Monthly Review Press.

—— 1990. The Developmentalist Illusion: A Reconceptualization of the Semi-periphery. In William G. Martin (ed.) *Semiperipheral States in the World Economy*, pp. 18–25. Westport, Conn.: Greenwood.

—— 1994. *The Long Twentieth Century: Money, Power, and the Origins of Our Times*. London: Verso.

Barnet, Richard J., and John Cavanagh 1994. *Global Dreams: Imperial Corporations and the New World Order*. New York: Touchstone.

Bello, Walden 1996. Structural Adjustment Programs: 'Success' for Whom? In Jerry Mander and Edward Goldsmith (eds), *The Case Against the Global Economy*, pp. 285–293. San Francisco: Sierra Club.

Bello, Walden, with Shea Cunningham and Bill Rau 1994. *Dark Victory: the United States, Structural Adjustment and Global Poverty*. London: Pluto Press, with Food First and Transnational Institute.

Bienefeld, Manfred 1989. The Lessons of History and the Developing World. *Monthly Review* (July–August): 9–41.

—— 1992. *Rescuing the Dream of Development in the Nineties*. Paper No. 10. Falmer: Institute of Development Studies, University of Sussex.

Bonacich, Edna, Lucie Cheng, Norma Chinchilla, Nora Hamilton and Paul Ong (eds) 1994. *Global Production: The Apparel Industry in the Pacific Rim*. Philadelphia: Temple University Press.

Canak, William L. 1989. Debt, Austerity, and Latin America in the New International Division of Labor. In William L. Canak (ed.), *Lost Promises: Debt, Austerity and Development in Latin America*, pp. 9–27. Boulder, Colorado: Westview Press.

Corbridge, Stuart 1993. Ethics in Development Studies: The Example of Debt. In Frans J. Schuurman *Beyond the Impasse: New Directions in Development Theory*, pp. 123–139. London: Zed Books.

Cowen, M. P., and R. W. Shenton 1996. *Doctrines of Development*. London: Routledge.

Crook, Clive 1993. New Ways to Grow. A Survey of World Finance. *The Economist* (25 September): Special Supplement.

Davidson, Basil 1992. *The Black Man's Burden: Africa and the Curse of the Nation-State*. New York: Times Books.

Drainville, André C. 1994. International Political Economy in the Age of Open Marxism. *Review of International Political Economy* 1: 105–132.

Escobar, Arturo 1995. *Encountering Development: The Making and Unmaking of the Third World*. Princeton, NJ: Princeton University Press.

Friedmann, Harriet, and Philip McMichael 1989. Agriculture and the State System: The Rise and Decline of National Agricultures, 1870 to the Present. *Sociologia Ruralis* 29 (2): 93–117.

Gibbon, Peter 1996. Structural Adjustment and Structural Change in Sub-Saharan Africa: Some Provisional Conclusions. *Development and Change* 27: 751–784.

Gill, Stephen 1992. Economic Globalization and the Internationalization of Authority: Limits and Contradictions. *Geoforum* 23: 269–283.

Glain, Steve, and Peter Stein 1997. Worries Remain after Asian Markets Stage a Rebound. *Wall Street Journal* (30 October): A19.

Grosfoguel, Ramon 1996. From Cepalismo to Neoliberalism: A World-Systems Approach to Conceptual Shifts in Latin America. *Review* 19: 131–154.

Harris, Nigel 1987. *The End of the Third World*. Harmondsworth: Penguin.

Helleiner, Eric 1996. *States and the Re-emergence of Global Finance: From Bretton Woods to the 1990s*. Ithaca, NY: Cornell University Press.

Heredia, Carlos, and Mary Purcell 1996. Structural Adjustment and the Polarization of Mexican Society. In Jerry Mander and Edward Goldsmith (eds), *The Case Against the Global Economy*, pp. 273–284. San Francisco: Sierra Club.

Hobsbawm, Eric J. 1990. *Nations and Nationalism Since 1780: Programme, Myth, Reality*. Cambridge: Cambridge University Press.

—— 1996. The Future of the State. In Cynthia Hewitt de Alcántara (ed.), *Social Futures, Global Visions*, pp. 55–66. Oxford: Blackwell.

Korten, David 1996. *When Corporations Rule the World*. West Hartford, Conn.: Kumarian Press.

Lehman, David 1990. *Democracy and Development in Latin America*. Philadelphia: Temple University Press.

Lewis, Paul 1997. IMF Seeks Argentine Deal Linking Credit to Governing. *New York Times* (15 July): D1, D19.

Leys, Colin 1996. *The Rise and Fall of Development Theory*. Bloomington: Indiana University Press.

McMichael, Philip 1985. British Hegemony in the Nineteenth-Century World Economy. In Peter Evans, Dietrich Rueschemeyer and Evelyn Huber Stephens (eds), *States Versus Markets in the World System*, pp. 117–150. Beverly Hills, Cal.: Sage.

—— 1995. Globalization: Myths and Realities. *Rural Sociology* 61(1): 25–55.

—— 1996. *Development and Social Change. A Global Perspective*. Thousand Oaks, Cal.: Pine Forge Press.

McMichael, Philip, and David Myhre 1991. Global Regulation vs. the Nation-State: Agro-Food Systems and the New Politics of Capital. *Capital & Class* 43(2): 83–106.

McMichael, Philip, and Laura Raynolds 1994. Capitalism, Agriculture and World Economy. In Leslie Sklair (ed.), *Capitalism and Development*, pp. 316–338. London: Routledge.

Migdal, Joel S. 1986. *Strong Societies and Weak States: State–Society Relations and State Capabilities in the Third World*. Princeton, NJ: Princeton University Press.

Murray, D., and P. Hoppin 1992. Recurring Contradictions in Agrarian Development: Pesticide Problems in Caribbean Basin Nontraditional Agriculture. *World Development* 20: 597–608.

Myerson, Allen R. 1997. In Principle, a Case For More 'Sweatshops'. *New York Times* 22 June: 5.

Myhre, David 1994. The Politics of Globalization in Rural Mexico: Campesino Initiatives to Restructure the Rural Credit System. In Philip McMichael (ed.), *The Global Restructuring of Agro-Food Systems*, pp. 145–169. Ithaca, NY: Cornell University Press.

Ohmae, Kenichi 1995. *The End of the Nation-State: The Rise of Regional Economies*. New York: The Free Press.

Pacific Asia Resource Center 1993. *The People vs. Global Capital: The G-7, SAPs, and Human Rights*. New York: The Apex Press.

Palat, Ravi 1997. Pacific Century: Myth or Reality? *Theory and Society* 25: 303–347.

Panitch, Leo 1996. Rethinking the Role of the State. In James H. Mittelman (ed.), *Globalization: Critical Reflections*, pp. 83–113. Boulder, Colorado: Lynne Reinner.

Pauly, Louis W. 1997. *Who Elected the Bankers?* Ithaca, NY: Cornell University Press.

Polanyi, Karl 1957. *The Great Transformation: The Political and Economic Origins of Our Times*. Boston: Beacon Press.

Rich, Bruce 1994. *Mortgaging the Earth: The World Bank, Environmental Impoverishment and the Crisis of Development*. Boston: Beacon Press.

Ruggie, John Gerard 1982. International Regimes, Transactions and Change: Embedded Liberalism in the Post-War Economic Order. *International Organization* 36: 397–415.

Sachs, Wolfgang (ed.) 1992. *The Development Dictionary*. London: Zed Books.

Singh, Ajit 1992. The Lost Decade: The Economic Crisis of the Third World in the 1980s. *Contention* 2: 58–80.

South Centre, The, 1993. *Facing the Challenge: Responses to the Report of the South Commission*. London: Zed Books.

Strange, Susan 1994. *The Retreat of the State*. Cambridge: Cambridge University Press.

Teeple, Gary 1995. *Globalization and the Decline of Social Reform*. Toronto: Garamond Press.

Toye, John 1993. *Dilemmas of Development: Reflections on the Counter-Revolution in Development Economics*. Oxford: Basil Blackwell.

Wallerstein, Immanuel 1995. *After Liberalism*. New York: Vintage.

World Bank 1997. *World Development Report*. New York: Oxford University Press.

–5–

Cash for Quotas: Disputes over the Legitimacy of an Economic Model of Fishing in Iceland

Agnar Helgason and *Gísli Pálsson*

In response to ideological commitments and to economic and ecological problems, during the past three decades there has been a rapid extension of market approaches to many environmental goods formerly taken to be commonly owned in the West. The primary incentive for such actions derives from a well-known and pessimistic model of human behaviour. Commonly referred to as 'the tragedy of the commons' (Hardin 1968), this model reiterates an observation by Aristotle, that people tend not to look after that which they do not own (see McCay and Acheson 1987). Fuelled by this postulate, market approaches are currently being applied to pollution-generating industries with the allocation and marketing of emission permits (McCann 1996; Tietenberg 1994). Another instance of the extension of market forms, including private property rights and market exchange, to environmental goods in Western economies is systems of individual transferable quotas (ITQs). Such systems are characteristic, if not emblematic, constructs of neo-classical economic reasoning as it is applied in situations where production and the exploitation of resources has to be limited.

The implementation of ITQ management typically requires extensive changes to the institutional and conceptual framework of resource use, the most significant of which concerns the quantification and commoditisation of resource rights and their subsequent allocation to individuals. Such changes are held to result in a resource exploitation that is both ecologically sustainable and of optimal economic efficiency. Given the promise of such results, it is perhaps not surprising that ITQ systems have captured the imagination of many modern scholars and policy-makers. The editors of a collection of economic texts advocating ITQ management nicely convey the optimism and momentum associated with market-based solutions to environmental problems, suggesting that 'ITQs are a part of one of the great institutional changes of our times: the enclosure and privatisation of the common resources of the ocean' (Neher, Arnason and Mollett 1989: 3). Not only is the Western idea of ITQs increasingly exported to other parts of the world as a part of larger efforts to encourage modernisation and development, but an increasing number of resource regimes in the industrialised part of the world are now being modelled along these lines, including ocean fisheries in the United States, Canada, Australia, New Zealand and Iceland (see McCay 1995).

Economics, the discipline that provides the theoretical justification for ITQ systems, represents one of the most rigorous fields of the social sciences and the humanities. Only linguistics can claim a comparable status. In Western thought, in fact, the worlds of language and economics have often been regarded as analogous theoretical domains, as identical, orderly households. During the Middle Ages it became customary to speak of science as the 'reading of the book of nature' and, accordingly, the 'economy of nature' was presented as an inherently textual phenomenon (Pálsson 1995). Similarly, language has often been likened to the economy: Bourdieu (1977) applies the metaphor of the economy to 'linguistic exchanges' and Rossi-Landi (1983) presents language as 'work and trade'. The metaphors have gone back and forth (see Pálsson 1991: Chap. 1). A further parallel between linguistic and economic discourse is that both tend to assume a kind of Hardinian tragedy of the commons. If access to the linguistic commons is free for everyone, it is assumed, there arises a potential contradiction between the system and the individual. A tragedy of the linguistic commons occurs, since the speakers are unaware of the long-term consequences of their actions for the group and, ultimately, themselves.

More interestingly, given the context of this collection, the domains of the semiotic and the economic invite similar virtualist discourses, conflating reality and the models constructed to understand it. For autonomous linguistics, the theoretical position established by Saussure and reinforced by Chomsky and some others, language is a predetermined order of grammatical relations, a thing-in-itself given in advance of the act of speaking. The speaker, it is assumed, merely executes the rules of language, and whatever he or she has to say does not change the order of language. However, the linguistic rules established by the grammarians tend not to remain as virtual realities that identify the ways that a language really works. In addition, they tend to become virtualisms, as linguists seek to reinforce the linguistic order postulated by their analyses. Given sufficient political backing, that order becomes the 'real thing', so that everyday speech obeys the logic prescribed by normative grammarians. Descriptive rules become prescriptive. Despite its rhetoric of detachment and objectivity, neo-classical economics has much in common with autonomous linguistics and linguistic purism. Having modelled the dynamics of the market economy, neo-classical economists seek to reinforce the social order that it represents. The project of the economist, not surprisingly, is sometimes likened to that of the technician (see, for example, Mirowski 1994). Theorising and social engineering go hand in hand (see the discussion of Becker in Fine, this volume).

In what follows, we examine a case where an attempt was made to transform the reality of fishing in Iceland to bring it into accord with the virtual reality of neo-classical economics as expressed in the model of ITQ management. We discuss the social repercussions of the ITQ experiment, in particular the reactions to it from inside and outside the fishing industry. While a relatively small, albeit powerful, group of boat owners has embraced the ITQ model as an ideal form of reality, many Icelanders strongly object to its underlying principles and their social consequences. A central aspect of this objection seems to be a deeply-held concern that the social relations and significations previously associated with fishing rights were eradicated and replaced by social relations and significations associated with homogenised and commensurable exchange values and profit motives that are part of the world of commodities and monetary exchange (Helgason and Pálsson 1997). After two national fishermen's strikes and continual debate in the media and Parliament, the ITQ system's future seems highly uncertain.

We suggest here not only that economic life is considerably more complex than the virtual reality of neo-classical theorising allows, but also, and more importantly, that attempts to promote economically-efficient outcomes through the realisation of such neo-classical models can create more problems than they solve. A more empirically-based approach to prescriptive economic policy-making, one that takes heed of the social context in which policies are to be implemented, would undoubtedly have helped to avoid many of the problems associated with ITQ management in Iceland.

The Emergence of Fisheries Management

For most of Icelandic history, farmers and landowners occupied a central position in social and economic life, with fishing being regarded as merely a supplementary subsistence activity. In the nineteenth century, however, new markets for fish emerged, especially in Spain and England. As a result, fishing became a full-time occupation for many Icelanders, leading to the growth of fishing villages. As the focus of discussions on production gradually shifted away from the landed agricultural elite, fishermen, and particularly skippers, became the key figures of production discourse in this expanding market economy. Nowadays, fishing is by far the most important national and economic activity in Iceland, with most of the fish being caught within the 200-mile exclusion zone. Understandably, then, Icelanders are not indifferent to questions of property rights and rights of access to this most important of economic resources.

The importance of fishing does not only reflect the development of industrialisation and market production in Iceland, for it also played a key symbolic role in the Icelanders' campaign for independence from Denmark. In fact, fish stocks came to be perceived by activists as the economic pillar that would support an emergent Iceland. With the development of a market economy early in the twentieth century, domestic catches multiplied as boats and fishing gear became ever more efficient. There were problems on the horizon, however, as the activities of foreign fleets had also increased dramatically in Iceland's coastal waters. As a result, some of the most important stocks became heavily over-exploited, leading to indigenous demands for exclusive control over coastal waters.

Eventually, in 1948, four years after Iceland attained full independence, the government declared Iceland's exclusive right of access to the fish in its coastal waters and asserted the right to extend the fishing limits if necessary for the scientific protection of the stocks. By this time domestic and foreign exploitation of the fishing stocks had intensified substantially, heightening Icelanders' desire to appropriate the stocks as national property. The Icelandic government extended its fishing limits to 4 miles in 1952, to 12 miles in 1958 and to 50 miles in 1972. Finally, in 1976, after a series of minor international incidents usually referred to as the 'Cod Wars', Iceland claimed economic control of all resources within 200 miles of the coast, an event described by the Minister of Fisheries at that time as the final stage of the nation's struggle for independence (Bjarnason 1977; see also Brydon 1996).

Interestingly, the political rhetoric of the campaign for independence was closely linked to a vigorous discourse of egalitarianism. In previous times the normal Icelandic perception of the ocean had been one of a boundless common resource. While the beach belonged to the owner of the land, who also had privileged rights to resources of so-called 'net areas' (*netlög*, defined in terms of the depth at which a net of 20 meshes could be placed), generally the ocean was defined as a common resource (*almenningur*). The commons began at the point where a flattened cod could no longer be seen from land, this being the criterion used to define the 'fishing limits' (*fiskhelgi*). The principle of common use-rights has been applied to the resources of the sea for most of Icelandic history, and became particularly important during the campaign for independence. One example should suffice to convey the kind of sentiments this principle evoked. In 1926, commenting in the journal of the National Fisheries Association on the use of the national flag at sea, one Icelander urged fishermen to 'relish the rights conveyed upon [them] by the Icelandic nation, above and beyond the citizens of foreign nations', emphasising that within Icelandic waters they were 'the rightful heirs to the national estate' (*óðal*): 'The fishing territories are the common property of all Icelanders, to be jointly exploited by them without interference, according to the laws and regulations in force at each moment in time' (Bergsson 1926: 53–55).

The 200-mile exclusion zone put an end to large-scale foreign fishing in Icelandic coastal waters. The problem of over-fishing, however, was by no means resolved. The domestic fleet continued to grow, and it became apparent that some kind of restrictions on fishing would have to be enforced. Significantly, the first measures adopted were temporary bans on fishing on particular grounds, measures designed to affect producers equally. In theory, commoners retained equal rights to national resources, including fish. While there was always some degree of inequality in these matters, limitations on access tended to resonate with the egalitarianism that was so important in the rhetoric of independence. By 1982, however, Icelandic politicians and interest groups increasingly held that more radical measures would be needed to limit effort and prevent the collapse of the cod stock. At the annual conference of the Fisheries Association, most interest groups were rather unexpectedly in favour of an individual boat-quota system suggested by the Union of Boat Owners, which would divide a reduced catch within the industry itself on the basis of previous catches or 'fishing history' (*aflareynsla*). A fundamental departure from the egalitarian approach of traditional policy, this meant that some boats got higher quotas than others.[1]

The Icelandic quota system started in 1984. Although many skippers and fishers strongly disapproved of this rationing of access to the fishing stocks, they tolerated it because of an understanding that it was a temporary arrangement and that it would be discontinued once the fishing stocks had recovered. However, and much to the chagrin of skippers and fishers, the quota system was extended several times, first for one year, and then twice for two years at a time. However, there was another dimension to the quota system that few participants seemed to be aware of at the outset, although it was one that would come to dominate both the practice and the discourse of fishing in Iceland during the years to come. This was the exchange of quotas.

The Icelandic Experiment: An Economic Simulation

Quota systems originate from the field of resource economics, and from the economist's point of view the objective is not merely to enforce an upper limit on the catch, but to ensure maximum productive efficiency – effectively minimum costs and maximum profits. In order to achieve this, economists typically argue, fishing rights must emulate private property to the fullest extent possible (Árnason 1991; Neher, Árnason and Mollett 1989). In effect, this requires that quotas be incorporated into a market system as quantifiable, fully divisible and tradable goods. The allocation of quotas among producers creates conceptual boundaries around fishing rights, to which private property rights can then be attached, transforming them into commodities: individual transferable quotas.

---

1. A core aspect of quota management is the concept of the total allowable catch (TAC). On the basis of recommendations from fisheries biologists, the Minister of Fisheries decided annually how much of each species could be caught. Each vessel active in the fisheries was allocated a share of the TAC based on its fishing history. On the basis of this share, each vessel's annual catch could be determined. Hence, if its share of TAC in cod was 0.5 per cent and the TAC for the year was set at 100,000 tons, the vessel in question would be allowed to catch 500 tons.

The system introduced in Iceland was an ITQ system, although to begin with there were some restrictions on transactions with them. Quotas could be leased freely, but they could be bought or sold only as a block, by buying or selling the vessel to which they had been allocated. Fishing rights were thus given a new and transitional social identity by being associated with particular vessels, and hence were only partly commoditised. However, laws were passed in 1991 that lifted almost all restrictions on the transfer of ITQs and extended the system indefinitely, regardless of the future condition of the fishing stocks. The result of these changes was that ITQs formally became less transient in nature, fully divisible and thus more akin to permanent property rights. In other words, fishing rights became genuine commodities.

Commenting on these changes, an Icelandic economist and a leading proponent of the system claimed:

> For the first time, the fishing industry has agreed to a significant improvement in the fisheries management system without being threatened with the alternative of a financial disaster. This, I think, must be attributed to the potentially immense economic benefits of the [ITQ] system that have now become apparent to most of the participants in the fisheries (Árnason 1993: 207).

In fact, however, many in the industry, particularly skippers and fishers, strongly objected to these far-reaching changes. Even more significantly, a national survey in 1991 found that no less than 95 per cent of Icelanders wanted the fisheries to remain the common property of the nation (*Viðhorf til sjávarútvegsmála* 1991: 6). In the same survey, 87 per cent said that it was not fair that boat owners could profit from transactions with ITQs that had been allotted to them by the government free of charge. To give a further indication of the weight of opposition to the commoditisation of fishing rights, it is notable that another survey established that 60 per cent of boat owners believed that the buying and selling of ITQs was morally wrong (*Fiskifréttir* June 1990). As one boat owner, fiercely opposed to such transactions, put it: 'If it is efficient to steal from one and sell to another, then I reject such economic policy. ... It just will not do that the common property of the nation, like the fishing grounds, are being bought and sold by a few chosen individuals' (*Sjávarfréttir* June 1991: 36).

The events of 1991 marked a noticeable shift in emphasis, from the protection of fishing stocks to efficient production. The commodity status of ITQs became the crux of fisheries management. By thus altering the institutional framework of fishing, policy-makers and their economic advisers supposed that they could promote a social organisation of fishing that would not only ensure ecologically-sound exploitation of the fishing stocks, but would also maximise rents from the resource. As Árnason put it (1991: 411), 'profit maximising firms will not hold unused quotas. … [and] since the quotas are perfectly divisible and tradable in a perfect market, standard arbitrage arguments immediately yield the result that the total quota will always be allocated to the most efficient fishing firms in the most efficient proportions'.

This shift in the objectives of fisheries management also attested to an increased faith in the use of virtual realities to promote desirable outcomes. The ecological model that underlies stock size estimates and that is used to determine the annual total allowable catch presupposes complete knowledge of and ability to control the ecosystem. For obvious reasons, complete measurement of stocks is impossible. However, fisheries biologists presume they have an accurate idea of how the ecosystem of the fisheries functions and therefore knowledge of which variables they need to measure and how to measure them. On this basis they then propose an exact amount of fish that can be caught, consonant with sustainable growth of the fishing stocks. Given the validity of their models and measurements, fisheries biologists are able to fulfil an essential role as predictive and prescriptive scientists. (In fact, however, there are reasons to be sceptical about the validity of fisheries biologists' stock-size models; see Acheson and Wilson 1996; Pálsson 1998).

The project of the resource economist and manager is in many ways similar to that of the fisheries biologist. The job of the economist can be likened to that of an engineer, adjusting the socio-economic environment so as to accomplish optimum efficiency in production. The job is carried out within the virtual reality defined by their economic model: economic behaviour is presumed to be a natural constant, in that individuals will invariably react to changes in the supply and demand of economic goods and resources with instrumental rationality and self-interest. In contrast, the socio-economic environment is invariably regarded as an artificial and malleable cause of inefficiencies. Typically, these are held to result from restrictions on economic freedom, mainly in the extent of the exchangeability of things, in this case fishing rights. This is because the neo-classical model holds that the extension of commoditisation is a prime means to unearth the 'natural economy', the environment in which *homo oeconomicus* best operates.

This natural economy is a social vacuum, generated by disembedding people and things from 'restrictive' social relations and individual or collective moralities, the stuff of anthropological analyses and the primary causes of heterogeneity in social life (see Fine, Nelson, this volume). We have found it illuminating to present this interpretation of the economy in terms of the spatial metaphor of landscape (Helgason and Pálsson 1997). The disembedded economy represents a flat and homogeneous topography, where economic actors and goods are assumed to move about freely and in an entirely interchangeable way. Any deviations from this homogeneous and asocial space are assigned to the category of externalities, imperfections that need to be ironed out to ensure the maximum efficiency of outcome in that particular region of the economy (such as the commoditisation of fishing rights).[2]

Although neo-classical theory ordinarily treats individuals as homogeneous and entirely interchangeable, there is one important source of variability implicit in most economic models. That is, it is assumed that some actors will be more successful than others and hence, by inference, that individuals' actions in the economy will demonstrate what amounts to varying degrees of self-interest and rationality. Given this assumption, how can economists be sure that the commoditisation of fishing rights will lead to an optimally efficient outcome?

In order for the ITQ system to fulfil its primary objective of productive efficiency, it was essential that fishing rights should come to be perceived as commodities. In other words, ITQs needed to be seen exclusively as a means to maximise profits or to minimise losses, which economic actors must be willing to exchange freely. This perception of a commodity as solely a means to an end, without intrinsic value or meaning, is a fundamental characteristic of the neo-classical economist's virtual reality. To introduce this perception to the industry, however, it is not sufficient to pass laws that effectively define fishing rights as commodities; it is also necessary for participants in the industry to start using fishing rights as if they were commodities. Given that the appropriate legislation is in place, neo-classical theorists assume that this is an automatic process. Thus, those individuals who divorce fishing rights from their previous social identity will manage their economic affairs more rationally and be rewarded with higher levels of profit than will those who see fishing rights as having their old social identity. This selective process is guided by the invisible hand of the market, whereby those who make the highest profits will eventually buy out the less successful. The outcome, then, is a distribution of ITQs that generates the maximum overall economic efficiency of production in the industry and a prevalence of the commodity view of fishing rights. Questions of who the individual producers are, how many they are or how they go about their business are of little significance; all that is important is that the maximum level of economic rents is being produced.

Distributional questions and the existence of differential success in the economy are, however, sometimes addressed by economists. A special form of economic efficiency, allocative efficiency, provides economists with an answer to questions regarding the fairness and appropriateness of particular distributions of resources.[3]

---

2. Alternatively, externalities are regarded as mere economic noise, which can be ignored by applying the principle of *ceteris paribus*.

3. While conventionally only applied to the distribution of wealth and economic goods among consumers, the subject matter of welfare economics, increasingly the concept of allocative efficiency has been extended to the economic analyses of production, particularly in the field of resource economics (Saraydar 1989: 64–65).

According to economic theory, the greatest level of allocative efficiency is achieved when resources are distributed among individuals in just proportion to their utility. Utility, in this context, refers to an individual's needs, which, in turn, are determined by their subjective preferences and are manifest in their revealed preferences. Hence, in the context of the Icelandic fisheries, those who have the most need for ITQs should ultimately receive the largest shares. However, this raises the problem of how one measures and compares subjective needs and preferences. In other words, to take a real example, how would one compare the utility of an ITQ for a small-scale boat owner on the point of bankruptcy with its utility for a large and profitable fishing company?

Economists have given up trying to assess individual utilities as hopelessly subjective (England 1993; Sen 1987). Instead, they rely on a theoretical solution that seems objective, that of Pareto optimality. Based on utilitarian ethical theory, this assumes that the desirability of a particular distribution of resources is a function of net changes in the aggregate utility of a group of individuals. Given any initial distribution of a particular resource, one starts with the assumption that all individuals would like to increase their share rather than see it diminished. One result of this is that any involuntary redistribution of resources can not lead to a net increase in overall utility. In contrast, any distributional change that results in at least one person's being better off without anyone else's being worse off marks an increase in overall utility, and is a move towards Pareto optimality (see LeGrand 1991; Sen 1987).

According to orthodox economic theory, such distributional changes can only be achieved through market exchange. Because such exchange is, by definition, voluntary, and because both parties behave in a rational and self-interested manner, market exchange will only take place when both parties expect to benefit in some way. (Interestingly, in this case neo-classical economists rarely allow for variability in degree of rationality and self-interest.) Each transaction is a revealed preference, which signifies that some subjective preferences and needs have been satisfied, resulting in an increased aggregate utility. Thus, the invisible hand of the market inevitably achieves a state of greater allocative efficiency (Nelson 1993; Sen 1987). The more the activity in the market, the more efficient the outcome will be, and since everyone is, by definition, getting what they want, this redistributional process is, by definition, fair.

The axioms of productive and allocative efficiency lie at the heart of ITQ management and provide economists with a comprehensive and consistent model of what will happen and how people will react when fishing rights are transformed into commodities. One conclusion based on the model is that ITQ management will be welcomed by most producers as an opportunity to increase their profit. Another is that the notion of fishing rights as commodities will prevail in the industry, and as operators adapt to the new institutional reality of the fisheries there will be a rapid redistribution of fishing rights as the successful buy out the less successful, the expected reaction to this process being general indifference or enthusiasm. Yet another expectation is that the overall productive efficiency and satisfaction of industry members will increase in proportion to the extent of the exchange of fishing rights that takes place.

Some Social Consequences of ITQ Management

Since the introduction of ITQ management in 1984, and particularly since the 1990 legislation that made fishing rights true commodities, the Icelandic fishing industry has undergone a radical transformation. ITQs have become increasingly concentrated in the hands of large, vertically-integrated companies, while the number of smaller operators has diminished (for a detailed account of these structural changes, see Helgason 1995; Pálsson and Helgason 1995). In 1991 there were 1,155 ITQ-holders, among whom 16 'giants' (those with more than 1 per cent of the ITQs) controlled about a quarter of the total Icelandic quota. By early 1997, the number of ITQ-holders had decreased to 706, with 22 giants controlling about half the quota.

However, in spite of the confident predictions deriving from the virtual reality of productive and allocative efficiency models, a large majority of participants in the fishing industry and the Icelandic public are deeply concerned about the concentration of fishing rights in the hands of a few large companies. In public discourse the owners of the biggest companies are habitually referred to as 'quota-kings' (*kvótakóngar*) and 'lords of the sea' (*sægreifar*). The editor of *Vikingur*, a journal for fishers, voicing the concerns of fishers in general, put it this way:

> Before you know it the whole national fleet will be in the hands of ten to fifteen individuals, who will then also 'own' all the fish in the waters around Iceland. Thus a new aristocracy will have emerged, an aristocracy that decides where fishermen and employees of the fishing plants will live, what they earn and what rights they are to have (Valdimarsson 1990).

Clearly, under the ITQ regime the right to fish can no longer be associated with the principle of egalitarianism. Indeed, complaints are often raised that while fishing rights were traditionally the birthright of all Icelanders, now that they have become commodities they will be inherited by the holders' descendants like any other private property. An ex-skipper, who now runs a processing plant, put it like this:

> These property rights will be inherited by the descendants of the men who were lucky enough to have fished [owned boats] during those fateful years [when ITQ allocations were determined]. … we can imagine one day in the year 2000 that a 10-year-old girl or

boy, for example in Reykjavík, has become the principal heir to living fish in the sea ... because their grandfather, a boat-owner from the West-country, has just passed away (Hermansson 1991).

The concentration of ITQs in the hands of large companies can not be explained as the result of an inherent drive towards productive efficiency resulting from the commoditisation of fishing rights, or as the result of a widespread acceptance of the new social identity of fishing rights. Instead, there are two primary explanations for the differential success of actors in acquiring ITQ holdings. The first is a devaluation of ITQ shares. In Iceland the actual amount of fish a boat owner can catch each year depends on a combination of the size of the ITQ share (a figure that only changes when ITQ shares are bought or sold) and the size of the total allowable catch set annually by the Ministry of Fisheries, a figure that can vary from year to year for each species of fish depending on the recommendations of fisheries biologists. The result is that if the total allowable catch is reduced, ITQ shares become devalued and boat owners can catch fewer tons of fish per ITQ share that they hold.

This aspect of the ITQ system is highly relevant for the distributional changes outlined above. Following bleak estimates of the fish stocks in Icelandic waters by marine biologists, the Ministry of Fisheries made recurrent cuts to the total allowable catch from 1988 to 1995, particularly in cod, economically the most important species that is subject to ITQ management. As a result, many small companies found themselves left with insufficient annual catches to keep their boats active throughout the fishing year. To give some indication of the extent of these devaluations, a small-scale operator who controlled an ITQ share in cod of 0.1 per cent could catch approximately 254 tons of cod in 1987, 200 tons in 1991 and only 106 tons in 1994. Obviously, larger companies were also affected by these cuts; but many of these operators seem to have had more success in adapting to the situation. Indeed, our results indicate that while many small companies were forced to sell their ITQ shares and leave the system, the larger companies reacted by buying up this new supply of permanent fishing rights (Helgason 1995; Pálsson and Helgason 1995). From the buyer's point of view this is money well spent, given that the stocks will eventually revive and afford higher total allowable catches. In that event, ITQ shares would engender much higher annual catches and would become significantly more valuable.

Owing to the devaluation of ITQ shares, it became increasingly difficult for many small-scale operators to continue fishing as they used to. This occurred at the same time as larger companies were increasingly sending their trawlers to fish in international waters, where ITQs are not required. Thus a state of affairs emerged where a number of companies with large ITQ holdings were able to keep their vessels in action without using their quotas. These companies then leased their

ITQs out to those who did want to use them, operators of small-scale, inshore vessels with few or no ITQ holdings of their own.

These transactions typically involve long-term contracts between large ITQ-holders and smaller operators, where the former provide the latter with ITQs in return for a proportion of the proceeds. One such arrangement, usually referred to as 'fishing for others' (*veiða fyrir aðra*), is becoming more widespread. Here, the supplier of the ITQs is a large, vertically-integrated company that controls a processing plant and two or more trawlers, which are sent to fish in international waters. The company contracts to transfer its ITQs to a smaller operator's boat. The latter then fishes the ITQs and delivers the catch to the suppliers' processing plant for a price 40–50 per cent below the prevailing market price. Understandably, the lessee boat owners can not make the same level of profits when fishing for others that they could when fishing their own ITQs. They try to compensate for this by reducing the wages of fishers.

The typical lessee owns a relatively small vessel with a meagre supply of ITQs, or owns a 'eunuch' (*geldingur*), a boat that has virtually no ITQs of its own and depends on leased ITQs. Through ITQ leasing, boat owners with small ITQ holdings manage to prolong their fishing operations throughout the year. For the lessors of ITQs, participation in these new relations of production represents a rather lucrative business. By leasing its ITQs, a company can free itself from the expenses of actually catching the fish, while still procuring up to half of the market value of the catch. Moreover, the arrangement helps supply the company's processing facilities, while allowing its vessels to pursue other assignments in international waters, bringing even more fish to be processed. These new relations of production have become increasingly pronounced in recent years (Pálsson and Helgason 1995). These developments have led fishers to augment existing feudal metaphors by referring to the ITQ system as a tenancy system (*lénskerfi*). In this conception the quota-kings are likened to medieval landlords, with the fishing grounds as their estate (*óðal*). Conversely, fishers and small-scale lessee operators become the 'tenants' or 'serfs' (*leiguliðar*), who are granted access to the fishing grounds on the condition that they hand over their catch to the lessor's processing plants. The lessor not only controls how many tons a tenant boat is allowed to fish, but also controls the duration and location of each fishing trip. As one skipper put it, 'one must give in to almost every demand, because the quota-king makes all the rules, sets the price and everything'.

Contesting the Model: Controversy over the Social Identity of Fishing Rights

The emergence of profit-oriented ITQ leasing indicates a shift in the concept-ualisation of fishing rights, a shift that coincided with a growing perception among certain producers within the industry that ITQs were not just use-rights but were also, in effect, property that could be exchanged solely for profit. This new social identity of fishing rights is the other major factor that explains the apparent success of the larger companies, combined with their ready access to capital through the Icelandic banking system. The approach to business of the large, vertically-integrated companies is very different to that of the smaller operators, in that they tend to hold long-term economic goals, attempting to maximise their profits by adjusting to the system and exploiting all possible nooks and crannies that it offers. For them, the system provides new opportunities to make profits, and consequently they tend to endorse ITQ management with enthusiasm. These companies, then, react to the commoditisation of fishing rights in the way expected by neo-classical theory. In contrast, the smaller operators tend to perceive the ITQ system as an obstacle to their traditional way of fishing. These producers attempt to adjust the system to their way of doing things, fishing their quotas whilst waiting for the ITQ system to be abolished and replaced by something more akin to the 'old way'. More importantly, however, the smaller operators and, it seems, the majority of Icelanders vehemently object to the new commodity identity of fishing rights.

The transformation of the social identity of fishing rights, from the status of common property to commodity, has turned out to be one of the most contentious issues associated with ITQ management in Iceland. As we have already explained, common rights in fish are deeply embedded in Icelandic history and national identity. Traditional Icelandic conceptions of common rights in fish incorporate the notion that fish can only be transformed into commodities through the act of catching (see Pálsson 1991: 44–46). In contrast, the idea that individuals or companies can own and sell rights to fish that have yet to be caught or even spawned, the crux of ITQ management, horrifies many fishers. One voiced these concerns in an interview: 'I think that [un-caught fish] can never be counted as property. They can't do that. I don't believe that boat owners can appropriate animals that are not yet born as their property, like calves that have not yet been conceived.'

This opposition to the commodity identity of fishing rights should not be taken to mean that fishers and the general public are opposed to market production *per se*; far from it. The Icelandic fishing industry has been market-oriented for many decades, and when it comes to selling the catch, the most vociferous opponents of the ITQ system are very much in favour of the free market as a regulating device. It is very specifically the commoditisation of fishing rights and the consequences of this process that are being rejected.

Icelandic fishers and many of the general public attempt to resist profit-oriented exchange through a vigorous discourse that brands offending boat owners as immoral 'quota-profiteers' (*kvótabraskarar*). In particular, it is the profit-oriented monetary exchange of ITQs that is condemned. Such transactions bring into focus the new commodity nature of fishing rights, one which raises their exchange value over their use value. In the words of one fishers' representative: 'We have nothing against boat-owners who trade equivalent amounts of quotas in different fish species ... but we will not tolerate quota-profiteering [*kvótabrask*], where boat-owners make money from selling what they don't own.' Voicing similar concerns, one skipper complained: 'The system has strayed from its original purpose, now that it is possible to buy [un-caught] fish in the sea. There are almost as many speculators on dry land as there are fishermen' (*Dagur*, 25 August 1991). These businessmen, or 'quota-kings' as they are sometimes called, are pictured spending hours sitting in front of computer screens, wholly divorced from the productive process, profiteering with ITQs.

An important prerequisite for the rationalisation and distancing process, on which the success of the ITQ system depends, was that fishing rights would emerge in the economy devoid of their previous symbolic baggage. Clearly, however, the disembedded commodity identity of fishing rights has not prevailed in the Icelandic fishing industry, or indeed in the nation in general. For most Icelanders fishing rights are not and can not be viewed solely as a means to create economic rents, but remain very much embedded in their history and national identity. For these people, fishing rights represent egalitarian use-rights, a licence issued by the nation to go out to sea and create value through the act of fishing and selling the catch. The notion that value can be created by exchanging un-caught fish, the central notion of ITQ management, is conceived as highly unnatural.

This discourse of resistance seems to highlight the issue of agency and a labour theory of value (see Gudeman and Rivera 1990; Helgason and Pálsson 1997; Weiss 1996). In the case of the Icelandic ITQ system, the allocation of fishing rights to boat owners has resulted in a privileging of capital over labour, shifting power from sea to land and widening the economic rift between boat owners and their employees. Commenting on a young boat owner who had given up fishing and turned to renting out his ITQs, one fisher remarked, 'he isn't working and that's unnatural, a young man like him!' In the words of another fisher, 'it necessarily adds a devilish aspect to the system when people can rent their quota and then just relax in bed'. These and related statements testify to a powerful concept of work, bodily experience and labour value that resonates with the so-called medieval house view of production and exchange, wherein the merchant and the usurer were held not to be creating anything, but immorally breeding money from money (Simmel 1990).

Opposition to the ITQ system is neither trivial nor is it likely to peter out as people grudgingly accept the benefits of this alleged modernisation of the industry. In January of 1994, Icelandic fishers held a national strike protesting against the ITQ system, under the slogan 'No More Profiteering!' (*Braskið burt!*) The strike effectively shut down the fishing industry for two weeks, a predicament of grave importance for a nation that derives almost 70 per cent of its national income from exporting fish. Ultimately, the strike was terminated by temporary laws that forced fishermen back to work. Fishermen went on strike again in May 1995, this time for four weeks. Currently the dispute is unresolved, with rumours of new strikes surfacing every once in a while. Moreover, regular rumblings in the Parliament and the national media ensure that the continued existence of the ITQ system is, at best, precarious.

Conclusions

Contrary to the economic and social success story predicted by economists, the ITQ system has become one of the most contentious and tumultuous issues in Icelandic political history. Whilst the fate of the system depends on a continuing political contest, the ITQ system remains a panglossian virtual reality for its adherents and architects, who failed to foresee the scale of opposition. Indeed, it seems that their approach renders them blind to the convolutions of the moral and social environment within which the ITQ model is supposed to function. When pressed to consider the possibility of opposition to ITQ management, one leading Icelandic resource economist said that it could only be founded on 'traditional values and vested interests rather than rational arguments' (Árnason 1993: 206–207), whilst another cites 'the human capacity for misperceiving what is in one's best interest' (Hannesson 1994: 7). Leaving aside the question of how economists can ignore the revealed preference of fishermen for strike action rather than the ITQ system, economically the extent and severity of resistance has quite possibly dissipated any overall financial gains that might have been achieved through the reduction of fishing effort resulting from the ITQ system.

It is sometimes argued that all scientific disciplines simplify reality in one way or another through the use of specialised models and that such simplification is a prerequisite for analysis. Models are a way of conceptualising certain aspects of reality; thus, all disciplines perceive their part of the world as some kind of virtual reality. Devons and Gluckman (1964: 220) advocated such a point of view in their early discussion of the relationship between anthropology and economics:

> It is quite common for psychologists and sociologists to criticise economists on the grounds that they use basic assumptions about human motivations which are quite unreal and unjustifiably naïve. Yet it is uncommon to find any analysis of how these assumptions may affect the validity of the conclusions reached by economists. Usually these critics implicitly assume that, if the assumptions are 'wrong' or 'unreal', then it necessarily follows that the theory based on them will be mistaken and misleading. This may seem a reasonable view to take, but it is an essential part of our argument that it is an erroneous view.

Advocating what can only be described as an enforced fragmentation of the social sciences, these scholars argue that a scholar is 'entitled to disregard the researches and conclusions of ... other disciplines as irrelevant to his problems' (Devons and Gluckman 1964: 165–166).

We believe that this conception is entirely misplaced. The case we describe here shows that an anthropological perspective on economic life in the West may be essential to help avoid the exaggeration of problems to which prescriptive economic policy is directed. Earlier we referred to some of the similarities of economics and linguistics. The theoretical constructs established by both grammarians and resource economists, we argued, tend to attain lives of their own. Having modelled the real world, the modellers seek to reinforce the order postulated by their analyses, and, as a result, reality resonates with the models. There are important differences, however, between linguistics and economics.

For one thing, the solutions to Hardinian 'tragedies' of language and nature may not be the same. Neo-classical economics tends to opt for privatisation, emphasising the importance of property rights. Thus, it is argued, over-fishing is inevitable as long as the fishing grounds are defined as common property. Consequently, the only realistic alternative, euphemistically called 'rights-based' fishing (see Macinko 1993: 946), is a system of individual transferable quotas. Linguists, in contrast, tend to have mixed feelings about changing everyday language, the ultimate object of their analyses, in the process of recording it; this is the 'observer's paradox' of ethnolinguistics. Linguists know all too well that while they arrive on the scene to listen to language 'as it is', their mere presence unavoidably shapes the course of linguistic events and, therefore, their representation of speech. Economists are notorious for their lack of such sensibilities. Despite their rhetoric of detachment and objectivity, in practice economists tend to assume, as if they were following a strong version of what might be called a speech-act theory of the economy, that the economy is constituted in the act of naming it. Presently, the act of naming is the privileged exercise of economists. Perhaps it is time for anthropologists to rediscover the social and moral designation of the economy.

References

Acheson, James M., and James A. Wilson 1996. Order Out of Chaos: The Case for Parametric Fisheries Management. *American Anthropologist* 98: 579–594.

Árnason, Ragnar 1991. Efficient Management of Ocean Fisheries. *European Economic Review* 35: 408–417.

—— 1993. The Icelandic Individual Transferable Quota System: A Descriptive Account. *Marine Resource Economics* 8: 201–218.

Bergsson, K. 1926. Sýnið fánann. [Show the national flag!] *Ægir* 19(4): 53–54.

Bjarnason, Matthías 1977. Ávarp Matthíasar Bjarnasonar svarújátvegsráðherra. *Ægir* 70: 339–341.

Bourdieu, Pierre 1977. The Economics of Linguistic Exchanges. *Social Science Information* 16: 645–668.

Brydon, Anne 1996. Whale-Siting: Spatiality in Icelandic Nationalism. In Gísli Pálsson and E. Paul Durrenberger (eds), *Images of Contemporary Iceland: Everyday Lives and Global Contexts*, pp. 23–45. Iowa City: University of Iowa Press.

Dagur (Akureyri), 25 August 1991.

Devons, Eli, and Max Gluckman 1964. Conclusions: Modes and Consequences of Limiting a Field of Study. In M. Gluckman (ed.), *Closed Systems and Open Minds: The Limits of Naivety in Social Anthropology*, pp. 158–261. London: Oliver and Boyd.

England, Paula 1993. The Separative Self: Androcentric Bias in Neoclassical Assumptions. In Marianne Ferber and Julie A. Nelson (eds), *Beyond Economic Man: Feminist Theory and Economics*, pp. 37–53. Chicago: University of Chicago Press.

Fiskifréttir (Reykjavík), June 1990 to November 1991.

Gudeman, Stephen, and Alberto Rivera 1990. *Conversations in Colombia: The Domestic Economy in Life and Text*. Cambridge: Cambridge University Press.

Hannesson, Rögnvaldur 1994. Rights Based Fishing: The Role of Property Rights in Fisheries Management. Presented at the 82nd Statutory Meeting of the International Council for the Exploration of the Sea, 22–30 September, St John's, Newfoundland.

Hardin, Garett 1968. The Tragedy of the Commons. *Science* 162: 1243–1248.

Helgason, Agnar 1995. The Lords of the Sea and the Morality of Exchange: The Social Context of ITQ Management in the Icelandic Fisheries. MA dissertation, Department of Anthropology, University of Iceland.

Helgason, Agnar, and Gísli Pálsson 1997. Contested Commodities: The Moral Landscape of Modernist Regimes. *Journal of the Royal Anthropological Institute* 3: 451–471.

Hermansson, Halldór 1991. Fiskveiðistefnan og friðurinn. *Morgunblaðið* (Reykjavík) (25 June).

LeGrand, Julian 1991. *Equity and Choice: An Essay in Economics and Applied Philosophy*. London: Harper-Collins.

McCann, Richard J. 1996. Environmental Commodities Markets: 'Messy' versus 'Ideal' Worlds. *Contemporary Economic Policy* 14 (July): 85–97.

McCay, Bonnie J. (ed.) 1995. Property Rights and Fisheries Management. *Ocean and Coastal Management* 28 (1–3): special issue.

McCay, Bonnie J., and James M. Acheson (eds) 1987. *The Question of the Commons: The Culture and Ecology of Communal Resources*. Tucson: University of Arizona Press.

Macinko, Seth 1993. Public or Private? United States Commercial Fisheries Management and the Public Trust Doctrine, Reciprocal Challenges. *Natural Resources Journal* 32: 919–955.

Mirowski, Philip 1994. *Natural Images in Economic Thought: 'Markets Read in Tooth and Claw'*. Cambridge: Cambridge University Press.

Neher, Philip A., Ragnar Arnason, and Nina Mollett (eds) 1989. *Rights-Based Fishing*. Dordrecht: Kluwer Academic.

Nelson, Julie A. 1993. The Study of Choice or the Study of Provisioning? Gender and the Definition of Economics. In Marianne A. Ferber and J. A. Nelson (eds), *Beyond Economic Man: Feminist Theory and Economics*, pp. 23–36. Chicago: University of Chicago Press.

Pálsson, Gísli 1991. *Coastal Economies, Cultural Accounts: Human Ecology and Icelandic Discourse*. Manchester: Manchester University Press.

—— 1995. *The Textual Life of Savants: Ethnography, Iceland and the Linguistic Turn*. Reading: Harwood Academic.

—— 1998. The Birth of the Aquarium: The Political Ecology of Icelandic Fishing. In Tim Gray (ed.), *The Politics of Fishing*. London: Macmillan. (Forthcoming.)

Pálsson, Gísli, and Agnar Helgason 1995. Figuring Fish and Measuring Men: The Individual Transferable Quota System in the Icelandic Cod Fishery. *Ocean and Coastal Management* 28 (1–3): 117–146.

Rossi-Landi, Feruccio 1983. *Language as Work and Trade: A Semiotic Homology for Linguistics and Economics*. South Hadley, Mass.: Bergin and Garvey.

Saraydar, Edward 1989. The Conflation of Productivity and Efficiency in Economics and Economic History. *Economics and Philosophy* 5: 55–67.

Sen, Amartya 1987. *On Ethics and Economics*. Oxford: Basil Blackwell.

Simmel, Georg 1990. *The Philosophy of Money*, Second edition. (Edited by David Frisby; translated by Tom Bottomore and David Frisby.) London: Routledge.

Sjávarfréttir (Reykjavík), June 1991.

Tietenberg, Tom 1994. *Environmental Economics and Policy*. New York: HarperCollins.

Valdimarsson, Sigurjón 1990. Ritstjórnargrein (editorial), *Sjómannablaðið Víkingur* (Reykjavík) 1: 5.

Viðhorf til Sjávarútvegsmála 1991. *Þjóðmálakönnun, June 1991*. Reykjavík: Institute of Social Science, University of Iceland.

Weiss, Brad 1996. *The Making and Unmaking of the Maya Lived World: Consumption, Commoditization, and Everyday Practice*. Durham, NC: Duke University Press.

$-6-$

The Transnational Capitalist Class
Leslie Sklair

This chapter attempts to rethink the concept of the capitalist class in terms of the increasing abstraction of economic institutions and a concern with the ways that this abstraction is espoused as a model of the way things ought to be, the virtualism of the class. As theories of the capitalist class as a ruling class in one country, those of Domhoff (1967), Connell (1977) and Useem (1984) seem to me the most useful starting-places. However, I argue that globalisation makes this class more abstract, reflecting its changing structure and dynamics. Also, I start to explore the question of the extent to which the capitalist class, which all the above primarily analyse in terms of single countries (US, Australia, UK), is the ruling class in the global system, the transnational capitalist class (TCC). This argument conceptualises class in capitalist society in terms of relations to the means of production, distribution and exchange; it resists the neo-Weberian attempt to separate class, status and command (despite the persuasive arguments of Scott 1996); it highlights the central role of the capitalist class in the struggle to commoditise everything, and so render everything more abstract.

While the class and ruling-class literature is well known, even if highly contentious, theories of globalisation are less so. Therefore it is necessary to spell out in more detail my own conception of globalisation and the capitalist global system theory from which these hypotheses are derived. Since the 1980s there has been a great deal of attention paid to globalisation by scholars (Waters 1995 provides a useful introduction) and practitioners, notably in the business literature and material from the corporations (Kanter 1996).

It is important at the outset to distinguish between national–international and transnational–global approaches to globalisation. This distinction signals the difference between state-centrist approaches based on the pre-existing, even if changing, system of nation-states and global approaches based on transnational forces and institutions, where the state is one among several key actors and, in some theories of globalisation, no longer the most important (see Ross and Trachte 1990; Sklair 1995).[1] Not all writers are clear about this distinction, with resultant confusions.

---

1. Robinson (1996: 367–368) has argued that it is necessary to distinguish 'nation-state' centrism from 'state' centrism and that global system theory needs a fourth set of transnational practices, namely

The global system theory propounded here is based on the concept of transnational practices, practices that are abstracted from national class systems in that they cross state boundaries and do not necessarily originate with state agencies or actors. Analytically, they operate in three spheres, the economic, the political and the cultural-ideological. These are superimposed each on the others rather than being separate spheres. The whole is what I mean by the global system. While the global system, at the end of the twentieth century, is not synonymous with global capitalism, what the theory sets out to demonstrate is that the dominant forces of global capitalism are the dominant forces in the global system. The building-blocks of the theory are the transnational corporation (TNC), the characteristic institutional form of economic transnational practices; a still-evolving transnational capitalist class in the political sphere; and, in the culture-ideology sphere, the culture-ideology of consumerism.

The TCC is not necessarily the ruling class. The assumption on which my argument is based is that the TCC is the ruling class in the global capitalist system, a fairly obvious proposition. That global capitalism dominates the global system as a whole is less obvious; indeed, it is a rather contentious claim. Most of the attempts to theorise what might be seen as a global ruling class – notably the international bourgeoisie (more or less a staple of dependency theorists), the Atlantic Ruling Class (van der Pijl 1984), the corporate international wing of the managerial bourgeoisie (Becker *et al.* 1987), the international corporate elite (Fennema 1982), and answers to the question: 'Who rules the world?' (Goldfrank 1977) – have given pride of place to those who own and control the TNCs. Another source of insight into a global ruling class has emerged from the Gramscian turn in International Relations. Cox (1987: 271) writes of 'an emerging global class structure' and Gill (1990: 94ff.) identifies a 'developing transnational capitalist class fraction'. While all these grapple with the issue of state–global relations they do not, in my view, make the extraordinarily difficult decisive break with state-centrism that is necessary if we are to move forward. The key issues are the ways in which the capitalist class relates to the 'national interest' and 'national economy' and, in terms of this collection, the degree to which the capitalist class is being abstracted from a national political and economic context. Globalisation means that increasingly capitalists seek to transcend the national in search of the global. As an attempt to build on this rich literature, the concept of transnational practices and its political form, the TCC, is a step towards consolidating the theoretical link

---

transnational state practices. While I appreciate this point, I still maintain that the only way to avoid state-centrism, which I believe is fatal to any genuine theory of globalisation, is to conceptualise the political in terms of the TCC. Transnational state practices are the business of globalising state bureaucrats, not the state as such. The struggle between globalising and localising state bureaucrats, then, becomes a key site in which the hegemony of the TCC is mediated.

between globalisation and the ruling class and providing some evidence that these concepts have genuine empirical referents.

The Transnational Capitalist Class

The TCC is the characteristic institutional form of political transnational practices in the global capitalist system. It can be analytically divided into four main fractions: TNC executives, globalising bureaucrats, globalising politicians and professionals, and consumerist elites (merchants and media). My argument is that those who dominate these groups, taken together, constitute a *global* power elite, ruling class or inner circle in the sense that these terms have been used to characterise the class structures of specific countries (see Domhoff 1967; Scott 1996; Useem 1984). The TCC is opposed not only by those who reject capitalism as a way of life and an economic system, but also by those capitalists who reject globalisation. Some localised, domestically-oriented businesses can share the interests of the global corporations and prosper, but most can not, and perish. Influential business strategists and management theorists commonly argue that to survive, local business must globalise (for example, Kanter 1996). Inward-oriented government bureau-crats, politicians and professionals who reject globalisation and espouse extreme nationalist ideologies are comparatively rare, despite the recent rash of civil wars in economically marginal parts of the world. And while there are anti-consumerist elements in most societies, there are few cases of a serious anti-consumerist party winning political power anywhere in the world.[2]

The TCC is transnational (or global) in the following respects.

(a) The economic interests of its members are increasingly globally linked rather than exclusively local and national in origin, and hence are increasingly abstracted from their pre-existing contexts. As *rentiers* and as executives, their property and shares and their corporations are becoming more globalised; as ideologues, their intellectual products serve the interests of globalising rather than localising capital. This follows directly from the shareholder-driven growth imperative that lies behind the globalisation of the world economy and the increasing difficulty of enhancing shareholder value in purely domestic firms. The richest and most powerful corporations in the world, with few exceptions, tend to be globalising in terms of foreign economic activities, aspirations to world-class operations and the rhetoric

---

2. It has been argued, in the context of consumerism and the middle class in Asia, that 'the smaller capitalists and the petty bourgeoisie have resisted the internationalisation of their economies and are prepared to support governments that take a nationalist and populist line' (Robison and Goodman 1996: 13). It is difficult to reconcile this with their consumerist ideology and practices, based as they are on imported consumer goods and services. Patricio Silva (1995) shows that the *festival consumista* of the Pinochet regime in Chile persuaded the masses that globalising neo-liberal policies were in their best interests.

and practices of global corporate citizenship and global visions. For many practical purposes, economic activity around the world is still organised in the context of discrete national economies. However, the TCC increasingly conceptualises its interests more abstractly, in terms of specific markets that may or may not coincide with a specific nation-state, and in terms of the global market, which clearly does not.[3] Van der Pijl (1993: 30) traces the point when the context-bound 'national identity' of the corporations 'had to be abandoned' to the 1970s, and while few would go this far, there is sufficient evidence to show that the global corporation of today is not the same as the multinational corporation of the past.

(b) The TCC seeks to exert economic control in the workplace, political control in domestic and international politics and cultural-ideological control in everyday life through specific forms of global competitive and consumerist rhetoric and practice, devices that not only reflect their abstract view of the world but are also virtualisms, for they serve to make reality conform to that abstract vision. The focus of workplace control is the threat that jobs will be lost and, in the extreme, the economy will collapse unless workers are prepared to work longer and for less in order to meet foreign competition.[4] This is reflected in local electoral politics in most countries, where the major parties have few substantial strategic (even if many tactical) differences, and in the sphere of culture-ideology, where consumerism is rarely challenged.

(c) Members of the TCC have outward-oriented global rather than inward-oriented local perspectives on most economic, political and culture-ideology issues. The growing TNC and international institutional emphasis on free trade and the shift from import substitution to export promotion strategies in most developing countries since the 1980s are virtualisms that have been driven by members of the

---

3. I define 'domestic firms' as those serving an exclusively national market, employing only local co-nationals, whose products consist entirely of domestic services, components and materials. If you think that this is a ridiculously narrow definition for the realities of contemporary economies then you are more than half-way to accepting my concept of globalisation. Apart from small localised firms, the exceptions are mainly what are now commonly termed state-owned enterprises and quasi-monopolistic utility and services corporations (see any issue of the *Fortune* Global 500 for the 1990s). The facts that state-owned enterprises are being run more like TNCs or are being privatised and frequently sold to TNCs and that the quasi-monopolies are being rapidly deregulated, enhances rather than detracts from my central argument. For an application of this argument to the TNCs in California, see Sklair (1998).

4. This is being termed 'the race to the bottom' by radical critics (see Brecher and Costello 1994; Ranney 1994). While this is not new – capitalists have always fought against reductions in the length of the working day and increases in wages – its global scope is unprecedented. This is regularly noted, from the normally globalising *Economist* (in 'Profits of gloom', 28 September 1996), which asserts that most of the extra profit generated by information technology and globalisation is going straight to the owners of capital at the expense of wages, to the Indian *Economic Times* (4 March 1997), which notes that as globalisation makes India richer, the peasants get poorer.

TCC working through government agencies, elite opinion organisations and the media.

Some of the credit for this apparent transformation in the way in which big business works around the world is attached to the tremendous growth in business education since the 1960s, particularly in the US and Europe, but increasingly all over the world. In 1990 there were at least 184 business schools in the US offering postgraduate degrees in international business. Their abstract orientation is illustrated by a spokesman for the Wharton School: 'We wanted to be a school of management of the world that just happens to be headquartered in Philadelphia' (Carey 1990: 36). (Of Wharton students on various postgraduate business programmes in 1990, between 26 and 40 per cent were from outside the US.) Research on INSEAD in Paris suggests that business schools are beginning to have a significant impact on the behaviour and ideology of European executives as well (Marceau 1989). There is now a huge literature in the popular and academic business press on the making of the global manager and the globalisation of business and management (see Warner 1996: *passim*) that confirms that this is a real phenomenon and not simply the creation of a few 'globaloney' myth-makers.

(d) Members of the TCC tend to share similar life-styles, particularly patterns of higher education (increasingly in business schools) and consumption of luxury goods and services, which generates their own social, but not local, context. Integral to this process are exclusive clubs and restaurants, ultra-expensive resorts in all continents, private as opposed to mass forms of travel and entertainment and, ominously, increasing residential segregation of the very rich secured by armed guards and electronic surveillance, from Los Angeles to Moscow, from Manila to Beijing.

(e) Finally, members of the TCC seek to project abstracted images of themselves as citizens of the world as well as of their places of birth. Leading exemplars of this phenomenon include Jacques Maisonrouge, French-born, who became the chief executive of IBM World Trade in the 1960s (Maisonrouge 1988); the Swede Percy Barnevik, who created Asea Brown Boverei, often portrayed as spending most of his life in his corporate jet (Taylor 1991); the German Helmut Maucher, head of Nestlés far-flung global empire (Maucher 1994); David Rockefeller, said to be one of the most powerful men in the United States (Gill 1990); the legendary Akio Morita, the founder of Sony (Morita and Reingold 1987); and Rupert Murdoch, who actually changed his citizenship to pursue his global media interests (Shawcross 1992).

The concept of the TCC implies that there is one central inner circle that makes system-wide decisions and that it connects in a variety of ways with members of the TCC in each locality, region and country. Despite real geographical and sectoral conflicts, the whole of the TCC shares a fundamental interest in the continued accumulation of private profit. What the inner circle of the TCC does is to give a unity to the diverse economic interests, political organisations and cultural and ideological formations of those who make up the class as a whole. As in any social class, fundamental long-term unity of interests and purpose does not preclude shorter-term and local conflicts of interest and purpose, both within each of the four fractions and between them. The culture-ideology of consumerism is the fundamental value system that keeps the system intact; but it permits a relatively wide variety of choices – for example, what I term 'emergent global nationalisms' (see below). These are a way of satisfying the needs of the different actors and their constituencies within the global system. The four fractions of the TCC in any geographical and social area, region, country, city, society, community, perform complementary functions to integrate the whole. The achievement of these goals is facilitated by the activities of local and national agents and organisations that are connected in a complex global network.

A crucial component of this integration of the TCC as a global class is that most of its senior members will occupy a variety of interlocking positions. These are not only the interlocking directorates that have been the subject of detailed studies for some time in a variety of countries (Mizruchi and Schwartz 1987; Scott 1990: Vol. 3; Stokman, Ziegler and Scott 1985), but also connections outside the direct ambit of the corporate sector, which constitute a 'civil society', as it were, servicing the state-like structures of the corporations. Leading corporate executives serve on and chair the boards of think tanks and charities, scientific, sports, arts and culture bodies, universities, medical foundations and similar institutions (Domhoff 1967; Scott 1990: Vol. 1, Pts 2, 3; Useem 1984). It is in this sense that the claims 'the business of society is business' and 'the business of our society is global business' become legitimated in the global capitalist system. Business, particularly the TNC sector, then begins to monopolise symbols of modernity and postmodernity like free enterprise, international competitiveness and the good life, and begins to transform most, if not all, social spheres in its own image.

While they are all members of a single, global class and share important characteristics, each fraction of this class has its own specific characteristics. These can be analysed in terms of their economic base, their political organisation and their culture and ideology.

TNC Executives

The most important fraction of the TCC comprises the leading executives of the world's biggest TNCs. The executives of these corporations wield power to the extent that they control parts of the global economy, and their actions and decisions can have fundamental effects globally and on the local communities in which their corporations are active in any capacity. This group may also include the leading executives of companies that, while not themselves among the biggest TNCs, are of strategic importance for the global economy.

The economic base of these executives is their corporate salaries and their privileged access to shares and other financial rewards in the companies they work for either directly or as members of boards.[5] The executives of the TNCs are paid relatively large salaries compared with workers in responsible positions in other economic spheres. While actual remuneration naturally differs from company to company, industry to industry and country to country, it is probably true to say that, with the exception of individual sporting and entertainment superstars, corporate executives have the highest salaries of any employed group.

The political organisations of the corporate elite are the peak business associations and bodies that connect business with other spheres (governments, global politics, social issues and so forth) operating at various levels. These include the Business Roundtable in the US (Burch 1981), the CBI in Britain (Grant and Marsh 1977), similar bodies in Europe (Charkham 1994) and Japan (Lynn and McKeown 1988) and a truly global network of interlinked Chambers of Commerce. The political organisation of business has been the subject of academic and occasionally public debate in many countries (Domhoff 1980; Scott 1990: *passim*). For the period relevant to the globalisation of the capitalist class, from the middle of the 1960s to the present, the peak organisations of big business have been mainly national, though there is evidence of increasingly significant global linkages. For example, they connect with international organisations like the OECD and agencies of the UN, which play an important role in establishing global norms for business, trade and governance. All major business sectors are also organised in trade and industry associations, nationally and internationally. The major corporations, not surprisingly, dominate these associations and often are influential in setting the rules for global production and trade, rules that help bring the world into conformity with the global image.[6]

The culture and ideology of TNC executives is an emerging consumerism, where global brands and tastes, abstracted from their pre-existing contexts, are promoted in the effort to turn all cultural products into commercial opportunities. It is important to distinguish here between the individual preferences and life-styles of executives, which might vary considerably, and the culture and ideology of the class as a class. Irrespective of how individual executives live their lives, there is no doubt that global marketing and selling have become the ideological rationale for the system as a whole. This does not, however, preclude modifying these global

---

5. This bland statement conceals a furious dispute over the managerialism thesis of Berle and Means and the classic refutation by Zeitlin, reprinted in Scott (1990: Vol. 2, Pts 1, 2).

6. The current (1997) negotiations over a Multilateral Agreement on Investments being finalised at the OECD are strong evidence for this line of argument.

formulae to suit local tastes, as happens frequently in, for example, the fashion and fast foods sectors. The same can be said for more specific political tastes with respect to the neo-liberal agenda. The top leadership of big business tends to be less reactionary on social and labour issues than, for example, small business and some of the think tanks and other institutions that corporations help to finance. 'It is this sense of partial detachment from the narrow concerns of the individual firm and partial attachment to the broader concerns of the classwide business community that centrally characterizes the inner circle's outlook' (Useem 1984: 111). More systematic research is clearly needed on the global implications of this issue.

Globalising Bureaucrats

The idea of globalising bureaucrats, a critical reaction to state-centrist conceptions of ruling class alliances, is intended to highlight the struggles that take place within all states between the outward-oriented globalisers and the inward-oriented nationalists. These struggles are expressed in a variety of ways (notably, more or less liberal or restrictive foreign investment regimes and trade policy, official multiculturalism or chauvinism) and through a variety of institutional forms (more or less intrusive foreign economic relations agencies, more or less powerful inter-governmental agencies).

While the major international organisations (notably the World Bank, the IMF, the World Trade Organization, and GATT) are still mainly driven by representatives of their most powerful members, it is less clear that, for example, the World Bank can be said to be driven by the 'national interests' of the US. For example, in his detailed account of the life and work of the first President of the World Bank, Oliver (1995: 187) comments that George Woods was a 'New York banker, not a Washington bureaucrat', the implication being that bankers, unlike bureaucrats, are driven largely by the profit motive.[7] A study of the very different historical traditions of the systems of corporate governance in five of the world's largest economies concludes: 'Companies need to be truly *inter*national from top to bottom if the sterility and antagonism of economic nationalism are to be avoided' (Charkham 1994: 343). The old Marxist argument that the workers have no nation has to be turned on its head. Today it is globalising capitalists who have no nation,

---

7. I maintain this, despite the apparent US–Japanese conflict of interest over World Bank policies as analysed by Wade (1995). While Wade makes many telling points, he neglects to consider the argument that it is not the interests of the US and Japanese states that were at issue but the interests of different sectors of big capital as represented by various agents (notably globalising bureaucrats) in the US and Japan. The doyen of Japanese progressive economists, in a chapter on 'The March of Corporate Capitalism', sees a definite 'globalization trend' in Japan (Tsuru 1993: 192–204), and this is confirmed if we examine the annual reports and other publications of many of the major Japanese corporations.

and it is the demands of the global market, not national interests, that drive the global capitalist system. Meanwhile the working class, and the labour movement that purports to represent it, calls on 'its' state, politicians and business leaders to protect it against the ravages of globalisation. The growth of powerful regional trading blocs like NAFTA, the European Union and APEC, far from undermining this argument, points to the increasing weakness of individual nation-states in the face of the globalising agenda.

Globalising bureaucrats fulfil a governance function for the global capitalist system at the local, national, interstate and eventually global levels where individual states are not directly involved. Typically, these people are to be found dealing with or actually working in national, regional and local growth coalitions led by corporate investment. These include national bureaucracies responsible for external economic relations (exports, investments in both directions, market-driven aid agencies); international organisations, notably the World Bank, IMF, OECD, WTO, regional development banks and some agencies of the UN; and organisations like the Bilderberg Group (Thompson 1980), the Trilateral Commission (Gill 1990; Sklar 1980), the International Industrial Conference organised every four years by the Conference Board and the Stanford Research Institute (Townley 1990) and the Davos meetings of the World Economic Forum, which bring together the four fractions of the TCC and their foot-soldiers every year. The senior personnel in the major philanthropic foundations (notably Ford and Rockefeller) also fall into this category. The top ranks of the globalising bureaucracies thus combine career bureaucrats with retired corporate executives (putting their marketing skills to use 'in the public service') and the upwardly mobile *en route* to top TNC jobs (Kowalewski, Letko and Leonard 1991).

Remuneration in the public sector is considerably less than in the TNC sector, except in cases where corruption permits illegal enrichment.[8] Salaries and perquisites for most government employees in most countries appear to be relatively modest in comparison with those in the private corporate sector, but there are frequent opportunities for augmenting earnings from directorships, fees and other sources, if not concurrently then almost certainly later for senior officials. While public service rules sometimes restrict outside earnings, these do not last for ever and do not cover all the privileges that such positions engender.[9] Globalising bureaucrats frequently move to the business sector, working directly for the

8. This is, of course, not restricted to the poorest parts of the world, as cases involving corporations in the US, Europe, Japan and South Korea clearly illustrate.

9. Since the start of the wave of denationalisations and quasi-privatisations of state-owned enterprises in the 1980s, a new category of corporate executives has been created. These are often the same people who ran the state-owned enterprises, and their links with the TCC will repay further study.

corporations whose interests they may have been indirectly serving (or impeding) as public employees.

The agencies in which globalising bureaucrats work are, in a sense, their political organisations, and in many countries particular local and national government agencies can be identified with, for example, open-door policies that further the interests of the global capitalist class (whoever else's interests they may also further). Globalising bureaucrats also work politically through corporatist agencies that combine representatives of the state, business and labour.[10] Such agencies, particularly those with regulatory functions, are often dominated by big business.

The culture and ideology of state and private-sector globalising bureaucrats tend to be more complex than those of TNC executives. Their dominant ideology appears to be in a process of transformation. What had been a more context-oriented state interventionism is turning into a more abstract neo-liberalism that privileges the unrestricted operation of the free market. This neo-liberalism holds that a country's best interests are served by playing a full part in the global economy, the growth of which, in turn, depends upon unfettered competition. The neo-liberal dogma that this can only be fully achieved in an entirely market-driven system provides the economic theory for this assumption, the framework for the virtualism of policies that seek to implement the neo-liberal vision by destroying systems of tariff protection and labour regulation, forcing all firms and their workers to become internationally competitive.[11]

The ideology is reinforced daily by cultural practices cohering into what can be termed an emergent global nationalism. This is a kind of virtualist's nationalism, one that subordinates the nation to the global economy. It seeks to make each country an integral part of the global capitalist system while maintaining its identity by marketing national competitive advantages of various types through its own global brands (for example, American fast foods and entertainment, Japanese cars and electronics, French wines and perfumes, Italian furniture) and tourism (now the most important hard-currency-earning industry in an increasing number of local and national economies).[12]

10. See Tolchin and Tolchin (1993) on these in city, state and federal governments in the US and my own discussions of Australia (Sklair 1996) and elsewhere (Sklair 1995).

11. It is worth noting (a) the contradiction for globalising bureaucrats implicit in another dogma of neo-liberalism, that the state should basically never intervene in the economy, and (b) the key role of globalising bureaucrats in the struggle between capital and labour, invariably favouring business, in many if not all countries. These issues are discussed in Lang and Hines (1993).

12. Wallis (1991: 90) shows how art is used to 'sell nations' through major exhibitions on Mexico, Indonesia and Turkey. The last coincided with the ending of a ban on imported cigarettes, permitting the expansion of Philip Morris, a major sponsor, into Turkey. The marketing of cities (see Ashworth and Voogd 1990) is also of great relevance here.

Globalising Politicians and Professionals

Globalising politicians and professionals are a diverse group of people who perform a variety of personal and technical services for the TCC.

Globalising Politicians. Few politicians are independently very wealthy, though in most electorally-based political systems politicians who want to be successful need wealthy backers. The failure of left-wing politicians to sustain programmes of genuine reform within (let alone radical challenges to) capitalist hegemony anywhere in the world since the 1970s helps explain why most successful politicians in most countries tend to be globalising to a greater or lesser extent, even when they hide behind nationalist rhetoric. Politicians from both conservative and social-democratic parties commonly come from and return to the corporate sector and globalising bureaucracies in various capacities. In most representative democracies, elected politicians and officials must respond to the interests of their local constituents; but these interests are more often than not defined in terms of the interests of the corporations that provide employment and make profits locally.

As one of the most open countries in the world in terms of public access, research on these issues is most advanced in the US. Research on Political Action Committees (Useem 1984) and local corporation–politician connections (Domhoff 1996; Stern 1988; Tolchin and Tolchin 1993) attests to a phenomenon that is probably even more widespread in countries where there is less public scrutiny of such relationships. Empirical research also confirms the important thesis that the corporate sector is well-represented in the higher non-elective offices of state by those who return to the corporations after their periods of public service (Domhoff 1980; Scott 1990: Vol. 1).

While there have been several impressive contributions to the literature on government–business relations in capitalist countries, there has been little research specifically on the relationships between TNC executives and government.[13] Like the globalising bureaucrats, capitalist politicians and those in non-capitalist parties have been increasingly persuaded that their 'national interests' lie in the accelerated growth of the global economy through unfettered competition and free trade in a more or less extreme version of transnational neo-liberalism (Overbeek 1993). As politicians, necessarily responsive to the often contradictory vested interests of a variety of constituencies, members of this group rarely adopt a fully-fledged version of the emergent global nationalism of the globalising bureaucrats. They are characterised more by a rich cultural mix, often reflecting regional factors, especially within federal systems of government. However, at base, they share to a greater or

13. The major exceptions are network studies of various types, for example, Domhoff (1980, 1996), Mizruchi and Schwartz (1987) and Useem (1984) .

lesser extent the orthodoxies of a globalising neo-liberalism against the localising tendencies of their opponents.

Globalising Professionals.   Top business professionals, notably corporate lawyers and consultants, command substantial salaries in most countries and it is safe to assume that some of them derive other benefits from the companies with which they routinely do business. These professionals, as a group, have attracted a good deal of attention in recent years. This is largely due to the growth of two phenomena, which, while not exclusive to the era of globalisation, have spread rapidly since the 1960s. These are, first, the business services industries, ranging from information technology to management consulting, financial services and public relations of various types (Aharoni 1993) and, second, the rise of the think tanks, particularly those associated with the neo-liberal free trade and free enterprise agendas (see Alpert and Markusen 1980; Cockett 1995; Marchak 1991). The dominant elites in these institutions are among the most visible members of the TCC. They are organised politically in their own professional organisations, in the corporatist organisations noted above and in think tanks and universities, where they market more or less research-based information and policy to corporations and govern-ments. As they are largely funded by government departments, TNCs and private capitalists, their independence is often a matter of dispute. The culture and ideology of these professionals is a complex mix of global nationalism and neo-liberalism. The global networks of business consultants like Arthur Anderson and McKinsey, and Burson-Marsteller, the largest PR firm in the world, contain many individuals who have worked in business services, government advisory bodies, major corporations and think tanks, sometimes several at the same time.

In a notable study of the Trilateral Commission, an elite organisation that has played host to a galaxy of ruling-class stars and that appears to be of particular significance for a globalising agenda, Gill (1990) tries to develop a Gramscian analysis connecting the hegemonic needs of modern capitalism, the creation of a TCC fraction and the internationally-oriented Trilateralist thrust. Gill argues that organisations like the Trilateral Commission 'are able to develop a general class consciousness and cohesion. The process involves rotation of corporate leaders into and out of the American executive branch [and] a relationship between the transnational class fractions discussed earlier and steering patterns in American capitalism' (Gill 1990: 165). While many might doubt that such organisations really do have the power and influence that those who write about them claim and, more specifically, might doubt that the Trilateral Commission can bear the theoretical weight of Gill's analysis, he nevertheless puts forward a strong argument that the corporate elites in the US and elsewhere are active in a very wide range of organisations and activities that are not directly concerned with the balance sheets of their corporations. These organisations are of particular interest in so far as some of them have been identified with the propagation of the neo-liberal agenda (Cockett 1995). While the new-right think tanks, a prime source of virtualism, are not excessively well-endowed financially, by targeting elite opinion they have much more influence than their modest resources would indicate. They certainly provide a professional forum that is culturally and ideologically hospitable for both aspiring younger and retiring older members of the TCC. What I have termed globalising politicians and professionals are certainly working on the front line for the corporate elite.

Another context in which globalising professionals service the interests of capital is as members of what Evan (1981) calls International Scientific and Professional Associations (ISPAs) and Haas (1992), rather more conceptually, calls epistemic communities. Clearly not all of these are capitalist or globalising; perhaps most of the leaders of these associations or communities are hostile to global capitalism. However, there is enough evidence of the corroding effects of the corporate sponsorship of research, commercially-motivated networking and academic institution-building to suggest that even the most epistemic of communities find themselves from time to time being persuaded of the correctness or relevance of the corporate case for other than strictly cognitive reasons. If these professionals, mainly scientists of various types, can be mobilised in defence of the projects of big business and global capitalism, the impact on public opinion can be considerable.[14]

Consumerist Elites (Merchants and Media)

Consumerist elites are generally TNC executives, but they are so important for global consumerist capitalism that they require special treatment. Like other TNC executives, their economic base is in salaries and share capital and their culture and ideology is a cohesive culture-ideology of consumerism. However, the specificity of the members of the media elite lies in their political organisation, more specifically their means of political expression through the television and radio networks, newspapers, magazines and other mass media they own and control. The retail sector, particularly the ubiquitous shopping malls that are springing up all over the world, can in this sense be regarded analytically as part of the mass media. Through the medium of advertising the links between media and merchants and the entire marketing system (raw materials, design, production, packaging, financing, transportation, wholesaling, retailing, disposal) become concrete. In the apparently inexorable increase in the global connectedness of the mass media and

14. The role of the epistemic community of food scientists in the British beef saga of the 1990s (and the processed foods industry in general) would make an excellent case study of the TCC in action.

consumerism we can chart the ways in which the TCC appears gradually to be imposing its hegemony all over the world.

Global system theory argues that consumerist elites play a central role in capitalist hegemony. The practical politics of this hegemony is the everyday life of consumer society and the promise that it can be reality for most people in the world. This is certainly the most persistent image projected by television and the mass media in general. In one sense, therefore, shopping is the most successful social movement, product advertising in its many forms the most successful message, consumerism the most successful ideology of all time.

In his absorbing paper on 'The Magic of the Mall', Goss (1993) points out that shopping is the second most important leisure-time activity in the US (after watching television, much of which promotes shopping anyway). 'Shopping has become the dominant mode of contemporary public life' (Goss 1993: 18). While this is true at present only for the First World and perhaps some privileged elites elsewhere, the rest of world appears to be following rapidly (Findlay, Paddison and Dawson 1990).

Like capitalism, the process of taking the purchase of necessities of consumption out of local market-places, redefining this as shopping and relocating it increasingly into the more controlled environments of supermarkets and malls, did not just happen. The transformation of the built environment and the re-negotiation of the meaning of shopping from satisfaction of basic needs for the masses into a form of mass entertainment, a major leisure activity, is one of the greatest achievements of global capitalism. This transformation has been achieved in an amazing variety of ways, from advocacy advertising, where large corporations take out expensive adverts to persuade people of the virtues of free enterprise (Sethi 1977), to the 'commercialized classroom' (Knaus 1992); from advertorials, where sponsors pay for insertions that look like editorial content in the mass media (Stout, Wilcox and Greer 1989), to 'the ultimate capital investment', strategic philanthropy (Kyle 1990).[15] Advertising agencies have for some time been surveying the global consumer (Englis 1994) and extending the geographical scope of their regular global brand-preference rankings.

The point of the concept of the culture-ideology of consumerism is precisely that, under capitalism, the masses can not be relied upon to keep buying when they have neither spare cash nor access to credit, and, less obviously, even when they do have spare cash and access to credit. The creation of a culture-ideology of consumerism, therefore, is bound up with the self-imposed necessity that capitalism must be ever-expanding on a global scale. This expansion crucially depends on selling more and more goods and services to people whose basic needs (a somewhat

---

15. For a useful Japanese perspective on this issue, see 'Corporate Philanthropy' (*Tokyo Business Today*, May, 1990: 30–34). This item has an interesting list of Japanese corporate donations to universities, a theme that Domhoff, Useem and others discuss for the US and the UK.

ideological term) have already been comfortably met, as well as to those whose basic needs have not been met.

Consumerist elites play a part in the regular business groups in most countries and globally, but they also have dedicated organisations for their own purposes. Through their ownership and control of television channels, radio stations, newspapers, magazine and book publishers, advertising agencies, public relations firms, film and video production and distribution networks, shopping centres and other retail outlets, they spread the culture-ideology of consumerism as the normal environment of everyday life for the vast majority of people in the First World, and increasingly over most of the rest of the world. The global project of capitalist consumerism would not be possible without them, which is precisely the reason why the processes of globalisation date from the 1960s onwards, paralleling the technological revolutions that made modern mass media possible. So, in a fundamental sense, the television channels and mass newspapers and magazines of those who control the media have the same general form as the political organisations of the rest of the TNC executives, with the dramatic and power-enhancing difference that there is a massive ready-made, and apparently receptive, audience for the messages that they wish to propagate.

Having specified the structure of the TCC in general, it is important to note that the particular places where this class operates in the unfolding era of globalisation all have their peculiarities, even though they are broadly similar in fundamentals in so far as they are parts of the global capitalist system. So the homogenising effects of globalisation (one defining characteristic of the phenomenon) and the peculiarities and uniqueness of history and culture are always in tension. This tension creates a globalising dialectic. Its thesis is the historical local context of communities, real and imagined, of all types, the relatively recent invention of the nation-state being the most prominent in the modern era. Its antithesis is the emerging global, the abstract, of which the global capitalist system driven by the TCC is the dominant, though not the only, force. Its synthesis is as yet unformulated.

Capitalist Crises and the Transnational Capitalist Class

All ruling classes in all social systems not characterised by pure democracy have to ensure their power to sustain the normal processes of interaction. So police forces, courts of law, armies, Gods (religious and secular), super-ego, posterity and other mechanisms of social control play their part to defend the integrity of the social system, to permit accommodation to change, and even (on occasion) to ensure the success of unavoidable revolutions in human affairs. All ruling classes have a siege mentality to some extent (Sklair 1997: 517–519), which explains why they have armies and police forces and other agents of physical and social control. However, there are two specific reasons why the siege mentality of the TCC (or, more accurately, its immediate predecessors) is particularly sensitive. First, the old ideological certainties of the divine rights of kings, emperors, gods and sacred texts have, of course, seriously diminished in the twentieth century; and second, the rise of democratic polities of various kinds in recent decades has exposed ruling classes all over the world to much more public scrutiny than ever before, though rarely to effective democratic control.[16]

The theoretical-historical foundations of this argument and line of research originate in Gramsci's attempt to construct a theory of hegemony and ideological state apparatuses (Gramsci 1971). Much of the voluminous *Prison Notebooks*, written from 1929 to 1935, can be read as a continuous critique of the assumption, not difficult to gather from the Marx–Engels classics, that ruling classes generally rule effortlessly until revolutionary upsurges drive them from power and make everything anew. As many scholars inspired by, sympathetic with and hostile to Marxism have pointed out, the general impression of the Marxist classics is of a rather deterministic sociology, one that says that men make history but not in circumstances of their own choosing, and puts the emphasis on the latter rather than the former.

It is no accident that Gramsci is associated both with a more cultural and less deterministic interpretation of Marxism and with the concept of hegemony, for they do connect. Gramsci made the connection through the role of the intellectuals in the creation and sustenance of hegemonic forms for the ruling class. He argues:

> The hegemony of a directive centre over the intellectuals asserts itself by two principal routes: 1. a general conception of life, a philosophy . . . which offers to its adherents an intellectual 'dignity' providing a principle of differentiation from the old ideologies which dominated by coercion, and an element of struggle against them; 2. a scholastic programme, an educative principle and original pedagogy which interests that fraction of the intellectuals which is the most homogeneous and the most numerous (the teachers, from the primary teachers to the university professors), and gives them an activity of their own in the technical field (Gramsci 1971: 103–104).

While much of this still seems quite valid, it suggests too much of a one-way process, the 'directive centre' asserting its hegemony over the intellectuals. Research on intellectuals suggests a more dialectical process, in which distinct groups of intellectuals, inspired by the promise or actual achievements of global capitalism, articulate what they perceive to be its essential purposes and strategies, often with

16. While it is generally agreed that global capitalism delivers more genuine democracy and rule of law than any other large-scale system yet put into practice, the level of cynicism about actually-existing democracies appears to be growing all the time all over the world. For a penetrating analysis of this see Robinson (1996).

support and encouragement from the corporate elites and their friends in government and other spheres, particularly the media. In a study that is of great relevance to the present discussion of a global ruling class, Cockett (1995) shows how about fifty intellectuals of various types in the UK carried out an anti-Keynesian neo-liberal counter-revolution from the 1930s to the eventual triumphs of Thatcher–Reaganism in the 1980s.[17]

Cockett shows clearly and in convincing detail how the revolution begun by Hayek and others in the 1930s was kept alive by public and private meetings, conferences, academic and more popular publications, lobbying of various types, feeding the media, assiduous contacts with the politically powerful (or soon to be powerful) and, with the exception of mass demonstrations, all the trappings that are the daily fare of social movements research. This is not an idealist account of social change in which the power of ideas eventually turns the tide. On the contrary, it is a much more subtle argument, in which the bearers of powerful ideas that have few powerful adherents work away until the material forces begin to change in their direction (the crises of capitalism and state power in the 1970s feeding the widespread disillusionment with Keynesian and welfare-state solutions to these crises and the legitimation crisis in general).

Enter Gramsci, again. 'A "crisis of authority" is spoken of: this is precisely the crisis of hegemony, or general crisis of the state' (Gramsci 1971: 210). Writing in the 1930s from a fascist prison, Gramsci saw the latest 'crisis of hegemony' as resulting from the First World War and the Communist advances since then, and would undoubtedly have seen the next crisis of hegemony for international capitalism as resulting from the Second World War. Since then, theories of capitalist crisis (fiscal crisis of the state, crisis of welfare, crisis of de-industrialisation and environmental crisis are just a few of the contenders) have been articulated from all sides. These have generally been seen as crises that need global as well as national solutions (Ross and Trachte 1990). The collapse of communism and capitalist triumphalism, paradoxically, have increased the pressures on the capitalist system to solve all the problems of the contemporary world, quickly and globally.

My argument is that the global capitalist project is gaining ground as the emerging solution to all these crises and, as befits a hegemonic crisis of the first order, the solution is a new conception of global hegemony, 'in other words, the possibility and necessity of creating a new culture' (Gramsci 1971: 276). But while Gramsci was thinking of a new socialist order, for the 1990s this raises the prospect of an

---

17. Cockett (1995: 306) says that 'the internationalization of the work of the British "think-tanks" was one of the most extraordinary features of economic liberalism as it developed in the 1980s', but discusses the issue only in passing. For a more comprehensive, though less systematic, account see Marchak (1991), who argues that many in the new right are very suspicious of corporate capitalism.

'emerging supranational corporate agenda' (Ranney 1994) or 'transnational neo-liberalism' (Overbeek 1993).

The devastation of the 1970s – the oil shocks, the subsequent debt crises, the corporate restructuring and downsizing (the race to the bottom) and the apparent inability of politicians to deal with these problems in any way other than by means of short-term palliatives – suggests that the local effects of globalisation increase the pressures on the TCC to deliver what the culture-ideology of consumerism promises, more private possessions leading to better and happier lives for all. However, the pressure is usually refracted through the political system and government attempts to get to grips with the problems of unemployment, deskilling, job insecurity, international competitiveness, law and order, immigration and emigration, and multiculturalism. The culture-ideology of consumerism raises expectations that can be satisfied in at least two ways: redistribution of resources (this tends to be the social-democratic localising solution) and increasing the size of the cake to be distributed (the neo-liberal globalising solution). An unwelcome result of the Thatcher–Reagan neo-liberal experiments in the UK and US, copied widely throughout the world, has been the absolute enrichment of some combined with the relative impoverishment or economic stagnation of many more in rich and poor countries alike.[18] This has produced an arrogant over-confidence in the over-privileged and a sometimes violent, sometimes fatalist, reaction in the under-privileged. This is, of course, not the first time this has happened.

The corporate elite has commonly and with good reason felt insecure, whether from physical assault (Gladwin and Walter 1980) or expropriation (Minor 1994), particularly in the foreign countries where they do business. Though both phenomena appear to have declined in the past decades, it is not very surprising that TNCs have routinely taken pre-emptive action to put their case before the public and the authorities with whom they have to deal. For many reasons, big business tends to be unpopular and its claims tend to be treated with a high degree of cynicism, so it often resorts to indirect ways of creating support for its causes and influencing public policy (Dreier 1982; Rowell 1996). One of the most important ideological tasks of big business is to persuade the population at large that the business of society is business and so to create a climate of opinion in which trade unions and radical opposition groups (especially consumer and environmental movements) are considered to be sectional interests while business groups are not. This is, of course, a large part of the creation and maintenance of global capitalist (I would add, consumerist) hegemony.

There is a good deal of agreement among scholars that (as Communist Parties used to do in countries where they were illegal or circumscribed) big business

---

18. Feenstra (1996) argues in the *American Economic Review* that the real wages of less-skilled workers in the US have fallen dramatically since the late 1970s. This is true for many other countries.

often creates front organisations to propagate its messages. Many apparently straightforward civic organisations are, in fact, largely run by and funded by the corporate elite.[19] Most of the research on these phenomena has been carried out on business groups in the US and most focuses on the ways in which big business, both domestic (Domhoff 1996; Ryan, Swanson and Buchholz 1987) and foreign (Tolchin and Tolchin 1993), influences the US government and its various state apparatuses to legislate in the interests of capital. In Latin America, the case of the Chicago boys in Chile (and elsewhere) is well-known, and one study comes to this measured conclusion: 'available data reveal that policymakers have mainly interacted with the leadership of a few carefully selected conglomerates' (E. Silva 1996: 316; see also Jung 1988 on South Korea; MacIntyre 1994 on Asia).

Though they flirt with the now generally discredited conspiracy theory of capitalist hegemony, Eisenhower and Johnson [*sic!*] (1973) provide a useful checklist for studying the not-so-public sides of business–government relations in the US and, to some extent, elsewhere.

'Official conspiracies' are those institutionalized ways in which corporate interests shape and guide policies of the U.S. government . . . The main apparatus of official conspiracies consists of organizations controlled by members of the corporate elite class that sponsor research, commission studies, publish influential journals, issue reports, engage in formal and informal dialogues with government officials, formulate policy guidelines, see that their men [and, increasingly, women] are appointed to key government posts, etc. Such organizations dealing with foreign policy include: Corporate-controlled research-planning advising and report-issuing public affairs groups . . . Businessmen's organizations . . . Executives commissioned task forces, committees, and missions . . . Citizen (read business) advisory councils and committees . . . U.S. Representatives to U.N.-sponsored panels . . . Research Institutes . . . Foundations . . . (Eisenhower and Johnson 1973: 51–53).

Since the 1970s there have been many excellent studies documenting and analysing this phenomenon, notably on the Council on Foreign Relations (Shoup and Minter 1977) and its French equivalent (Domhoff 1981), on the Business Roundtable (Burch 1981), on business leaders in government (Useem 1980), and on the Trilateral Commission (Gill 1990; Sklar 1980). Domhoff (1996) makes the case for a pervasive corporate ruling class whose organisations steer the state in various policy directions. These findings have been replicated to some extent by research from other countries (see Scott 1990; E. Silva 1996).

19. Radical publications like *Multinational Monitor* and others associated with the name of Ralph Nader in the US frequently 'expose' such organisations. Rowell (1996) demonstrates this globally for the environmental field. Poole (1989) uses similar evidence to argue, paradoxically, that 'Big Business Bankrolls the Left'.

This fragility at the core of capitalism, the problem of business, is best illustrated in the heartland of capitalist hegemony, the US. In the 1970s, corporations there deliberately sought 'to reverse a dramatic decline in public confidence in big business which they blame on the media' (Dreier 1982: 111). To do this, business mobilised think tanks, university business-journalism courses, awards and prizes, advocacy advertising and increased sponsorship of culture, to encourage more favourable reporting and a *détente* between business and media. An important addition to Dreier's list is the development of 'Business Ethics' both as an area of academic research (in their survey article, Tsalikis and Fritzsche 1989 identify over 300 bibliographic items) and as a set of responses for big business under threat, elegantly exposed in, appropriately enough, an article in *Propaganda Review* by Graziano (1989).[20]

The reason for all this activity is that the capitalist class always faces the threat of challenge from below. No doubt big business is more popular in some places and times than it is in others, but the point is that capitalist hegemony needs constant support, attention and originality to sustain it.[21] This is no less true for capitalism in the global context than in the national.

The parallel developments of cheap global mass media and substantial increases in various forms of global business relations are simultaneous indicators of the unprecedented global reach of contemporary capitalism and the global exposure of its promises and performance. If the preceding analysis has provided evidence that a TCC is emerging and is beginning to act as a global ruling class in some spheres, it remains necessary to show concretely how this class is attempting to resolve the crises of global capitalism. And this is where the virtualism of the TCC can be judged against the reality of its practices and their real-life consequences.

20. Anti-big business sentiment has existed in the US and elsewhere since at least the nineteenth century (Galambos 1975; Piott 1985) and the envy-based polemic of von Mises (1956). Lipset and Schneider (1983) argue that the major institutions (business, labour and government) all suffer from a 'confidence gap' in the US. For the view of an influential capitalist ideologue, see Rand (1967). Boies and Pichardo (1993–1994), in their work on the Committee on the Present Danger as an 'elite social movement organization', update this literature and make some conceptual innovations. The rarity of research on how big business organises to sustain its hegemony, compared with oppositional social movements, mirrors the rarity of research on the capitalist class itself, compared with other classes.

21. Evidence from other countries on the opposition to big business and capitalist hegemony can be gleaned from the general social movements literature. In an informative book on Australia, Browning (1990) claims that the left is organised in an anti-business global network, a common and not unreasonable claim of capitalist-inspired ideologues.

Acknowledgement

This chapter is based on Sklair (1997). I am grateful to James G. Carrier for his suggestions and editorial work.

References

Aharoni, Yair (ed.) 1993. *Coalitions and Competition: The Globalization of Professional Business Services*. London: Routledge.

Alpert, Irvine, and Ann Markusen 1980. Think Tanks and Capitalist Policy. In G. William Domhoff (ed.), *Power Structure Research*, pp. 173–197. London: Sage.

Ashworth, Gregory J., and H. Voogd 1990. *Selling the City: Marketing Approaches in Public Sector Urban Planning*. London: Belhaven Press.

Becker, David G., Jeff Frieden, Sayre P. Schatz and Richard L. Sklar 1987. *Post-imperialism*. Boulder, Colorado: Lynne Rienner.

Boies, John, and Nelson Pichardo 1993–1994. The Committee on the Present Danger: A Case for the Importance of Elite Social Movement Organizations to Theories of Social Movements and the State. *Berkeley Journal of Sociology* 38: 57–87.

Brecher, Jeremy, and Tim Costello 1994. *Global Village or Global Pillage: Economic Reconstruction from the Bottom Up*. Boston: South End Press.

Browning, Bob 1990. *The Network: A Guide to Anti-Business Pressure Groups*. Victoria: Canonbury Press.

Burch, Philip H., Jr 1981. The Business Roundtable: Its Make-up and External Ties. *Research in Political Economy* 4: 101–127.

Carey, Patricia 1990. The Making of a Global Manager. *North American International Business* (June): 36–41.

Charkham, Jonathan 1994. *Keeping Good Company: A Study of Corporate Governance in Five Countries*. Oxford: Clarendon Press.

Cockett, Richard 1995. *Thinking the Unthinkable: Think-Tanks and the Economic Counter-Revolution, 1931–1983*. London: Harper-Collins.

Connell, Robert W. 1977. *Ruling Class, Ruling Culture*. Cambridge: Cambridge University Press.

Cox, Robert W. 1987. *Production, Power, and World Order: Social Forces in the Making of History*. New York: Columbia University Press.

Domhoff, G. William 1967. *Who Rules America?* Englewood Cliffs, NJ: Prentice-Hall.

—— (ed.) 1980. *Power Structure Research*. London: Sage.

—— 1981. Provincial in Paris: Finding the French Council on Foreign Relations. *Social Policy* (March–April): 5–13.

—— 1996. *State Autonomy or Class Dominance? Case Studies on Policy Making in America*. Hawthorne, NY: Aldine de Gruyter.

Dreier, Peter 1982. Capitalists vs. the Media: An Analysis of an Ideological Mobilization among Business Leaders. *Media, Culture and Society* 4: 111–132.

Eisenhower, David, with Dale L. Johnson 1973. The Low Profile Swings a Big Stick. In D. L. Johnson (ed.), *The Chilean Road to Socialism*, pp. 42–71. New York: Anchor Books.

Englis, Basil (ed.) 1994. *Global and Multinational Advertising*. Hillsdale, NJ: Lawrence Erlbaum.

Evan, William M. 1981. *Knowledge and Power in a Global Society*. London: Sage.

Feenstra, Robert C. 1996. Globalization, Outsourcing, and Wage Inequality. *American Economic Review* 86: 240–245.

Fennema, Meindert 1982. *International Networks of Banks and Industry*. The Hague: Martinus Nijhoff.

Findlay, Allan M., Ronan Paddison and John A. Dawson (eds) 1990. *Retailing Environment in Developing Countries*. Andover: Routledge, Chapman and Hall.

Galambos, Louis 1975. *The Public Image of Big Business in America, 1880–1940: A Quantitative Study in Social Change*. Baltimore: Johns Hopkins University Press.

Gill, Stephen 1990. *American Hegemony and the Trilateral Commission*. Cambridge: Cambridge University Press.

Gladwin, Thomas N., and Ingo Walter 1980. *Multinationals under Fire*. New York: Wiley.

Goldfrank, Walter 1977. Who Rules the World? Class Formation at the International Level. *Quarterly Journal of Ideology* 1: 32–37.

Goss, Jon 1993. The 'Magic of the Mall': An Analysis of Form, Function, and Meaning in the Contemporary Retail Built Environment. *Annals of the Association of American Geographers* 83: 18–47.

Gramsci, Antonio 1971. *Selections from the Prison Notebooks*. (Edited and translated by Q. Hoare and G. N. Smith.) London: Lawrence and Wishart.

Grant, Wyn, and David Marsh 1977. *The Confederation of British Industry*. London: Hodder and Stoughton.

Graziano, Loretta 1989. How Business Ethics Became 'Issues Management'. *Propaganda Review* (Summer): 29–31.

Haas, Peter 1992. Introduction: Epistemic Communities and International Policy Coordination. *International Organization* 46: 1–35.

Jung Ku-Hyun 1988. Business–Government Relations in the Growth of Korean Business Groups. *Korean Social Science Journal* 14: 67–82.

Kanter, Rosabeth Moss 1996. *World Class: Thriving Locally in the Global Economy*. New York: Simon & Schuster.

Knaus, H. 1992. The Commercialized Classroom. *Multinational Mónitor* (March): 14–16.

Kowalewski, David, Thomas Letko and Robin Leonard 1991. Revolving Doors, Corporate Performance, and Corruption of Markets. *Critical Sociology* 18 (Spring): 93–108.

Kyle, Ann 1990. The Ultimate Capital Investment. *California Business* (1 July): 36–41.

Lang, Tim, and Collin Hines 1993. *The New Protectionism*. London: Earthscan.

Lipset, Seymour Martin, and William Schneider 1983. *The Confidence Gap: Business, Labor, and Government in the Public Mind*. New York: The Free Press.

Lynn, Leonard, and Timothy McKeown 1988. *Organizing Business: Trade Associations in America and Japan*. Washington, DC: American Enterprise Institute.

MacIntyre, Andrew (ed.) 1994. *Business and Government in Industrialising Asia*. Ithaca, NY: Cornell University Press.

Maisonrouge, Jacques 1988. *Inside IBM: A European's Story*. (Translated by Nina Rootes.) London: Collins.

Marceau, Jane 1989. *A Family Business? The Making of an International Business Elite*. Cambridge: Cambridge University Press.

Marchak, M. Patricia 1991. *The Integrated Circus: The New Right and the Restructuring of Global Markets*. Montreal: McGill–Queens University Press.

Maucher, Helmut 1994. *Leadership in Action: Tough-Minded Strategies from the Global Giant*. (Translated by B. J. Perroud-Benson.) New York: McGraw-Hill.

Minor, Richard 1994. The Demise of Expropriation as an Instrument of LDC Policy: 1980–1992. *Journal of International Business Studies* 25: 177–188.

Mizruchi, Mark S., and Michael Schwartz (eds) 1987. *Intercorporate Relations: The Structural Analysis of Business*. Cambridge: Cambridge University Press.

Morita, Akio, and Edwin Reingold 1987. *Made in Japan: Akio Morita and Sony*. London: Collins.

Oliver, Robert 1995. *George Woods and the World Bank*. Boulder, Colorado: Lynne Rienner.

Overbeek, Henk (ed.) 1993. *Restructuring Hegemony in the Global Political Economy: The Rise of Transnational Neo-Liberalism in the 1980s*. London: Routledge.

Piott, Steven 1985. *The Anti-Monopoly Persuasion: Popular Resistance to the Rise of Big Business in the Midwest*. Westport, Conn.: Greenwood Press.

Poole, W. 1989. How Big Business Bankrolls the Left. *National Review* (10 March): 34–39.

Rand, Ayn 1967. America's Persecuted Minority: Big Business. In *Capitalism: The Unknown Ideal*, pp. 44–62. New York: New American Library.

Ranney, David 1994. Labor and an Emerging Supranational Corporate Agenda. *Economic Development Quarterly* 8 (February): 83–91.

Robinson, William 1996. *Promoting Polyarchy*. Cambridge: Cambridge University Press.

Robison, Richard, and David S. G. Goodman (eds) 1996. *The New Rich in Asia: Mobile Phones, McDonald's and Middle-Class Revolution*. London: Routledge.

Ross, Robert J., and Kent C. Trachte 1990. *Global Capitalism: the New Leviathan*. Albany: SUNY Press.

Rowell, Andrew 1996. *Green Backlash: Global Subversion of the Environmental Movement*. London: Routledge.

Ryan, Mike, Carl Swanson and Rogene Buchholz 1987. *Corporate Strategy, Public Policy and the Fortune 500: How America's Major Corporations Influence Government*. Oxford: Basil Blackwell.

Scott, John (ed.) 1990. *The Sociology of Elites*. Three volumes. Aldershot: Edward Elgar.

—— 1996. *Stratification and Power: Structures of Class, Status and Command*. Cambridge: Polity.

Sethi, S. Prakash 1977. *Advocacy Advertising and Large Corporations*. Lexington, Mass.: D. C. Heath.

Shawcross, William 1992. *Murdoch*. Sydney: Random House.

Shoup, Laurence, and William Minter 1977. *Imperial Brain Trust: The Council on Foreign Relations and United States Foreign Policy*. New York: Monthly Review Press.

Silva, Eduardo 1996. From Dictatorship to Democracy: The Business–State Nexus in Chile's Economic Transformation, 1975–1994. *Comparative Politics* 28: 299–320.

Silva, Patricio 1995. Modernization, Consumerism and Politics in Chile. In D. Hojman (ed.), *Neo-Liberalism with a Human Face? The Politics and Economics of the Chilean Model*. (Monograph Series, No. 20), pp. 118–132. Liverpool: Institute of Latin American Studies, the University of Liverpool.

Sklair, Leslie 1995. *Sociology of the Global System*. Second edition. Baltimore: Johns Hopkins University Press.

—— 1996. Conceptualizing and Researching the Transnational Capitalist Class in Australia. *The Australian and New Zealand Journal of Sociology* 32: 1–19.

—— 1997. Social Movements for Global Capitalism: The Transnational Capitalist Class in Action. *Review of International Political Economy* 4: 514–538.

—— 1998. Globalization and the Corporations: The Case of the California *Fortune* Global 500. *International Journal of Urban and Regional Research*: forthcoming.

Sklar, Holly (ed.) 1980. *Trilateralism: The Trilateral Commission and Elite Planning for World Management*. Boston: South End Press.

Stern, Philip 1988. *The Best Congress Money Can Buy*. New York: Pantheon.

Stokman, Frans N., Rolf Ziegler and John Scott (eds) 1985. *Networks of Corporate Power: A Comparative Analysis of Ten Countries*. Cambridge: Polity Press.

Stout, P., G. Wilcox and L. Greer 1989. Trends in Magazine Advertorial Use. *Journalism Quarterly* 66: 960–964.

Taylor, William 1991. The Logic of Global Business: An Interview with ABB's Percy Barnevik. *Harvard Business Review* (March–April): 90–105.

Thompson, Peter 1980. Bilderberg and the West. In Holly Sklar (ed.), *Trilateralism: The Trilateral Commission and Elite Planning for World Management*, pp. 157–189. Boston: South End Press.

Tolchin, Martin, and Susan Tolchin 1993. *Buying into America*. Washington, DC: Farragut.

Townley, Preston 1990. Global Business in the Next Decade. *Across the Board* (January–February): 13–19.

Tsalikis, John, and David Fritzsche 1989. Business Ethics: A Literature Review with a Focus on Marketing Ethics. *Journal of Business Ethics* 8: 695–743.

Tsuru, Shigetsu 1993. *Japan's Capitalism: Creative Defeat and Beyond*. Cambridge: Cambridge University Press.

Useem, Michael 1980. Which Business Leaders Help Govern. In G. William Domhoff (ed.), *Power Structure Research.*, pp. 199–225. London: Sage.

—— 1984. *The Inner Circle: Large Corporations and the Rise of Business Political Activity in the US and UK*. New York: Oxford University Press.

van der Pijl, Kees 1984. *The Making of an Atlantic Ruling Class*. London: Verso.

—— 1993. The Sovereignty of Capital Impaired: Social Forces and Codes of Conduct for Multinational Corporations. In Henk Overbeek (ed.), *Restructuring Hegemony in the Global Political Economy: The Rise of Transnational Neo-Liberalism in the 1980s*, pp. 28–57. London: Routledge.

von Mises, Ludwig 1956. *The Anti-Capitalistic Mentality*. Princeton, NJ: Van Nostrand.

Wade, Robert 1995. Japan, the World Bank, and the Art of Paradigm Maintenance: *The East Asian Miracle* in Political Perspective. *New Left Review* 217 (May–June): 3–36.

Wallis, Brian 1991. Selling Nations. *Art in America* (September): 85–91.

Warner, Malcolm (gen. ed.) 1996. *Encyclopedia of Business and Management*. London and New York: Thompson Business Press.

Waters, Malcolm 1995. *Globalization*. London: Routledge.

−7−

Virtual Capitalism: The Globalisation of Reflexive Business Knowledge
Nigel Thrift

The analysis of capitalism is beset by scripts that prevent us from seeing many of the new things that are going on. These scripts are typified by a recent paper by Altvater and Mahnkopf. For these two authors, the triumph of the world market comes on apace, forced by various mechanisms that have intensified a tendency to global disembedding, in which the market has increasingly become separated from its social bonds.[1] These mechanisms are of four types. First, money takes on a new, more aggressive stance, as 'there emerges a global financial system as a monetary sphere uncoupled from the real economy' (Altvater and Mahnkopf 1997: 450). Second, the economy becomes globalised, as 'commodification envelops the global system' (1997: 451). Third, temporal and spatial coordinates are compressed by the expansion and acceleration of money and other forms of commodification. We live, therefore, in a world time of 'all-encompassing contemp-oraneity' (1997: 456) produced by new means of transportation and communication. Fourth, these developments produce new environmental stresses and strains, as natural resources are used up and not replaced.

Elsewhere, I have taken strong exception to these kinds of scripts (see Thrift 1995, 1996a). Their tone is that of the seer, able to navigate the currents of history with aplomb. Their assumptions are often mistaken, based on bad or outmoded historical research, and on long-standing intellectual habits like technological determinism, the pervasiveness of which has only recently been acknowledged. These scripts, in other words, tell their stories with a kind of supernatural confidence that is more appropriate to the old Norse sagas than to the soap operas of everyday economic life.

I want to take issue with such scripts, by starting to write a different one. I will begin in the same place as Altvater and Mahnkopf, the triumph of the global market, but then draw rather different lessons. Instead of seeing this triumph as the apogee of capitalism, I will suggest that what it points to is just how tentative, tendentious

---

1. Bob Jessop has kindly pointed out to me that Altvater and Mahnkopf's recent (1996) German book contains a more nuanced account of these mechanisms.

and uncertain global capitalism really is. The world that capitalism has wrought is, exactly as Marx pointed out, one of chronic uncertainty and instability. Capitalism is, in other words, hoist with the petard of its own success.

Capitalist firms exist in a world that they increasingly regard as inherently uncontrollable, and in a kind of self-fulfilling prophecy, that regard itself helps bring about that lack of control (Thrift 1997). How, then, can firms establish some control of their circumstances? I will argue that their vision of uncertainty has pushed those who run capitalist firms into taking a virtual turn (Carrier 1997*a*; Miller 1996), a turn towards 'theory' but, as I shall make clear, towards a *quite particular form of theory*.

I pursue this question in two ways in this chapter. In the first part, I will consider the *practical* forms of theory, based upon the dictates of the moment, that are crucial to the running of capitalist organisations. In the second part I build on this base by considering the rise of reflexive management theory over the course of the twentieth century. This is a form of virtualism that, as I point out, has its own self-reproducing institutional dimension, which is itself undergoing its own form of globalisation, as I will underline by using the example of Asia. However, as I note in my conclusion, the term 'virtual' needs some qualification in the case of capitalism.

My chief source of inspiration for what I say here is work on concrete material practices, of the sort investigated in recent research on material culture, the sociology of science and actor-network theory. This body of work grounds theory in specific arenas of practice. By situating knowledge in context, it questions what might be meant by terms like 'concept' and 'idea', terms that, though often bandied about as the very stuff of theory, are always ingrained in practices (Thrift 1996*b*).

Practical Capitalism

I need to start by describing briefly my understanding of the global capitalist economy, which is very different from that of writers like Altvater and Mahnkopf, who constantly confuse the logic of theory with the logic of practice. First, I do not think that the capitalist economy has become progressively more disembedded, in the sense of more abstract and more abstracted. However, I think it has become more distanciated (Giddens 1991), structured through time and over space by all manner of machines and other devices; but this has produced a multitude of times and spaces that interact in complex ways with each other. This distanciation has produced a thickening of communication: in many senses, capitalist firms live in a more intimate and connective world than ever before. Second, I do not think that money is something apart from a 'real' economy, on which, by implication, it acts as a social corrosive. Rather, money acts in complex ways, depending upon the networks in which it is deployed. In other words, it is not one thing, but many different instruments working to many different purposes (Leyshon and Thrift 1997). Third, I do not think that we live in a time of all-pervasive contemporaneity. To echo my first point, all manner of times are constructed by the particular networks that thread their way differently around the world. Some of these times are fast, some are slow; there is no mean (Thrift 1997). Fourth, I dissent from Leslie Sklair's stance in this collection, for I do not think that the capitalist economy has become globalised in any strong sense. The world capitalist economy is 'profoundly mixed' (Mann 1997: 480). It is a raucous conglomeration of competing priorities, some transnational, some not. In other words, my world capitalist economy is a tentative creation, constantly generating new networks that sometimes survive and sometimes do not. The fact that it is full of tools of ordering does not mean that it is ordered. The fact that it uses fast technologies does not mean that it is fast. The fact that it has its ideologies does not mean it is ideological. Rather, its existence demonstrates the multiple, multiplex ways in which profit can be sought out and realised (Latham 1997).

How, then, might we think about theory in capitalism, rather than the theories *about* capitalism that abound? Let us start with a picture: Hans Holbein's famous painting of *The Ambassadors* (1533). In this painting is a sign of the new confidence in business and trade, a sign that is also one of the reasons for that confidence. The sign, placed significantly under the globe, is one of the first books for business people, a German work, the cover of which translates as 'A New and Well Grounded Instruction in All Merchant's Arithmetic in Three Books compiled by Peter Apian, Astronomer in Ordinary at Ingolstadt' (Conley 1996; Foister, Roy and Wyld 1997; Latour 1988).

Academics have treated this and similar signs as betokening the first stirrings of political economy. Being academics, they have tended to see the birth of political economy as a pivotal event: the beginnings of a discourse, a textual outfitting of the world, which constitutes notions of economy (Foucault 1970). Similarly, they have tended to assume that one of the descendants of political economy, economics, is the theoretical language of business. They have thought that, over the years, economics has provided the theoretical backbone of business. Thus the world is made into a reflection of theory.

But I have become less and less convinced by this kind of story. No one can deny that political economy and economics have been important in the world, but I am not at all sure how important they have been in business. They *are* important as discursive elements of states, justifying action in producing arenas that the state enacts as 'economic'. On the whole, however, I think that capitalist firms play to different drums. I make this judgement for four reasons.

First, much economics has never been quite as important in business as is often made out to be. It is true that economics is taught to MBA students, sometimes in profusion, as at the hard-line economics business schools like Stanford, and at many German business schools. It is also true that many business people have been taught some formal economics. But what strikes me is how little economics is ever *used* in business (a similar point is made in Chapman and Buckley 1997). The exception is financial economics. This is used in financial markets and is one of the backbones of corporate finance; more generally it appears in audit operations and in standard measures like ROCE (return on capital employed). But such economics seems to function mostly as legitimation, a discursive principle that can be referred to, but that often bears about as much relation to the conduct of business as the high court judge does to the shoplifter.

The second reason I doubt that political economy and economics are important in firms is that capitalist business is performative (Thrift 1997). By this I mean that it is a practical order that is constantly in action, based in the irreversible time of strategy (Bourdieu 1977). Whilst it has its contemplative aspects, based in the time of learned knowledge, it is chiefly an order of the moment, and a means of crafting the moment. Tasks have to be carried out. Reports have to be made. Plans for the next two years cannot be made in two years' time. There is no 'if only . . .' (Boden 1994).

The third reason is that capitalist business is based in a material culture that ranges from the vast number of intermediaries required to produce trade, through the wide range of means of recording and summarising business, to the different layouts of buildings that discipline workers' bodies. These devices and arrangements are not an aid to capitalism; they are a fundamental part of what capitalism is. My point here is hardly unusual, for there are elements of it in the work of Braudel, and more recently it has been taken up by actor-network theorists (Latour 1986, 1993). However, only recently have researchers begun to work through its consequences.

The fourth and final reason is that capitalist business is based in a notion of 'theory' that is of a different order from more formal theory; it is based on problematising and problem spaces rather than a succession of scholarly theories that roll by and are judged according to particular criteria of correctness. The difficulty is that academics tend to marginalise and demean such theory on a number of grounds: its lack of formality; its source in social groups that are regarded as practical rather than theoretical; its closeness to technological devices; its allegiance to the empirical; its fixation on the moment. In turn, however, the denigration of such theory can be seen as a problem for more formal notions of theory, since

these problematising voices tend not to be much concerned with 'epochal' theories or systems, or with abstract conceptions of society and yet, some suggest, it is these voices that have often proved decisive, setting the terms under which sociological theories can place themselves 'in the time' or, alternatively, shaping the criteria which strip their truthfulness away (Osborne and Rose 1997: 80).

So, I want to interpret the sign of Peter Apian's book in a different way; not as one of the first sightings of political economy, but as one of the first sightings of new forms of practical business theory, based on what I will call the promotion of intelligence and competence within specific problem spaces. Such thinking on 'how to solve' specific problems, usually by modest example, has a long but only partially-told history in business, and more generally (Osborne and Rose 1997).

I argue that, in the sphere of business, three different but related variants of this theory exist, each with its own specialist communities that produce and disperse these intelligences and competences. Such communities include not only specific kinds of people, but also specific kinds of devices, vital parts of the means of producing and distributing intelligence. Elsewhere, these spheres have been referred to by terms like 'regimes of calculation' (for example, Porter 1995). For my purposes, however, this conjures up too great a sense of a pursuit of objectivity through numerical means. I prefer, then, to call them 'theoretical networks'.

Bookkeeping

The first such theoretical network I call bookkeeping. Until recently, the history of accounting was something of a backwater, but in the last ten years it has grown markedly, which makes it easier to present a brief history of this network. Its early growth was based on three practices. The first of these was the abacus or counting board.

> By the late eleventh and twelfth centuries, treatises on elementary calculations were, by and large, treatises on the use of the counting board, and there was a new word, *abacus*, meaning to compute. In the sixteenth century counting boards were so common that Martin Luther could offhandedly refer to them to illustrate the compatibility of spiritual egalitarianism and obedience to one's betters (Crosby 1996: 44).

But the counting board was a device for computing, not recording.

> Its users of necessity erased their steps as they calculated, making it impossible to locate mistakes in the process except by going back to the beginning and repeating the whole sequence. As for permanently writing down the answers, that was done in Roman numerals (Crosby 1996: 111).

Thus, another important practice, which allowed not only better calculation but also better recording, was imported from Arabic Spain in the twelfth century. This was calculation using Arabic numerals, called 'pen reckoning'. Even given the usefulness of these numerals, it took three hundred years for them to become current throughout Western Europe, even though they allowed calculating and recording to be done with the same symbols, and did not erase themselves as calculation occurred, and so could be checked.

The final element of this first theoretical network is double-entry bookkeeping. Living in a blizzard of transactions as they did, merchants and other business people had to have some sense of how to track each transaction. This problem was solved by the evolution of a two-column system of debits and credits, probably originating in Venice at the end of the thirteenth century. This was supplemented by the practice of entering each entry twice, keeping what was, in effect, a double account. This procedure spread across Europe, chiefly through manuals and bookkeeping practice (Robson 1992).

Nowadays, the bookkeeping network is most often associated with the computer, but it is important to understand the extent to which automated practices of bookkeeping have evolved gradually. Thus, tabulating and calculating machines were introduced in the 1880s into accounting departments, later supplemented by punch-card systems and various electro-mechanical devices for sorting and analysis (Yates 1994). Thus, by the time the computer appeared, the protocols of automated bookkeeping had already been established.

Written Procedures

A second theoretical network consists of the crystallisation of organisational practice in written procedures, as codes and algorithms, organisational values, opinions and rhetorics, as well as skills, are frozen into devices like operating manuals, company rules and procedures, company handbooks, posters and the like. The network has its origin in two devices. The first is instruction manuals, dating from the sixteenth century. These are the first attempts to objectify practical knowledge (Thrift 1984). The second is the recording and compiling of lists, and then reports, which collect and draw up information that could not have been written down hitherto.

List-making has frequently been seen as one of the fundamental activities of advanced human society, as necessary for coordinating activity across time and space, and it is associated with the development of complex organisational structures and infrastructures (Yates and Orlikowski 1992). Similarly, the creation of lists brings with it substantial political and conceptual changes in the classes of things that they inventory (Bowker and Star 1994: 188–189). Thus, Jack Goody (1971, 1987) has argued that the first written records are lists of things; Michel Foucault (1970) and Patrick Tort (1989) have claimed that the production of lists revolutionised science in the nineteenth century and led directly to modern science; Bruno Latour (1987) has proclaimed that the prime job of the bureaucrat is to compile lists that can be shuffled and compared. These authors have helped turn our attention away from dazzling end-products of list-making: Hammurabi's code, mythologies, the theory of evolution, the welfare state and so on. They have instead described the work involved in making these productions possible. They have done so by dusting off the archives and discovering piles and piles of lowly, dull, mechanical lists.

Negotiations over the content of the list become reified in the lists themselves, and often take quantitative form, especially if the items listed are numerous, costly or critical for other operations. This reification does not preclude making judgements using those lists, but these now involve multiple actors, including individuals, organisations and technologies; decisions remain, but now entail bureaucracies as well as the individuals making the judgements (Bowker and Star 1994: 188–189).

From the middle of the nineteenth century, the production of lists and instruction manuals was facilitated by the development of new office technologies that not only recorded, copied, duplicated and stored information, but, through these different activities, effectively created it. In particular,

> mass-produced typewriters appeared in 1874, aimed at a large market of court reporters, authors and other specialised users. Typewriters operated by experienced typists could produce documents at three times the rate of pen and paper, thus increasing the speed and lowering the cost of producing them. Beginning in the 1880s and 1890s, firms adopted the typewriter just in time to slow the already rising costs of their increased internal and external written communication (Yates 1994: 32).

At the same time, prepared forms became common. These reduced the time spent recording information and encouraged consistency and made it easier to retrieve information. (Around 1900, the tab function was added to typewriters precisely in order to aid the typist in typing tables and filling out forms.) Duplicating activity was also becoming easier. Carbon paper, hectographs and stencils were used to produce large numbers of copies, culminating in the invention of the mimeograph late in the 1890s. Filing systems also became more common, with the introduction of vertical filing at the Chicago World's Fair in 1893. In turn, these inventions allowed the production of systems of indexing and organising that were much lauded in management periodicals and textbooks. The card file also became more common and had many of the same effects. Thus, by the time of the computer, many business procedures, codes and algorithms had already emerged and needed only to be adapted to the new medium (Pellegram 1997).

In some cases, values, opinions, rhetorics and skills are frozen in the written word or number; but it is just as likely that they are encapsulated in visual representations. These are the graphs, maps, charts and diagrams that envision the organisation and give it its position in the 'economy' (Buck-Morss 1995). For example, graphs were widely adopted in the early twentieth century to make information more accessible and compelling to those using it. While graphic representations of data had existed for at least a century, they had been used primarily for government statistics and later for experimental data in science and engineering. Advocated by systematisers and engineers-turned-managers, graphs gained considerable popularity as a way to make the information gathered and analysed available to decision-makers in an efficient and compelling form (Yates 1994: 36).

Often these visual representations sink into the background, serving no other purpose than to provide a stance from which to act into the world. For example:

> After a 90-minute session at Andersen [Consulting], which involved a particularly complicated diagram, the question was asked: 'Why do you draw so many charts?' After a moment of thought, the reply came 'I don't know. Everyone here does' (O'Shea and Madigan 1997: 85).

Visual representation keeps evolving. Much has been made of the impact of the computer; but perhaps the most potent tools of the last few decades have been the humble flipchart, the overhead projector and the slide projector, all used in a vast number of different situations to produce, organise and represent the thinking of groups. That said, in the last twenty years a new crystallisation of organisational practice has become possible through the development of computer software of a bewildering range and variety, which imposes standards but also offers choices. In turn, software has become intelligent in its own right, and capable of producing complex representations.

Humanist Management

The third network is the most recent, even though its pre-history can be traced back to Robert Owen or to Quakers like the Cadburys and Rowntrees. Its modern origin is usually identified as managerial experiments in the 1940s and 1950s in Britain and the United States arising out of psychology. In Britain, it emerged from the work of psychologists like C. S. Myers and Elliott Jacques at the Tavistock Institute, as well as from the work of Eric Trist on coal mines in Haighmoor. In the United States it emerged from the invention of training groups and the founding of the National Training Laboratories (NTL) by psychologists like Lewin, Lippitt, MacGregor and Argyris, in Bethel, which then spread widely.

From these beginnings there developed an alternative tradition of management, one that stresses human interaction and self-fulfilment as general elements of organisational success. Indeed, one might argue that this network has, to a considerable degree, developed in direct opposition to the other two networks, as a conscious effort to supplement, extend or even undermine them. Kleiner (1996) shows how this network was built in piecemeal fashion from all manner of sources until the 1970s, depending upon the enthusiasms of particular managers and corporate whim. But in the period since the 1970s, it has become highly successful as the inculcation of 'soft' management skills like team leadership, creativity, emotional thinking and the like.

This network has been successful for four reasons. First, it was able to find a home in institutional bases like business schools and, increasingly, management consulting firms. Second, it was able to promote itself through the media, with which it is strongly linked, especially through inspirational books for managers and on business growth and the like (Carrier 1997*b*; Crainer 1997*b*; Micklethwait and Wooldridge 1996; Thrift 1997). Third, it has been able to produce believers who have considerable investments in the network, especially in the human-resources sector that it has largely driven. Fourth, and finally, it has been able to produce and make general its own interactional devices. These include all manner of transactional trainings and therapies (Brown 1997; Heelas 1996), as well as far more mundane but equally effective means of interaction. Thus, business lunches and seminars and conferences are now regarded as a background hum in business; but they all had to be invented. For example, social events and seminars as means of selling to businesses were probably invented by Marvin Bower of McKinsey as a way of selling services. The first such event was held in 1940 and was called a 'clinic dinner'. Conferences about business strategy (which are also marketing tools) probably originated with Bruce Henderson of Boston Consulting in the 1960s. They were used as a means of starting or maintaining relations with top corporate management (O'Shea and Madigan 1997).

The three networks I have described are not necessarily opposed to each other. They interact in most business organisations, sometimes in opposition, sometimes in uneasy co-existence, sometimes in concord.[2] And out of this interaction, new practices are produced. For example, one of the most significant new practices in recent times has been new forms of business indicator. These can be interpreted in a number of ways. They can be seen as the movement of bookkeeping culture into the humanist network, as an example of the rise of 'audit culture' (Power 1997; Strathern 1996). Equally, however, they might be seen as the spread of humanist forms into bookkeeping networks. Probably, however, they are a new, hybrid form.

Thus, the 'balanced scorecard' approach (Kaplan and Norton 1997) aims to complement standard financial indicators with a whole range of other indicators

---

2. None of this is to say that old ways of divided and decidedly non-humanist management do not survive, and are not powerful. For example, see Grove (1996) and Jackson (1997*a*) on Intel. But, even here, such ideas can be turned into a new management fad.

of business success that stress 'softer' attributes like leadership, human resource management, business process management, customer and market focus, information utilisation and quality, all of which are, in turn, broken down into further indicators. For example, in one British financial services firm,

> score cards are displayed on desktop machines in each branch. Each branch manager can only see information for his or her branch, each area or regional manager can only see information for the relevant area or region and so forth. The headline screen displays a distillation of statistics for each area – for example, the customer services survey uses 50 items, but these are compressed into just five components. A further 70 screens can, however, be accessed for further levels of data (van de Vliet 1997: 80).

Each of the indicators has to be effective if the whole is to work, and each indicator is meant to correspond with 'a "defined desired state", "written in an active, almost emotional way", to create a positive mental image' (van de Vliet 1997: 80). Another example is the rise of 'relational software', systems that instantly call up a client's personal details, and thereby allow high levels of personal interaction. Again, this example can be interpreted in two ways, as a movement of the bookkeeping culture into the humanist network, or vice versa. More probably, again, it is a hybrid.

Reflexive Capitalism

> These days it seems like any idiot with a laptop computer can churn out a business book and make a few bucks. That's certainly what I'm hoping.
>
> (Adams 1996: ix)[3]

The key point of my chapter is that capitalist theory is of a practical bent. However, it is interesting that, over the last thirty years or so, capitalist business increasingly has taken a more reflexive, virtual turn. This turn is not a total one. It is concentrated in larger firms and the more dynamic of the smaller ones. But that it exists can no longer be doubted.

Some words of caution are necessary, however. First, much of what I will describe here has direct antecedents in practical theory. Thus the seminar, which is now so essential to the practices of reflexive capitalism, is an outgrowth of previous practices. Similarly, many of the books and guides that circulate in such profusion in business are really only developments of company procedures and guides. Second, reflexive theory and practical theory remain closely linked. Whilst the language of the reflexive turn is often stratospheric, the fact is that it has to be

---

3. Ironically, Scott Adams's 'Dilbert' cartoon series has become a major business-publication industry in it own right.

connected to practical theory if it is to be sold on in quantity. In other words, reflexive theory is likely to be commoditised at an early stage and must stand up to the rigours of the market.

The reflexive turn is based on a body of management theory that has arisen from a number of sources. To begin with, management theory has clearly had a long history of its own. For example, even at the turn of the twentieth century there was the systematic management movement in the United States and, a little later, the scientific management of F. W. Taylor; the *Management Review* was founded in 1918; the *Harvard Business Review* in 1922; the American Management Association in 1925. By the end of the First World War, Arthur D. Little, originally an engineering firm, included management advice amongst its services; James McKinsey started his consulting firm in 1925.

Arguably, however, management theory came into its own after the Second World War through the incorporation of a large and eclectic body of knowledge. This included organisation theory, economics and actual business practice (including, most especially, the use of case studies as exemplars of success) on the one side, and on the other it included 'softer' sources of inspiration, including sociology and psychology. Currently, its most visible manifestation is the 'business fad' (Huczynski 1993; Shapiro 1995; Thrift 1997). In the past, such fads have included management by objectives, quality circles, just-in-time manufacturing and, most famously of late, business process re-engineering (Hammer and Champy 1992; Coulson-Thomas 1997) and core competences (Hamel with Prahalad 1994). More recent fads have included the balanced scorecard (Kaplan and Norton 1997), the living company (de Geus 1997) and, most particularly, knowledge as capital (Nonaka and Takeuchi 1995). For example, 1997 saw a a number of books published with exactly the same title: *Intellectual Capital* (including Edvinsson and Malone 1997; Stewart 1997). These marketable philosophies are the basic quanta of business knowledge, not least because their impact on consultants' fortunes can be enormous.[4] They are the means of tapping the moment by creating the spirit of the moment. They are

part of a tried and tested formula that evolved after Tom Peters, a McKinsey and Co. consultant, gathered wealth and fame in the wake of *In Search of Excellence*, published some 15 years ago and the most successful business book of modern times. The response: Get an article in the *Harvard Business Review*, pump it up into a book, pray for a best-

---

4. For example, with the success of Norton and Kaplan's balanced scorecard, Renaissance Solutions grew from 76 professionals with revenues of $13 million in 1994 to 221 professionals with revenues of $52 million in 1996. Small wonder, then, that periodically there are scandals, such as CSC Index's purchases of copies of a book they had published, Treacy and Wiersema's *The Discipline of Market Leaders* (1995), in order to get it into best-seller lists.

seller, then market the idea for all it is worth through a consultancy company (O'Shea and Madigan 1997: 189).

Whilst fads come round like the seasons, they are only the most visible part of the system of reflexive business knowledge. Many other knowledges circulate as well, chiefly through the unremitting hum of courses and seminars.

How has this autopoietic system been able to come about? There are four different reasons. The first of these is an interlocking institutional arrangement that I have described elsewhere (Thrift 1997). It consists, to begin with, of the business school. Business schools have, of course, existed for some time: Wharton, the first business school, was set up at the University of Pennsylvania in 1881; the University of Chicago and the University of California both established under-graduate schools of commerce in 1899; Stern (New York), Amos Tuck (Dartmouth) and Harvard followed in the next decade (Mark 1987; Micklethwait and Wooldridge 1996). They have boomed, however, since the 1960s. Currently, more than 75,000 students are awarded MBAs every year in America, fifteen times the number in 1960, and every year 250,000 people around the world sit the GMAT entrance examination for MBA courses (Micklethwait and Wooldridge 1996). The business school has produced new, more reflexive knowledge in three ways. First, it has systematised and then reproduced existing business knowledge. For example, the case-study method at one time so beloved of Harvard Business School can be used as a means of reflecting back on business. Second, it has synthesised existing academic knowledge and fed it into businesses. For example, the primary route for much organisation theory into business has been from journals like the *Administrative Science Quarterly* into the business school and so into business. Third, it has produced new knowledge by producing new modes of interchange and knowledge creation. For example, the presence of more mature MBA students who already have business experience means that academic knowledge is tested against that experience.

Another element of the institutional arrangement supporting reflexive capitalism is the management consultancy (Table 1), which, like the business school, has grown massively since the 1960s. Consultants trade in reflexive knowledge and do so more and more conspicuously. For example, Arthur Andersen, with revenues of $3,115 million in 1996 and an international staff of about 44,000 consultants, has its own 'university', the former girls' school at St Charles, Illinois, which is now known as Andersen Consulting College. There, it trains consultants by the thousands and, increasingly, promotes conferences and video conferences.[5] And, since

5. For example, in 1988 Andersen Consulting College established an electronic school of the future, and is mounting conferences on 'Learning for the 21st Century', with speakers such as Russell Ackoff, Deepak Chopra, Marva Collins, Edward de Bono, Peter Drucker, Morton Egol, Stephen Jay Gould and Thomas Kelly.

Table 1 Top 25 Management Consulting Firms, 1996

	Management consulting revenues ($M's)		Consultants World-wide	Revenue per consultant
	World	United States	No.	($000's)
Andersen Consulting	3,115	1,590	43,808	71
McKinsey & Co	2,100	800	3,944	532
Ernst & Young	2,100	1,400	11,200	188
Coopers & Lybrand Consulting	1,918	1,005	9,000	213
KPMG Peat Marwick	1,380	770	10,764	128
Arthur Andersen	1,380	766	15,000	92
Deloitte & Touche	1,303	821	10,000	130
Mercer Consulting Group	1,159	707	9,241	125
Towers Perrin	903	659	6,262	144
A. T. Kearney	870	530	2,300	378
Price Waterhouse	840	481	6,230	135
IBM Consulting Group	730	530	3,970	184
Booz-Allen & Hamilton	720	540	5,685	127
Watson Wyatt World-wide	656	417	3,730	176
The Boston Consulting Group	600	180	1,550	387
Gemini Consulting	600	218	1,470	408
Arthur D. Little	574	299	1,939	296
Hewitt Associates	568	538	3,807	149
Aon Consulting	473	318	4,370	108
Bain & Company	450	240	1,350	333
American Management Systems	440	300	2,960	149
Woodrow Milliman	350	188	1,150	304
Grant Thorton	306	66	886	345
Sedgwick Noble Lowndes	262	78	3,142	83
The Hay Group	259	119	1,035	250

Source: Wooldridge 1997

Andersen believes in the growth of an 'infocosm', consultants communicate through a computer communications system called Knowledge X-Change, aimed at integrating the organisation's business knowledge. Most recently, it has established a 'thought leadership' centre near its technology centre in Palo Alto.[6] But there is a rub:

> Whatever the product – downsizing, growth, or something else – consultants need to sell ideas. The problem is that what consulting has to sell isn't always new, and certainly isn't always fresh. It is an unusual industry because it builds its knowledge base at the

6. To illustrate the closeness of the relationship, management consultants are increasingly forming alliances with business schools and business thinkers (see Wooldridge 1997).

expense of its clients. From a more critical perspective, it is not much of a stretch to say that consulting companies make a lot of money collecting experience from their clients, which they turn around and sell in other forms, sometimes not very well disguised, to other clients (O'Shea and Madigan 1997: 13).

A final element of the institutional arrangement supporting reflexive capitalism is the management guru. Though they had existed before (Peter Drucker is a case in point), management gurus came into their own early in the 1980s with the rise of new types of high-energy management theorists, led by Tom Peters (Micklethwait and Wooldridge 1996). Many of these consultants now have their own, very successful consulting companies (as in the case of Michael Porter's Company, Monitor). Management gurus are high-profile embodiments of management fads, whose business is to produce and, more importantly, to *communicate* these fads by performatively energising their audiences.

Thus far I have described the first general reason for the rise of reflexive capitalism, the institutional framework that supports it. A second reason has been the growth of the business media. Reflexive business theory is intimately associated with those media, for management has become a cultural industry. In particular, business fads depend upon media to make them visible and generate their audiences (Jackson 1997b). This link has, of course, been present for a long time. For example, Marvin Bower published a handbook of McKinsey management philosophy, *Supplementing Successful Management*, in the 1940s. However, the significant association of business theory with the media dates from the success of Peters and Waterman's *In Search of Excellence*, published in 1982, the book that demonstrated the size of the market. Since then, each year has seen a flood of management books, tapes and videos.

> In 1991 McGraw Hill published 25 [business] titles; in 1996 it published 110. Marketing budgets at the esteemed . . . Harvard Business School Press are estimated to have almost doubled in the last four years. In the UK alone 2931 business titles were published in 1996, compared with a paltry 771 in 1975 (Crainer 1997b: 38).

Sometimes ghost-written,[7] the books can relate management to almost any aspect of human life, from jazz (Kao 1997) to computer hacking (Phillips 1997).

7. The American company Word Works has effectively cornered the market for ghost-writing: 'a look through the business best sellers reveals that Word Works have been involved in a large percentage of the big sellers of the last ten years' (Crainer 1997b: 38), including books by Hammer and Champy (1992), and by Treacy and Wiersema (1995).

The business media consist of a number of institutions. To begin with, there are the various institutions that publish books, business journals and the business pages of other periodicals. And, increasingly, there are the producers of radio and television programmes and videos. For management theory to spread, it must become interwoven with the media, and books that sell widely take on their own momentum, becoming the subject of presentations by business gurus and being actively marketed by the management consultants who have been involved in producing them. Similarly, increasing numbers of journals are being published by management consultants in order to spread their ideas, such as the *McKinsey Quarterly, Strategy and Business* (Booz and Allen) and *Transformations* (Gemini). Another set of institutions consists of media consultants and press officers who interact with the media, attempting to sell ideas to them. A symbolic date for this set of institutions was the appointment, in 1980, of a press officer by Bain and Company, the last significant consulting firm to resist the press. Even they were forced to recognise the necessity of media publicity, a necessity underlined by the recent, widespread use of advertising by some management consultants; 'Robert Duboff of Mercer Management says that "ten years ago, if I'd suggested we advertise, I'd have been shot; five years ago I'd have been whipped"' (Wooldridge 1997: 16). Then, finally, there is the audience for business ideas. About this audience we know very little (see Thrift 1997), but there can be no doubt that it is extensive and rapidly growing.

A third reason for the development of reflexive capitalism has been the growth of new business practices, as well as the transformation of some older ones. Of these, three stand out. One is the area of human resources. Human resources managers have become a staple of most firms since the 1970s. Another is the growth of marketing, spurred on by the simultaneous growth of computers and psychology. In particular, since the beginnings of consumer psychology in the 1940s and 1950s, marketing has taken on a more clearly psychological tinge (see Miller and Rose 1997). The final practice is the growth of interest in leadership, communication and other 'soft skills'. Recently, for example, there has been much interest in emotions and emotional leadership (for example, Cooper and Sawaf 1997).

A fourth reason is simply momentum. For example, more and more people in business have been taught reflexive management in business schools, and they provide a ready audience for related management ideas. Again, such people are likely to demand reflexive management when they attain positions of responsibility, and thus pull in more people skilled in reflexive theory. Similarly, a growing number of managers have themselves worked in management consultancies and, in any case, 'bosses who have had a taste of management theory, either at business schools or working for consultancies, may be more inclined to listen to consultants than those who have not' (Wooldridge 1997: 4).

Nigel Thrift

'Good Ideas have Flight': The Globalisation of Reflexive Capitalism[8]

What is clear is that this institutional arrangement is rapidly globalising, together with the management ideas that mobilise it. It is worth considering in some detail how reflexive capitalism is journeying and, in order to achieve this, I want to concentrate on the example of Asia.

Asia, of course, has some business traditions that depart from conventional Western practice. To begin with, for thousands of years it has had extensive trade networks. For hundreds of years it has had significant theoretical networks, based on the use of the abacus and indigenous forms of bookkeeping, which are only now being analysed fully (Goody 1996). Its economic ethics (such as 'rationality') have been varied, and though they may have been based on the family more than have Occidental economic ethics, equally, as Carrier (1995), Goody (1996) and others have pointed out, this depiction has often suited both East and West as signals of their difference (as for example, in notions of collectivist and individualist spirits of capitalism).

While Asia's business history has been a different one, it is worth remembering that this is a relative judgement. Asia has still shared much of its economic history with the rest of the world: it has never been a closed economic zone. Thus, it is no surprise that Asia has been drawn into the practices of reflexive capitalism. Asian firms have experienced a massive increase in physical and electronic communication, and therefore in general inter-connection. They have experienced the problems of economic success, such as the increasing scale of business organisations, the need to ensure management succession in what have been family-run firms[9] (Dumaine 1997; Hiscock 1997a, 1997b) and a general shortage of managers.[10] In these circumstances, it is not surprising to find the reproduction of the institutional set-up of reflexive capitalism in Asia.

8. John Clarkson, Chief of Boston Consulting Group, cited in Wooldridge (1997: 15).

9. Thus, even the most patriarchal of the large family-run Asian businesses have been hiring professional managers for some time. Now they are hiring and firing specific kinds of managers. 'As an example, (Richard) Li tells how he recently had to choose between two managers in one of his Asian operations. One was old school – very loyal but with no specific skills, the other knew the industry intimately and was creative and bicultural. Li fired the former and gave the job to the one with the specific knowledge. Says he: "it is much more difficult in Asia to remove top managers. But when you have a dramatic technological change or a sharp change in a market, then I believe the model of change makes it necessary to fire someone"' (Dumaine 1997: 45).

10. On one reckoning, by 1996 there were 80,000 foreign joint-ventures in China. If each requires four managers, then even this small sector of the Chinese economy needs nearly a third of a million managers. China produces 300 MBAs a year. Even adding in Chinese students who study overseas and American-born Chinese, there is a massive gulf between supply and demand, underlined by high managerial salary inflation and rapid managerial turnover (Micklethwait and Wooldridge 1996).

Table 2 Top 25 Asia-Pacific Business Schools, Ranked by Quality of MBA

Rank	School	Full-time Enrolment
1	Melbourne Business School	200
2	University of New South Wales (Sydney)	228
3	Indian Institute of Management (Ahmedabad)	392
4	Chinese University of Hong Kong	90
5	International University of Japan (Niigata)	126
6	Asia Institute of Management (Manila)	389
7	Indian Institute of Management (Bangalore)	380
8	National University of Singapore	147
9	Indian Institute of Management (Calcutta)	463
10	Australian National University (Canberra)	42
11	Nanyang Technical University (Singapore)	50
12	University of Queensland (Brisbane)	138
13	Hong Kong University of Science and Technology	60
14	Macquarie Graduate School of Management (Sydney)	12
15	Chulalongkorn University (Bangkok)	200
16	Monash Mt Eliza Business School (Melbourne)	350
17	Asian Institute of Technology (Bangkok)	300
18	University of Adelaide	20
19	Massey University (Palmerston North, NZ)	30
20	Royal Melbourne Institute of Technology Business Graduate School	30
21	Jamnalal Bajaj Institute of Management Studies (Bombay)	240
22	Curtin University of Technology (Perth)	98
23	Lahore University of Management Sciences	70
24	University Sains Malaysia (Penang)	30
25	De la Salle University (Manila)	44

Source: Information in the September 1997 issue of *Asia Inc*.

The business school is a fairly recent invention in Asia, with most dating from the late 1960s or 1970s. Many Asians still attend business schools outside Asia; indeed, until recently the demand for MBAs could not have been satisfied from within Asia (see Figure 1). But Asia now has many business schools, with the number expanding all the time, and more and more Asians are attending them (see Table 2), as well as the large number of Asian business colleges, distance learning schemes and the like that offer credentials.[11] Many of the business schools are

11. For example, Vietnam hosts a number of business courses, of which the most substantial has been a Swedish-funded project to create a centre for management training at the National Economic University (NEU) in Hanoi. Students can pick from programmes including an MBA from Boise University, a distance-learning MBA from Henley Management College and a new NEU course that produced its first group of 36 MBA students in March 1998. It is worth nothing the pace of change. The first Vietnamese allowed to study an MBA abroad only got her degree (from India) in 1992. Even

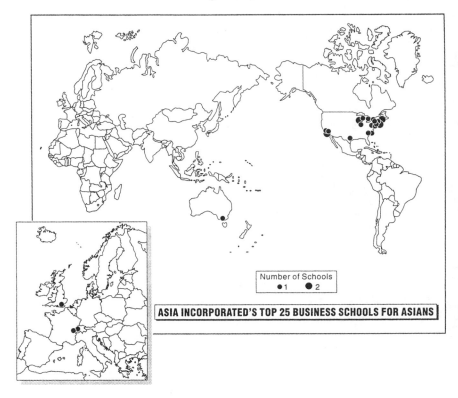

Note: Prepared from information in the September, 1997, issue of *Asia Inc.*

Figure 1 The 25 Leading Business Schools for Asians outside Asia

wildly over-subscribed, even though their fees are often well above average national incomes. For example, in India in 1996, 40,000 students took the entrance examinations for the six Indian Institutes of Management (at Ahmedabad, Calcutta, Lucknow, Bangalore, Calicut and Indore) but only 1,000 were accepted (*Financial Times*, 20 October 1997: iv). In China in the same year, there were 4,000 applicants for a twenty-month MBA course at the China Europe International Business School in Shanghai, but only 65 were accepted (Micklethwait and Wooldridge 1996; the number accepted on to the course increased to 120 in 1997).

The management consultant is another important part of the institutional arrangement in Asia. Until recently, expansion into Asia has been rather haphazard. For example, McKinsey is only now opening an office in Bangkok, while

---

now it is difficult to obtain an MBA outside Vietnam because of cost and difficulties in getting permission, but seven Fulbright MBA awards are made each year (Grant 1997).

BCG's Tokyo office opened before its London one because one of the partners, James Abbeglen, had a passion for Japan. Booz-Allen arrived in Indonesia in the early 1980s because the head of one of the country's biggest banks, BNI, had walked into the firm's New York office and asked them to work for him (Wooldridge 1997: 6).

Similarly, Asian expansion plans of most management consultant firms are uneven. For example, market penetration is still low in Japan. Further, these plans face a number of problems. First, establishing an intangible product in a market dominated by family firms who have often been suspicious of outsiders and their world is difficult. It can take a decade or more to establish a profitable branch office that is staffed by locals (Wooldridge 1997: 6). Second, recruitment and retention of staff is difficult when well-qualified people are scarce, and when training local recruits increases their market value and makes them difficult to keep. Third, while it is necessary to keep a balance of Western and local employees, it is not always easy to do so, as many clients in emerging markets would rather take advice from foreigners. In particular, 'Chinese family companies tend to put more faith in grey-haired westerners than in Chinese MBAs just out of business school' (Wooldridge 1997: 6). Fourth, it is difficult for consultants to publicise their activities: many Asian clients do not like their names used in firm publicity. In spite of these problems, management consultancies are expanding rapidly in Asia. For example, Andersen Consulting now has 4,000 people in Asia, while McKinsey's Indian Office is the company's fastest-growing (Micklethwait and Wooldridge 1996).

Management gurus also are becoming influential in Asia. Indeed, for many, it is one of their most important stamping grounds, as typified by books that are tailored to the market, like Naisbitt's *Megatrends Asia* (1995). A number of superstar gurus regularly tour the region. For example, Tom Peters currently charges $95,000 for a one-day seminar that usually lasts about seven hours (even in India!) (Crainer 1997*a*).

For many western gurus, Asian speaking tours offer much the same enticements that the musical variety do for elderly rock stars. The money is good ($25,000 a seminar), the audience large and relatively uncritical, and there is also a chance that you can find an Asian anecdote or two to spice up your performances back home (Micklethwait and Wooldridge 1996: 57).

Finally, Asian business media are extensive. Apart from business-oriented news-papers, the region contains a large and lively battery of magazine titles such as *Asia Inc*, as well as a large market for Western business titles.

Three kinds of ideas have been circulated in Asia by this mix of periodicals, travelling gurus, consulting firms and the like. One is the standard self-improvement theme, which emphasises leadership, self-discipline and other skills; and books on this theme sell well. For example, Zhang Ruimin is the President and Chair of the Chinese Haier Group, which employs 13,000 people in plants in China, Malaysia, Indonesia and the Philippines, chiefly in the manufacture of home appliances. The Haier Group is known for its aggressive management style, which has made Zhang Ruimin into one of the few famous managers in China (*The Economist*, 20 December 1997: 119). He told the *Financial Times* (3 November 1997: 16) that

> he has a profound interest in US business thinking – an avid reader of Western business books, Mr Zhang has just finished Peter Senge's *The Fifth Discipline*, which he appreciated for its emphasis on what he describes as the idea of 'a people-nurturing business'.

Another set of ideas has been the recurring business fads and fashions. For example, the bible of business process re-engineering, *Re-engineering the Corporation* (Hammer and Champy 1992), has sold 17 million copies world-wide, including 5 million copies in Asia. Whilst few companies have taken up the approach lock, stock and barrel, there have been Asian examples.

The third set of ideas has been based on the Asian, and especially Japanese, experience (see, most recently, Chin-Ning 1996; Hampden-Turner and Trompenaars 1997). In turn, these ideas have spawned Asian management gurus. The most notable of these are from Japan, such as Kenichi Ohmae (a former McKinsey employee) and, more recently, Ikujiro Nonaka,[12] whose book with Hirotaka Takeuchi, *The Knowledge-Creating Company* (1995), has become a business bestseller. However, there are also Korean gurus, such as Chan Kim (now at INSEAD).[13]

We can argue about the relative influence of these three kinds of idea on Asian managers, but they are beginning to have an effect. For example,

---

12. Symbolising the transnational nature of reflexive capitalism, Nonaka is the Professor of Knowledge Management at the Haas School of Business at Berkeley and Dean of Knowledge Science at Japan's Institute of Science and Technology in Hokuriku. His work, along with that of earlier gurus like Chris Argyris on 'organisational learning', has spawned the 'knowledge officer' in many organisations.

13. Interestingly, so far as I know no one has tried to make a management fad out of Chinese overseas capitalism, with its emphasis on family and relationships (Ong and Nonini 1997). However, this may change. For example, "relationship-building is the essence of strategy, not a by-product of it" says Tsun-yan Hsieh of McKinsey, a management consultancy' (*The Economist*, 29 March 1997: 87). *The Economist* article goes on to argue that Western firms find this idea hard to accept because of their organisational structure and tendency to move executives around, but an emphasis on networking is creeping into Western firms through the rise of relationship managers and the like.

in a massive pan-Asian survey of business people in 1995 roughly half of the respondents had bought a book by a Western management writer in the previous two years (although it was noticeable that roughly the same proportion admitted that they had not finished reading it) (Micklethwait and Wooldridge 1996: 57).

In turn, increasingly these ideas can no longer be seen as a purely Western cultural form. They are being produced simultaneously in many parts of the world, as the institutional arrangements of reflexive capitalism expand into all areas of economic growth, most especially Asia.

Conclusions

Reflexive theory is moving into the business world, producing a virtual sphere of operation that did not exist before, a sphere that complements practical business theory but still differs from it. However, there are two crucial differences between this virtual capitalism and virtualism in other spheres of life. First, as already noted, virtual capitalism will always be close to practical theory. Even though it now has its own institutional arrangements to support, spread and legitimate it, there are structural reasons why reflexive management theory must stay close to practice. Second, and related, reflexive business knowledge is *performative*.

All knowledge, of course, involves embodied performance, usually in defined contexts that are a part of that knowledge and of the trust in which it is held. However, reflexive business knowledge is of a particularly performative character. To begin with, it is based on specific training in the skills of interaction and presentation, training that is pronounced in nearly all of business life (see du Gay 1996; Kerfoot and Knights 1996). Further, embodied performance increasingly is central to the communication of business knowledge: the kind of performance found in the management seminar is a fundamental part of business life. At any one time at numerous sites around the world these studied interactions are taking place (Thrift 1997). In line with this, management theory, more than other forms of virtual knowledge, relies on a conglomeration of performed and book knowledge; and the two are not exclusive, but are parts of a chain of production and communication. Finally, management theory itself increasingly stresses the importance of embodied performance as an important aspect of the 'human capital' that businesses increasingly attempt to foster and harness. Thus, the process of social relationship must be managed as a commercial resource in its own right. In turn, this means more attention must be paid to the self and its ability to relate, through the body, to others.[14]

14. Ironically, basic insights from non-representational theory (Thrift 1996*b*) are well understood in parts of management theory. For example, von Krogh and Roos (1996) argue against 'representationism' and for an 'anti-representationistic' perspective.

In other words, it cannot be doubted that something akin to a virtual capitalism now exists, and that it is beginning to produce, perhaps for the first time, an international language of capitalism. But for all that, this virtualism is still resolutely based in the practical order of business.

Acknowledgements

I am pleased to be able to acknowledge the help and comments of a number of people on this paper, especially James G. Carrier, Jonathan Friedman, Bob Jessop, Danny Miller and Kris Olds.

References

Adams, Scott 1996. *The Dilbert Principle: A Cubicle's Eye View of Bosses, Meetings, Management Fads and Other Workplace Afflictions*. New York: Harper-Collins.

Altvater, Elmer, and Birgit Mahnkopf 1996. *Die Grenzen der Globalisierung: Politik, Ökonomie und Okologie in der Weltgesellschaft*. Munster: Verlag Westfälisches Dampfboot.

—— 1997. The World Market Unbound. *Review of International Political Economy* 4: 448–471.

Boden, Deirdre 1994. *The Business of Talk: Organisation in Action*. Cambridge: Polity Press.

Bourdieu, Pierre 1977. *Outline of a Theory of Practice*. Cambridge: Cambridge University Press.

Bowker, Geoffrey, and Susan Leigh Star 1994. Knowledge and Infrastructure in International Information Management. In Lisa Bud-Frierman (ed.), *Information Acumen: The Understanding and Use of Knowledge in Modern Business*, pp. 187–215. London: Routledge.

Brown, Michael F. 1997. *The Channeling Zone: American Spirituality in an Anxious Age*. Cambridge, Mass.: Harvard University Press.

Buck-Morss, Susan 1995. Envisioning Capital: Political Economy and Display. In Lynn Cooke and Peter Wollen (eds), *Visual Display: Culture Beyond Appearances*, pp. 110–141. Seattle: Bay Press.

Carrier, James G. (ed.) 1995. *Occidentalism: Images of the West*. Oxford: Oxford University Press.

—— (ed.) 1997*a*. *Meanings of the Market: The Free Market in Western Culture*. Oxford: Berg.

—— 1997*b*. Mr Smith, meet Mr Hawken. In J. Carrier (ed.), *Meanings of the Market: The Free Market in Western Culture*, pp. 129–157. Oxford: Berg.

Chapman, Malcolm, and Peter J. Buckley 1997. Markets, Transaction Costs, Economists and Social Anthropologists. In James G. Carrier (ed.), *Meanings of the Market: The Free Market in Western Culture*, pp. 225–250. Oxford: Berg.

Chin-Ning Chun 1996. *The Face, Black Heart: The Asian Path to Winning and Succeeding*. London: Nicholas Brealey.

Conley, Tom 1996. The Wit of the Letter: Holbein's Lacan. In Theresa Brennan and Martin Jay (eds), *Vision in Context: Historical and Contemporary Perspectives on Sight*, pp. 45–62. London: Routledge.

Cooper, Robert K., and Ayman Sawaf 1997. *Executive EQ: Emotional Intelligence in Business*. London: Orion Business Books.

Coulson-Thomas, Julian (ed.) 1997. *Business Process Re-Engineering*. London: Nicholas Brealey.

Crainer, Stuart 1997a. *Corporate Man to Corporate Skunk: The Tom Peters Phenomenon*. London: Capstone Publishing.

—— 1997b. Get Me a Writer! *Silver Kris* December: 36–38.

Crosby, Alfred W. 1996. *The Measure of Reality: Quantification and Western Society, 1250–1600*. Cambridge: Cambridge University Press.

de Geus, Arie 1997. *The Living Company*. London: Nicholas Brealey.

du Gay, Paul 1996. Organising Identity: Entrepreneurial Governance and Public Management. In Stuart Hall and P. du Gay (eds), *Questions of Cultural Identity*, 151–169. London: Sage.

Dumaine, Bernard 1997. Asia's Wealth Creators Confront a New Reality. *Fortune* (8 December): 42–55.

Edvinsson, Lief, and Michael S. Malone 1997. *Intellectual Capital: The Proven Way to Establish your Company's True Value by Measuring its Hidden Brainpower*. London: Piatkus.

Foister, Susan, Ashok Roy and Martin Wyld 1997. *Holbein's Ambassadors*. London: National Gallery Publications.

Foucault, Michel 1970. *The Order of Things: An Archaeology of the Human Sciences*. London: Tavistock.

Giddens, Anthony 1991. *Modernity and Self-Identity: Self and Society in the Late Modern Age*. Cambridge: Polity Press.

Goody, Jack 1971. *The Domestication of the Savage Mind*. Cambridge: Cambridge University Press.

—— 1987. *The Interface Between the Written and the Oral*. Cambridge: Cambridge University Press.

—— 1996. *The East in the West*. Cambridge: Cambridge University Press.

Grant, John 1997. Marxism meets the MBA. *Financial Times* (22 December): 11.

Grove, Anthony S. 1996. *Only the Paranoid Survive*. London: Harper-Collins.

Hamel, Gary, with C. K. Prahalad 1994. *Competing for the Future*. Boston: Harvard Business School Press.

Hammer, Michael, and John Champy 1992. *Re-Engineering the Corporation: A Manifesto for a Business Revolution*. London: Nicholas Brealey.

Hampden-Turner, Charles, and Leo Trompenaars 1997. *Mastering the Infinite Game: How East Asian Values are Transforming Business Practices*. London: Capstone Press.

Heelas, Paul 1996. *The New Age*. Cambridge: Polity Press.

Hiscock, Gary 1997*a*. Asia's Next Wealth Club. *World Executive's Digest* (December): 19–22.

—— 1997*b*. *Asia's Wealth Clubs: Who's Really Who in Business – The Top 100 Billionaires in Asia*. London: Nicholas Brealey.

Huczynski, Andrzej A. 1993. *Management Gurus: What Makes Them and How to Become One*. London: Routledge.

Jackson, Tim 1997*a*. *Inside Intel: How Andy Grove Built the World's Most Successful Chip Company*. London: Harper-Collins.

—— 1997*b*. Not all Rubbish. *Financial Times* (24 December): 14.

Kao, John 1997. *Jamming*. Boston: Harvard Business School Press.

Kaplan, Robert S., and David P. Norton 1997. *The Balanced Scorecard*. Boston: Harvard Business School Press.

Kerfoot, David, and Deborah Knights 1996. 'The Best is Yet to Come?': The Quest for Embodiment in Managerial Work. In David Collinson and Jeff Hearn (eds), *Men as Managers, Managers as Men: Critical Perspectives on Men, Masculinity and Management*, pp. 78–98. London: Sage.

Kleiner, Art 1996. *The Age of Heretics: Heroes, Outlaws and the Forerunners of Corporate Change*. New York: Doubleday.

Latham, Robert 1997. Globalisation, Market Boundaries and the Return of the Sovereign Repressed. Presented at the SSRC Conference on Sovereignty, Modernity and Security, April, Notre Dame, Indiana.

Latour, Bruno 1986. Visualisation and Cognition. In Hans Kuclick (ed.), *Studies in the Sociology of Culture Past and Present. Sociology of Knowledge* 6 (special issue): 1–40.

—— 1987. *Science in Action*. Milton Keynes: Open University Press.

—— 1988. Opening One Eye while Closing the Other . . .: A Note on Some Religious Paintings. In Gordon Fyfe and John Law (eds), *Picturing Power: Visual Depiction and Social Relations*, pp. 15–38. London: Routledge & Kegan Paul.

—— 1993. *We Have Never Been Modern*. Brighton: Harvester-Wheatsheaf.

Leyshon, Andrew, and Nigel J. Thrift 1997. *Money/Space: Geographies of Monetary Transformation*. London: Routledge.

Mann, Michael 1997. Has Globalisation Ended the Rise and Rise of the Nation-State? *Review of International Political Economy* 4: 472–496.

Mark, John P. 1987. *The Empire Builders: Power, Money and Ethics inside the*

Harvard Business School. New York: William Morrow.

Micklethwait, John, and Adrian Wooldridge 1996. *The Witch Doctors: What the Management Gurus are Saying, Why it Matters and How to Make Sense of It*. London: Heinemann.

Miller, Daniel 1996. *Capitalism: An Ethnographic Approach*. Oxford: Berg.

Miller, Peter, and Nicholas Rose 1997. Mobilising the Consumer: Assembling the Subject of Consumption. *Theory, Culture and Society* 14: 1–36.

Naisbitt, John 1995. *Megatrends Asia: The Eight Asian Megatrends that are Changing the World*. New York: Simon & Schuster.

Nonaka, I., and H. Takeuchi 1995. *The Knowledge-Creating Company: How Japanese Companies Create the Dynamics of Innovation*. Oxford: Oxford University Press.

Ong, Aihwa, and Donald Nonini (eds) 1997. *Ungrounded Empires: The Cultural Politics of Chinese Transnationalism*. New York: Routledge.

Osborne, Thomas, and Nicholas Rose 1997. In the Name of Society, or Three Theses on the History of Social Thought. *History of the Human Sciences* 10: 87–104.

O'Shea, James, and Charles Madigan 1997. *Dangerous Company: The Consulting Powerhouses and the Businesses they Save and Ruin*. London: Nicholas Brealey.

Pellegram, Andrea 1997. The Message in Paper. In Daniel Miller (ed.), *Material Cultures: Why Some Things Matter*, pp. 103–120. London: UCL Press.

Phillips, Nicholas 1997. *Reality Hacking*. London: Heinemann.

Porter, Theodore M. 1995. *Trust in Numbers: The Pursuit of Objectivity in Science and Public Life*. Princeton: Princeton University Press.

Power, Michael 1997. *The Audit Society*. Oxford: Oxford University Press.

Robson, Kevin 1992. Accounting Numbers as Inscription: Action at a Distance and the Development of Accounting. *Accounting, Organisations and Society* 17: 685–708.

Shapiro, Eileen C. 1995. *Fad Surfing in the Boardroom: Reclaiming the Courage to Manage in the Age of Instant Answers*. Reading, Mass.: Addison-Wesley.

Stewart, Thomas A. 1997. *Intellectual Capital: The New Wealth of Organisations*. London: Nicholas Brealey.

Strathern, Marilyn 1996. Cutting the Network. *Journal of the Royal Anthropological Institute* 2: 517–535.

Thrift, Nigel J. 1984. Flies and Germs: A Geography of Knowledge. In Derek Gregory and John Urry (eds), *Social Relations and Spatial Structures*, pp. 330–373. London: Macmillan.

—— 1995. A Hyperactive World? In R. J. Johnston, P. Taylor and M. Watts (eds), *Geographies of Global Change*, pp. 18–35. Oxford: Basil Blackwell.

—— 1996a. New Urban Eras and Old Technological Fears: Reconfiguring the Goodwill of Electronic Things. *Urban Studies* 33: 1463–1493.

—— 1996*b*. *Spatial Formations*. London: Sage.

—— 1997. The Rise of Soft Capitalism. *Cultural Values* 1: 29–57.

Tort, Patrick 1989. *La raison classificatoire: Quinze études*. Paris: Ambier.

Treacy, Michael, and Fred Wiersema 1995. *The Discipline of Market Leaders: Choose Your Customers, Narrow Your Focus, Dominate your Market*. New York: Addison-Wesley.

van de Vliet, Ann 1997. The Balanced Scorecard. *Management Today* (September): 23–31.

von Krogh, Georg, and Johan Roos 1996. *Managing Knowledge: Perspectives on Cooperation and Competition*. London: Sage.

Wooldridge, Adrian 1997. Trimming the Fat: A Survey of Management Consultancy. *The Economist* (22 March, Survey): 1–26.

Yates, Joann 1994. Evolving Information Use in Firms, 1850–1920: Ideology and Information Techniques and Technologies. In Lisa Bud-Frierman (ed.), *Information Acumen: The Understanding and Use of Knowledge in Modern Business*, pp. 26–50. London: Routledge.

Yates, Joann, and Walter J. Orlikowski 1992. Genres of Organisational Communication. *Academy of Management Review* 17: 299–326.

Conclusion: A Theory of Virtualism
Daniel Miller

In the Introduction to this volume, Carrier suggests that current changes in our world may be viewed as the legacy of a much longer history in which abstraction has been steadily emerging. These include both abstraction in economic practice and abstraction in ideas and values that are not simply a reflection of these changes in practice but may be closely associated with them. This should not lead us to simplify history into some smooth trajectory or evolutionary inevitability, nor to homogenise what are highly disparate regions whose particular histories must be regarded as equally authentic and not some version of a 'proper' overarching process. Anthropologists are particularly wary of simple notions of progress or modernity that work by classifying others as primitive or lacking in progress. But these caveats do not justify ignoring evident directionality in particular times and places. Furthermore, there are many new technologies and forms of communication that may make a larger and more generalised perspective warranted today in a way that it was not before. This is clear in the chapters of this collection, where discussions on topics ranging from the nature of a global capitalist class to the global effects of economic theory provide warrant for making what are dangerous but necessary generalisations. Carrier's Introduction and first chapter refer largely to a particular regional historical sequence that has had a unique impact and has been linked with parallel processes found elsewhere.

Here I intend to complement the Introduction. Seeing virtualism as a mould designed to create a new shape in the world and of the world leads us to enquire into both its causes and its consequences. Carrier tackles the first task, arguing that there is a particular historical sequence that might explain the rise of forms of abstraction today that can be accounted for in terms of the longer historical sequences that provided the potential for their emergence. By contrast, here I ask not where we have come from, but where we are going to; not so much the causes of virtualism, but its nature and consequences. Doing so provides the flux that is needed to fuse the hard-edged but independent mineral constructs of the previous chapters into a possible whole sculpture that would justify the transcendent category of virtualism.

This chapter is thus intended to have its own integrity as a 'story', but also to act as a conclusion to the volume as a whole. Doing so does not mean simply summarising the substantive chapters in the collection, some of which raise doubts about the possibility of effective virtualism or make points that contradict some of the claims I make here. In particular, many of the authors would probably see their work as closer to a conventional Marxist critique and would balk at my idea that we need to replace Marx's critique of capitalism with something else. This chapter also has a different focus from the chapters that precede it, in that it is concerned with the particular role of consumption in understanding the contemporary world, and I do not pretend to be clear myself as to how far the argument I make here works in relation to phenomena such as finance capital or, indeed, the virtualism of virtual reality within computer technologies.

My argument involves a high level of generalisation about an argument that is also a critique of high-level generalisations. Nevertheless, the justification for such a hazardous undertaking is given within the argument; and overall it is my belief that in the present the social sciences would benefit considerably from any theory that managed to clarify connections between features of our world that too often seem like isolated fragments whose simultaneous existence is no more than fortuitous. Even if my specific arguments do not appeal, I think that we do need to try to find an appropriate position from which to view our time. A struggle towards an enlightened, if not an Enlightenment, gaze still has much to be said for it.

A Defence of Grand Narrative

I want to tell a story. It is a particular kind of story, a grand narrative. With the rise of postmodernism and an academic sensitivity to cultural differences and pluralism over the past two decades, one of the main targets of criticism has become not so much political economy, but the way it had been developed by Marx, in particular through his use of Hegel. This tradition of political economy as grand narrative was rejected and replaced by many new areas of academic concern. These included cultural studies, literary studies, some branches of psychoanalysis (such as Lacanian) and a topic that will play a central role in this story, consumption.

Most of those interested in consumption saw it as a means to escape from the sins of grand narrative. This is because it implied a concern with the diverse fields of practice within which what otherwise might seem homogeneous phenomena, such as goods, services or media, become fragmented into the plural communities of consumption: different audiences might read the same text in opposing ways. It provided evidence not just for globalisation or homogeneity, but also for regional and local diversity. All of this is very welcome. My story has a somewhat perverse ambition, however, which is to use consumption in order to return to the tradition of a grand narrative. For a moment I put aside issues of diversity in order to see if there is any general direction in which history could be said to be moving.

The grand narrative, in its debt to Hegel, had many features that are now unpopular: it homogenised history as a normative sequence; it portrayed history as moving in a particular direction; it was idealist in that it weighed history against explicit concepts of rationality. I believe Hegel was prescient. While many of these features may not have been justified for his time, they may be rather more appropriate for our time. It is, thus, ironic that this tradition is being attacked at the very moment when history itself is coming into line with its own story. In making this claim I do not mean that history has an intrinsic direction, and certainly I do not avow a Western conceptualisation of progress. Rather I wish to suggest that today, rather more than at the time in which Hegel lived, there exist forces of such power and global reach that certain trends have become ubiquitous, and hence that we can talk meaningfully, perhaps for the first time, about history's having a direction.

Hegelians have always looked for dialectical features within historical processes. Briefly, they take all cultural phenomena as inherently contradictory processes, with a contradiction that creates its own subject. Humanity successively establishes new objective forms and institutions, for instance law or money. These create the possibility of new abstract and universalistic concepts, while at the same time generating more particularistic difference. At each cycle we reach a point when such forms and institutions become so autonomous from us, their creators, so driven by their own logic, that they become highly oppressive and dangerous to us. We need, therefore, to return to an understanding, which Hegel saw as a philosophical understanding, that these are indeed our own creations and that potentially we can expand ourselves by bringing them back to us, dialectically transcending the distance between universality and particularity, transforming them into that which strengthens rather than diminishes our humanity.

Marx exemplified these ideas. However, he moved the focus from philosophy to a series of material changes that had, indeed, achieved new forms of abstraction on the one hand, and particularity on the other. Of these, the most extreme example was capitalism. Marx focused on the growth of an autonomous logic to capitalism based on the original alienation of nature as private property. Capital had become a relentlessly-abstract force devoted to its own expansion, a force that threatened to destroy all cultural traditions and tear society apart in that quest. It produced a system in which commodities were not recognised as human creations, but had become enslaved to the autonomous logic of expanding capital. Marx represented this not as a consequence of immutable laws, but as a stage in the story of history. Since that time, many versions of dialectic theory have arisen, but those that are the more teleological and historical have fared less well than those that use the dialectic to create a relational perspective on social life (for a recent account, see D. Harvey 1996: 46–113).

From a dialectical perspective, it is clear that the one thing Marx would not be if he were alive today is a Marxist, since his sense of history was such that statements made in one century had to be superseded by a new understanding appropriate to the next historical moment. In short, Marx today, if he were to be consistent, would not be searching for capitalism, but for some different yet equivalent force relevant to the end of the twentieth century. He would expect that, if communism were not the end of history, then capitalism should have been superseded by some new, even more abstract and alienating, historical movement. One aim, then, in telling a story in this chapter should be to bring Marx up to date.

History is an unending process and can never be 'resolved' in the way that the concept of communism implied. Contradiction is not a characteristic of a phase of history, it is intrinsic to culture. We have always been and will always be living through attempts to resolve contradictions, attempts that must be partial because they create new contradictions in turn. After the triumph of capitalism as abstraction must come its negation. This negation need not diminish the actions of capitalism as an economic motor. However, the negation would seek to ameliorate the force of abstract capitalism, which oppressed humanity by reducing labour merely to its logical place within capitalist processes. Put in other words, capitalist universalism should create its own potential for a new particularism, such that workers could develop societies in ways never previously envisaged.

The editors of this volume both work within the discipline of anthropology; both have worked as ethnographers, a mode characteristic of the discipline. Ethnography in turn lends itself to its own, highly parochial 'local traditions' (Fardon 1990), in which what is respected is intensive knowledge about small groups of peoples. The orientation of this knowledge is ambivalent. It owes a great deal to positivism when anthropologists claim that long-term scholarly observation of repetitive action in the field makes that knowledge authoritative, but it is also relativistic when anthropologists claim that their knowledge is valid only for the small group of people studied, and should not be assumed to apply to their neighbours, let alone other regions. One would expect, then, that anthropologists would be deeply sceptical of grand narrative or any esoteric theory, while more sympathetic to postmodernist assertions of incommensurability. Many, if not most, do have such leanings. However, anthropology is a curious discipline in that it has also fostered many of the most general and theoretical models of human society, such as functionalism and structuralism. It is almost as though, safe in the grounded knowledge of particularity, anthropologists have thought that they can afford such models, while remaining sceptical of those who work only on theoretical models and lack the sense of the relativism that is essential if they are to be used judiciously. My pretensions follow such a trajectory. If this chapter is an attempt to discern the shape of the woods and landscapes of our moment in history, it is intended to be complemented always by a commitment to remain immersed ethnographically in the dense thickets and undergrowth that lie beneath.

A Story

I return to the story and its legacy from the writings of Marx. The narrative has unfolded much as might have been predicted, which is to say, in ways that Marx did not predict. Today we see something very different from the capitalist society that Marx experienced and described. In most regions, our lives are dominated by much more than simply our niche in the circulation of capital. Homogeneity exists at some levels, such as the global capitalist class that Sklair describes. However, the diversity of society that the ethnographer encounters is a complete repudiation of the homogenisation of society under early capitalism. We would expect there to be a diversity of routes constituting any such negation: trade unions in one place, the state in another. The result today is that we have many different forms of capitalist societies, unless, of course, you believe the postmodernist mantra that all current diversity is simply superficiality.

As ethnographers we experience cultural difference as profound. One cause of these differences is the regional inequality that is created by capitalism as a global system. As the literature on world-systems demonstrated, often development in some areas has been secured through underdevelopment in others. In other regions it has been localisation, rather than globalisation, that has led to capitalism's being subject to increasing contextualisation: German capitalism has many elements that distinguish it from that of Japan, and both are quite distinct from plantation systems in South America. The degree to which this has historically proved to be the case could hardly be clearer, in that we live in a marvellous period when the fastest-growing version of capitalism is the Chinese Communist variety (Smart 1997). If so, our grand narrative is a story not without some quite good jokes.

If China and South Asia do achieve high growth rates and, rather more doubtfully, find means to spread the benefits that accrue, then the more progressive elements of this story would seem to apply to the majority of the world population, though the large number of gaps forbids any simple evocation of a concept of progress.[1] For now, this story could be characterised as a clear taming of capitalism only for segments of populations within the countries that are most developed. In as much as this represents a historical tendency, then it probably achieved its fullest extent in Scandinavia in the 1960s, where powerful states achieved what I believe to be an unequalled ability to create from capitalism a machine for the service of human welfare through extremely tight forms of state control. We expect no perfection on this earth, and such state control may have had its less noble side, as in evidence

1. As the chapters by McMichael and Sklair make clear, the huge number of beneficiaries of these processes remain a minority population parasitic upon an oppressed majority. We are at a point, however, where changes in South and East Asia point to the possibility that this need not always be the case.

for the use of eugenics under Swedish social democracy. Even so, though capitalist, these were genuinely welfare states, and Scandinavian social democracy serves as an example of where history might have led us. I take these states as a benchmark that can be used in order to critique any counter-trends that may be discerned today, an actual, historical benchmark, and hence better than fanciful ones like utopian communism, against which we all stand equally condemned.

Scandinavia shifts our understanding of what capitalism could become. Instead of intrinsic contradictions between capitalist and worker, the region showed that states can create structures in which workers, either as partners or as holders of pensions and other assets, can become aggregate capitalists who retain an interest in profits being converted into mass welfare. Workers there enjoyed vast wealth and services previously not imaginable. The speed with which such transformations might take place are astonishing. There have been few more evocative portraits of the hell on earth that early capitalism could be than *Hunger*, in which the Norwegian novelist Knut Hamsun (1921) portrayed Oslo around 1900. By comparison, oil-rich Norway today provides its citizens with benefits that are prodigious.

Changes in the organisation of states and economies can only achieve a negation of early capitalism if they are matched by processes that enable people to draw from capitalism forms that can be used to enhance ordinary life. In my first attempt to contribute a footnote to this story (Miller 1987), I argued that even though institutions such as the state were crucial in these processes, there was one phenomenon above all that most fully expressed this historical negation, and this was consumption. My argument was that the very abstraction and universalism embodied in capitalism was most fully negated in a force that it had created, but that expressed with the greatest eloquence the possibilities of particularity and diversity brought down to the level of ordinary human practice, the very forms of experience that capitalism as abstraction had destroyed. Consumption plays this role theoretically and sometimes in actuality. It is here that the smallest social groups, even individuals, confront objects that, in their production, express the very abstraction of the market and the state. Yet, through purchase and possession, people can use those objects to create worlds that strive to be specific and diverse precisely because we wish to escape from our sense of alienation from the vast institutions of the market and the state.

For example, I found that impoverished householders on government housing estates in London used the potential of gender as exchange (between male DIY labour and female expertise in interior aesthetics) in order to create transformations in goods and services (specifically their kitchens) that made the development of their social relations the direct negation of the stigma attached to their situation at the lowest end of state services and market provision (Miller 1988). In more affluent circles it seemed to me that even the most critical and ascetic of the academics amongst whom I worked enjoyed in their daily consumption goods ranging from the services of restaurants to the latest forms of word processor, summer holidays and devices intended to help in securing the safety of children, goods that, when generalised as mass consumption, were clearly being voted for in practice even when they were to be condemned in theory; and they did not seem to regard themselves as superficial or passive in their enjoyment. If our academic perspectives are in any way to remain consistent with our private lives, then we have to acknowledge the benefits of capitalist commodities that accrue to those who can afford them.

Such observations on consumption are commonplace. What is required is a theory that does not simply conclude that the Marxist critique had been wrong. The solution is not to turn away from dialectical theory, but to employ it as the dynamic instrument that it was intended to be. The fault, then, lies with those who espouse Marxism but think that this requires the models and generalities Marx developed in the middle of the nineteenth century, because, for them, consumption under capitalism could only be an emanation of capitalism itself. However, were we to use dialectical theory properly, we should seek historical processes that were created by capitalism, processes that emerged as internal contradictions within capitalism and negated it. Mass consumption appears to fit the part. The contradictions within capitalism expressed as the opposed interest of capitalist and worker had become ameliorated when, by the middle of the twentieth century, ordinary workers achieved material benefits on a par with the capitalists of a century before. This need imply no change in the logic of capitalism itself, a highly amoral system of capital reproduction that offers little opportunity for the self-construction of the species being as the young Marx understood it. Similarly, powerful states and bureaucracies, essential to the construction of equality through complex tax and redistribution systems, had their own logic of dehumanising anonymity. Although necessary to achieve such objectives, these too are not appealing sources of identity, particularly after seeing how they were aestheticised by some fascist and communist states to become the focus of identity.

Consumption as negation is not, of course, accomplished through the mere accumulation of material forms. Rather, it requires the long-term process by which consumers appropriate goods and services in direct repudiation of the massive and unattractive institutional forces of capitalism, the state and, increasingly, science, which had created these goods. Only consumption as a process provides the flexibility and creativity that allow societies, small groups and even individuals to return to that act of self-construction of the species being that is the definition of human culture within dialectical theory. In a word, this century has shown that it is in consumption, and not, as Marx had argued, in production, that commodities can be returned to the world as the embodiment of human potentiality.

After outlining this model, I sought to characterise and exemplify these processes. Contrary to most writings on the subject, I have always believed that consumption is primarily a social achievement, not an individual one; that it is a cultural process that is hardly ever about individuals or subjectivities. My main example (Miller 1994, 1997) has been based on consumption and identity in Trinidad. I have tried to show how Trinidadians historically represent the extremes of capitalist alienation as slaves, as indentured labourers and as Third World migrants without local history or roots. I then explored their consumption of key symbols of alienation: Christmas, Coca-Cola, transnational corporations and the like. By contrast with the orientation of most academic writings, I have tried to show how, in consumption, these symbols of alienation become the very instruments through which the specificity of Trinidadian identity has been created as the negation of their historical legacy of alienation: Trinidadian Christmas; a black, sweet drink from Trinidad; Trinidadian-owned transnational corporations. My most recent ethnographic work on shopping in North London points in the same general direction (Miller 1998). Shopping has very little to do with individuals, with hedonism or even with materialism; it can be better understood as a ritual parallel to the structure of ancient sacrifice that is devoted to the construction of key relationships and the objectification of devotional love.

I do not mean these examples to imply that all consumption negates capitalism or the state. Rather, I present them to illustrate how, at one moment in history, it has the potential to do so. As part of a dialectical story, consumption may stand as the moment of negation of capitalism as the most powerful form of oppressive abstraction developed by humanity. But if it is to remain contemporary, a grand narrative constantly has to be re-written. If consumption has been used to counteract the effects of capitalism that Marx described, then I suspect Marx himself would be searching for what might be called the negation of the negation. There should be some new force emerging that is based on the contradictions of these earlier forces, perhaps the contradictions of consumption, a force that is now creating another institutional embodiment of human creativity as abstraction that will come to replace capitalism, a force that necessarily will be more extreme than capitalism, more abstract and more dehumanising, until it in turn can be negated. Marx today would surely be searching for this emergent formation.

I suggested that the high point in the taming of capitalism is to be found, not today, but twenty years ago in Scandinavian social democracy. Seen from the perspective of Western states, the last twenty years can only be regarded as regressive. We see a decline in the movement towards greater equality, a decline in faith in the welfare state, a decline in the sense of the progressive potential of consumption, a potential explored most visibly in the 1960s, with its explosion of creativity in music, clothing, life-styles and so forth. This regression is conceded even by those most in favour of classic economic perspectives. Just before Christmas 1997, *The Economist*, a periodical renowned for its neo-classical economics and opposition to the state, included a small note, 'Rising tide, falling boats'. It reported that in the United States the family income of the richest fifth of the population had increased by 30 per cent since the late 1970s, while the income of the poorest fifth had declined by 21 per cent, leaving the income of the former 19.5 times higher than the income of the latter. Further, in all but one state during this period, the income of the middle fifth had also fallen.

It does not take a great deal of imagination to translate these figures into human experiences: a wealthy community for whom the additional increases merely add to monies that are almost beyond their ability to spend, but that front claims about the country as a whole becoming 'richer'; while the poor, for whom every small shift represents a major constraint on their ability to realise their goals and values, have seen a terrifying fall in their ability to participate meaningfully in their own society. Similar things are likely to be happening elsewhere. South Asia and the east coast of China have seen the rise of a formidable middle class; but there are suggestions from the hinterlands that both areas face a rise in inequality comparable to that in the United States. For any perspective with even a smidgen of concern for human welfare, then, we live in regressive times. Why did this happen? What were the grounds for this reversal in our recent history? How do they serve to negate the progressive potential of consumption?

Economics beyond Capitalism

If the aim is to rise above the trees and attempt to discern the shape of the woods, then Trinidad offers a useful perspective precisely because it is situated on a periphery, where power tends to divest itself of some of its disguises (Gledhill 1994). Trinidad is in a curious situation. The constraints imposed on the major companies that had developed in order to exploit the island were based almost entirely on nationalism, given teeth by the 1973 oil boom, rather than any form of socialism. As a result there had been a clear local taming of capitalism, to some extent reversed in the recession that followed the decline in the price of oil. Capitalism in contemporary Trinidad had become surprisingly localised, including some powerful local transnational corporations that were starting to become complementary, rather than antagonistic, to state welfare politics. Trinidad was no ideal society, but this was a clear step up from colonialism, let alone from slavery.

This progressive process is currently being undermined, and, I suspect, negated, because of the arrival of structural adjustment.[2] As its causes and consequences

2. One reason to focus on structural adjustment is that it bears on Nelson's warning, in her chapter in this collection, that we should not presume that the discourse of economics has particular implications for practices in the world, which may be more resilient than neo-classical economists suppose. Structural adjustment shows precisely that it is most often the practice of economics as a powerful discipline that is destructive. While most academic disciplines produce abstractions that can be just as absurd as that of economics, they have not been granted the means to realise their models in the world.

are described at length in McMichael's chapter in this collection, here I need only say that structural adjustment is based on a series of models that were devised by economists working within some of the key institutions that were set up following the epochal meeting at Bretton Woods. These models, fostered most notably by the IMF and the World Bank, are purely academic, in the sense that they seem to pay no attention to local context. The measures for ending protectionism and abolishing currency control imposed on Trinidad would have been more or less the same if this had been Nigeria or the Ukraine. These sometimes fit the interests of capitalist corporations, but surprisingly often do not. This is because they are not the product of capitalism as an institutional practice of firms, or even a direct reflection of the interests of powerful countries, even the United States (though this is often claimed). I would argue instead that they are simply idealised and abstract models that represent the university departments of economics engaged in academic modelling.

As Thrift notes in his chapter, economics is not the 'theory' of working capitalism, which has had to remain thoroughly engaged and performative, while economics has not. So, while capitalism as a process by which firms seek to increase capital through manufacture and trade has become increasingly contextualised, complex and often contradictory (Miller 1997), another force has arisen that has become increasingly abstract. This force takes the shape of academics, paid for by states and international organisations and given the freedom to rise above context to engage in speculative modelling. While Marx had to tease out the abstract logic of capitalism, today the greater abstraction of academic economics is quite transparent and constantly confirmed by its practitioners. Social scientists may not think of academics as particularly powerful; but then *they* are not economists.

While capitalism engages with the world and is thus subject to the trans-formations of context, economics remains disengaged, so that structural adjustment in Trinidad could be not one iota Trinidadian. This is because economics has the authority to transform the world into its own image. Where the existing world does not conform to the academic model, the onus is not on changing the model, testing it against the world, but on changing the world, testing us against the model. The very power of this new form of abstraction is that it can indeed act to eliminate the particularities of the world. If we examine its details we find that all the changes that Trinidad was being asked to make were to remove what the economists call 'distortions'. For example, Trinidad was required to end subsidies to local companies because these distort the market in which those companies operate, making it deviate from the economist's ideal of the free market. The chapter by Helgason and Pálsson in this collection demonstrates, moreover, that this imposed remodelling of reality is by no means limited to developing countries.

So it is not that the economic model of the market represents capitalism, but that capitalism is being instructed to transform itself into a better representation of that model. If we look at the various forms of Thatcherism and Reaganomics, and their continuation under different names when their erstwhile opponents gain power, then what we find is what the Frankfurt school predicted, the rise of economics as the primary authority within politics. Just as capitalism had lost its ideological authority under a century of critique, it came to be replaced by a safer, more disengaged rhetoric.

The point that I have made briefly about Trinidad is supported by academics who study structural adjustment in detail. The most extreme view is found in the work of Susan George. Her argument anticipates what I say here, that institutions like the IMF transcend economic logic and represent some other kind of force. She says (George and Sabelli 1994) that the IMF and the World Bank resemble traditional forms of religion in the strength and insistence of their beliefs, in the purity of their model and in their inability to engage with the world despite a rhetoric of science and falsifiability. Other, less extreme writers are not far behind George in their condemnation. Perhaps the most concise statement of these views comes from Paul Mosely in a preface to a book by Frances Stewart. Mosely and Stewart are two of the most scholarly researchers on the topic, and their work is strongly placed within the discipline of development economics. Mosely says that

> there remains a lot of doubt about the state of the art in a number of areas, doubt which is magnified by the tendency of theory and practice to remain more separate from one another than in many branches of economics, or other sciences. One dramatic illustration of this has been the introduction of 'structural adjustment lending' by the World Bank and other international financial agencies in the last fifteen years, under which aid money has been offered in return for policy reform. In virtually all cases the justification offered for the policy reforms in question, e.g. privatisation, subsidy removal, trade liberalisation, has not been empirical evidence specific to the country in question but a priori theorising often based on an attempt to apply the general theorems of welfare economics without taking note of the conditions which have to be satisfied if these theorems are to apply, for example, perfect knowledge, no externalities, no economies of scale. The absence of empirical support for recommended reforms which often have serious political and social implications has led to justified scepticism, particularly in developing countries, about what social development has to offer in such a situation (preface by Mosely, in Stewart 1995: xi).

Mosely criticised economics for being too theoretical. In practice, however, the problem is exactly the opposite. It is that economists have applied their theories in practice with a sense of power that is unprecedented: no country in the world can hope to make more than a partial stand against them, and developing countries have virtually no means to combat these forces. If these theories had remained within the academic domain, the world would be much better off. As even the defenders of these policies have noted, the debt crisis had already cut a destructive swathe through development, so that their effect in some cases was to make an already bad situation still worse.

Structural adjustment provides a particularly clear case of the dominance of economic theory over politics, and indeed the dominance of economic theory over actually existing capitalism. In Trinidad, for example, local capitalism was remarkably robust and gaining dominance in the region. However, in order to combat the anticipated effects of structural adjustment, it had to shift direction in a number of significant ways, such as over-stretching its international base. Structural adjustment and similar policies pose the problems that they do in Trinidad and elsewhere because capitalism has, over a century and more, developed an organic form that by no means reflects the pure market orientation and practices that economists assume to be fundamental. (This point has been made forcefully within anthropology: Dilley 1992; Miller 1997; see especially Carrier 1997.) Critics who assume that economics is merely a branch of capitalism or is an extension of the global power of the United States are refuted by those such as George and Mosely, who have studied the institutions themselves. They show that, even though it purports to model capitalism, economics is actually an abstract modelling procedure, little affected by evidence – that it sometimes acts entirely against the interests of transnational capitalism and the major states.

The treatment of Trinidad as merely a distortion from a theoretical model, and the reduction of structural adjustment to an attempt to force all states into greater conformity with this model, is a consequence. To find the cause we need to look at the academic discipline that generated the model in the first place. The best way to appraise economics, as a leading character in this larger narrative, comes not from a portrayal of neo-classical economics, but from the extent and depth of the criticism that exists within the discipline of economics itself.

The internal critique of economics is vast and varied. Some of the most fundamental attacks are those that root the problem in the links between a particular epistemology and the subsequent pseudo-scientific genre that dominates the discipline (for example Ekins and Max-Neef 1992; Lawson 1997). Others acknowledge the social or embedded nature of preferences and behaviours, often referring back to social and moral issues in the neglected legacy of Adam Smith. Mayer (1993: 103–121) provides a useful distinction between the rise of theoretical modelling and the continuation of a more empirical tradition based on generalising data, but then adds the damning evidence that the findings of these empirical economists have demonstrated the falsity of most of the premises and assumptions behind neo-classical economics. Amongst the most influential critics is McCloskey (especially 1985), who has described the language and rhetoric of economics in a way that exposes the nature of its discourse as genre; and, in her contribution to this volume, Nelson provides a specific instance of this internal criticism. Structural adjustment programmes, on the other hand, show that what may seem to be just an academic concern with discourse can have vast consequences in the world.

It is significant that these extensive criticisms have had no real impact on the dominant trends in the discipline, indicating that neo-classical economics is effectively impervious to criticism, whether epistemological or empirical. Indeed, as Fine points out in his chapter in this collection, the same period that saw these internal criticisms has been characterised by a counter-movement that its own practitioners call 'economic imperialism' (Radnitzky and Bernholz 1987), a counter-movement that argues for the applicability of economic modelling to all other disciplines and to all aspects of social and cultural activity (see especially Tommasi and Ierulli 1995). In his discussion of the work of Becker, Fine shows how imperialist economics reduces analysis to tautologies of rationality that work by treating preferences in a highly parochial way and by refusing to consider the reasons behind them. This is the kind of logic that, if it were consistent (often it manages to be conveniently inconsistent), would argue that in a society where men are better paid, women should therefore stay at home in domestic labour. Furthermore, in divorce we should ignore our concept of natural rights, and children should be given to those who have the most resources to develop their potential – which, given their better pay, means men. Empirical studies of how people value children in financial terms (Zelizer 1985) show just how far Becker and his acolytes are from any understanding of the family and its rationality.

Economics, then, seems suited to be a key character in a dialectical story that suggests we look for an emerging institution that would negate the taming of many of the more abstract tendencies in capitalism. Compared to capitalism, economics is less grounded in the world and is therefore able to develop a form of abstraction that is still more impervious to criticism concerned with human welfare. Because it accomplishes a higher level of abstraction and decontextualisation than does capitalism, it breaks new ground in the self-alienation of a human institution from its role in the development of species being. As Mayer notes (1993: 29), many economists are said to baffle even physicists in the rigour of their quest for mathematical purity.

Virtualism

But in whose name is this being done? By what right do economists have this authority, this manifest power in the world? If this story is to remain consistent, then the answers to these questions must approximate the negation of the negation. That is, they must relate to the same force, consumption, that has emerged as the vanguard of history in its negation of capitalism as oppression. This is exactly what we find. The people and institutions proclaiming the inevitability of the market, from economists and politicians downwards, do so in the name of the consumer. Indeed, the whole point of the market is that it is supposed to be the sole process that can bring the best goods at the lowest prices to the consumer, the ultimate beneficiary. It is in the name of the consumer that distortions in the market, whether caused by government, trade unions or even actual consumers, are to be eliminated, for these prevent the realisation of that ideal state that best benefits the consumer.

The unique ability of the pure, free market to benefit the consumer is fundamental to economics, as presented in its primary textbooks. Thus, Sloman (1994: 1) notes that the main concern of economics is production and consumption, the latter being 'the act of using goods and services to satisfy wants. This will normally involve purchasing goods and services.' In an ideal free market, 'competition between firms keeps prices down and acts as an incentive to firms to become more efficient. The more firms there are competing, the more responsive they will be to consumer wishes' (1994: 21). Similarly, Stiglitz (1993: 30) says:

> This model of consumers, firms, and markets is *the basic competitive model*. Economists generally believe that, to the extent that it can be duplicated by market systems in the real world, the competitive model will provide answers to the basic economic questions of what is produced and in what quantities, how it is produced, and for whom it is produced that result in the greatest economic efficiency.

This is related to the principle of consumer sovereignty, that individuals are the best judges of what is in their own interests (1993: 191).

With the hindsight of history, a dialectical perspective makes this look almost inevitable. Since it was consumption as an expression of welfare that was the main instrument in negating the abstraction of capitalism, the move to greater abstraction had to supplant consumption as human practice with an abstract version of the consumer. The result is the creation of the virtual consumer in economic theory, a chimera, the constituent parts of which are utterly daft, as Fine has pointed out in several works (Fine 1995, this volume; Fine and Leopold 1993). Indeed, neo-classical economists make no claim to represent flesh-and-blood consumers. They claim that their consumers are merely aggregate figures used in modelling. Their protestations of innocence are hollow, however, because these virtual consumers and the models they inhabit and that animate them are the same models that are used to justify forcing actual consumers to behave like their virtual counterparts. Just as the problem with structural adjustment is not that it is based on academic theory but that it has become practice, so the problem with the neo-classical consumer is the effects that the model has on the possibilities of consumer practice. In some kind of global card trick, an abstract, virtual consumer steals the authority that had been accumulated for workers in their other role as consumers.[3]

---

3. The virtual consumer described here adds a particular twist to Nelson's arguments in this collection about the gendered nature of neo-classical economics. The other side of economic abstraction engendered as male, is the ubiquitous engendering of the consumer as female, borne out by the practice

Auditing and Virtualism[4]

The rise and power of economic theory as manifested in the authority of economic institutions such as the IMF and the World Bank is the primary example what here will be called virtualism; but it is by no means the only one. If the power of these institutions is part of a larger movement in history, then we can expect to see many parallel trends. The second candidate for virtualism is only too familiar to academics. In this case the ethnographic fieldworker need not stray much beyond the staff common room in order to accumulate the relevant evidence. If these last twenty years have indeed been the negation of the negation, then the cold winds of these changes should be felt even in such notoriously stuffy environments. In Britain, as in many other countries, the previous decades had seen an expansion of higher education, as also of medicine and welfare more generally. While hardly perfect, for inequalities certainly had not been eliminated, those decades clearly were improvements on the preceding era. More people were coming into education and the purpose of education was moving from esoteric research *per se* to giving students and others understanding, as well as knowledge.

In the last twenty years this movement has started to reverse, for what seems at first to be a rather curious reason. British academics bore each other endlessly with complaints about how they should spend their time in teaching or research, but actually seem to spend more and more of their time dealing with the paperwork generated by a variety of new institutional requirements that go under the common name 'auditing'. Paperwork once measured in pages is now measured by weight: teaching audits, research audits, audits of courses that may receive grants. These and too many others are the bane of academic life.

Academics will always grumble; but there has been a major shift in the use of time, confirmed by considering other institutions, such as the health service or local government. There has been a vast expansion of auditing, a curious result of a Thatcherite drive that, I suggest, sincerely believed in limiting centralisation and bureaucracy. Yet by its own actions, it increased substantially the resources going to management and homogenising bureaucracy. This contradiction between intention and result indicates that this historical process can not be understood as some simple expression of political will.

---

of consumption in most societies. As such, it was a largely feminine resistance through consumption that acted to negate the hard-edged capitalism of the male (see Miller 1995). That resistance now is being negated by the replacement of the actual female consumer with the virtual consumer.

4. In his chapter, McMichael presents a point of linkage between these two examples, arguing that bodies such as the IMF have become, in effect, the auditors of what is supposed to become a global self-regulated market.

This contradiction is a clear example of what Hegel understood as the inherent tendency of institutions created for human welfare to turn against us and become oppressive if they are allowed to follow their own autonomous logic of existence. The argument is given firm grounding by Power (1994, see also 1997) in his analysis of *The Audit Explosion*. He starts by noting the sheer extent of growth in auditing, now covering almost every branch of governance, from medical to criminal justice, from charities to corporate control. Partly as a result, about one graduate in twelve is now training in an accountancy firm (1994: 2). Power says that auditing can not be seen in isolation, but is part of the growth of 'new public management' (1994: 15), which stresses the definition of goals and the competition for resources within the organisation. Private companies have created a parasite that is equally bloodthirsty in the various forms of management consultancy, on which firms that describe themselves as 'cash-strapped' will spend huge sums. The growth of these consultancies is part of what Thrift (1997, this volume) calls 'soft capitalism' and what Salaman (1997) calls 'the new narrative of corporate culture'. These are based on an abstracted discourse that is likely to prove just as detrimental to these willing victims as the audit explosion is to public organisations. In his chapter, Thrift provides a detailed account of the long history behind what appears now as an explosion of virtual business knowledge and theory (see also O'Shea and Madigan 1997).

The character of this new form of discourse is important. 'One of the paradoxes of the audit explosion is that it does not correspond to more surveillance and more direct inspection. Instead, audits generally act indirectly upon systems of control' (Power 1994: 19). Thus, the audit process is really the control of control, so that legitimacy comes to depend more on being seen to be audited than on the actual audit outcome. One consequence is that auditing and the like tend to make organisations more opaque rather than more transparent. In adding another layer of control, they often create the very sense of loss of trust that they were supposed to counteract. Further, auditors are impervious to evidence that they are not actually improving organisation practice. Indeed, the failure of an institution that is audited almost invariably results in calls for more auditing, even when it is clear that the audit process and results made the organisation's problems worse. So, as with economics, auditing is a force that was originally attempting to understand organisations and help them but has become the slave of its own abstract and self-confirming logic.

The harmful abstraction of the audit culture is clear in higher education. Power (1997: 100) describes its effects on research, the production of knowledge: 'Scientists are changing research habits, and a whole menu of activities for which performance measures have not been devised have ceased to have official value. Editing books, organising conferences and, paradoxically, reviewing and facilitating the publications efforts of others fall out of account.' With respect to teaching, the passing on of that knowledge, Power (1997: 100) says: 'One of the unintended but predictable consequences of the RAE's [Research Assessment Exercises] has been to create incentives to teach less and write more.' More generally, 'the drift towards delivery philosophies of teaching, supported by hard managerial assumptions, is transforming teaching from a relationship into a transaction which can be made auditable in isolation' (1997: 103). Strathern (1997), an anthropologist and participant observer of the audit process, points to similar undesirable consequences: measures become reduced to targets, research quality is conflated with research departments, descriptions become prescriptions, any sense of contradiction or ambiguity is replaced by canons of clarity and itemisation, and the quality of teaching becomes reduced to the use of new information technologies (see also Gudeman 1998). Worst of all for a discipline whose strength lies in embedded knowledge and the study of context, Strathern (1997: 320) notes that the concern with transferable skills and the pressure to make intellectual work visible and measurable favour disembedded knowledge and attack the very qualities of complexity and sensitivity that anthropologists are taught to value.

All this points, then, to another parallel between auditing and economics. Their importance springs not so much from the theoretical nature of their arguments, but from their power over and practical effects on major institutions; and the major auditing firms hold substantial power over even the largest transnational companies (Montagna 1990). Certainly companies gain advantage from the knowledge that accountancy firms accumulate through their experience with different companies and practices; but this knowledge is part of a package, the primary intention of which is to restrict the aims and strategies of companies to that which can be quantified as financial benefits. This is the same sort of restriction that MacLennan (1997) describes in her study of the rise of various forms of cost–benefit criteria in American governmental regulatory policy. Cost–benefit analysis has become one of the primary means by which a strict market logic has been forced upon state bodies, which are thereby obliged to justify their regulatory proposals in financial terms, which means reducing them to those terms.

In whose name are these audits, consultancy reports and cost–benefit calculations required? They claim their legitimacy from what Keat, Whiteley and Abercrombie (1994) call *The Authority of the Consumer*. All these procedures are justified on the grounds that they benefit the consumer, whether as the actual recipient of the services or as the taxpayer getting value for money. This explains the sad, ironic comments about how those who once were students or patients are now consumers of health or educational services. Indeed, it is hard to imagine what political authority is left today that is not reducible to this hegemonic rhetoric of the consumer. Even the central state is becoming a consumer democracy.

So, benefit to the consumer is crucial to the legitimacy of the set of processes that I have called 'auditing'. Indeed, much of the announced benefit of health and education audits is the idea that they will destroy the privileged autonomy of older bureaucracies and allow the emergence of the consumer citizen, the appropriate judge of whether what is being offered is really of benefit (Walsh 1994). But just as Marx saw a sleight of hand in commodity fetishism, there is plenty of illusion here. One of the main reasons that governments have favoured auditing is that it justifies, in the name of consumer benefit, cutting costs. However, most commonly cutting costs is achieved by cutting services to consumers. Furthermore, as MacLennan (1997) points out, the same logic that enables auditors to act in the name of consumers reduces the ability of citizens to dispute those actions, to protest that there are important criteria other than value for money, supposedly the ultimate consumer good. In sum, policies justified in the name of the consumer citizen become the means to prevent the consumer from becoming a citizen, from determining the priorities of expenditure in the public domain.

Thus it appears that auditing is a sign of a shift to political virtualism. As Power notes (1997: 49),

> the executive arm of modern states raises funds through the legislature for mandated programmes. As supreme audit bodies have grown in significance, political accountability to the electorate has been more explicitly supplemented, if not displaced, by managerial conceptions of accountability embracing the need to deliver value for money.

Certainly the languages of governance seem to be shifting in a virtualist direction. Books that used to be about capitalism, a phenomenon imagined as being in a certain time and space, today are almost always about the market, which inhabits the time-less and space-less realm of economic models. Rose (1996) makes a related point, arguing that political considerations of 'society' increasingly have been replaced by 'community', an imagined entity that lends itself to virtualist treatment. In a sense, though, none of these are quite as problematic as what accounting does to the consumer, precisely because in this case there is no similar shift in language. The virtual consumer is simply called a consumer, so that the displacement of actual consumers leaves no trace.

The background to this narrative was an earlier argument that consumption as a practice is a negation of capitalism, and not an expression of it (Miller 1987). So, in turn, the present argument is that auditing is not what it claims to be, an expression of consumption or of the authority of the consumer. Rather, it is a negation of consumption, a negation of a negation. After all, the academic complaint is that auditing leads to deteriorating teaching and research, since the time available to spend on actual persons and projects is eaten away by the demands of auditing itself. Although there may be token consumer representation, auditing is primarily a managerial exercise that is allied to a strict market logic of cost and benefit. The paradox is that, while consumption is the pivot upon which these developments in history spin, the concern is not the costs and benefits of actual consumers, but of what we might call virtual consumers, which are generated by management theory and models. To the degree that virtual consumers come to displace actual consumers, resources that might have been used to turn abstract capital into welfare are moving backwards, fuelling the still more abstract models that are generated academically and in the institutions of auditing.

My argument, thus, is that structural adjustment in Trinidad and the rise of auditing in Britain are symptomatic not of capitalism, but of a new form of abstraction that is emerging, a form more abstract than the capitalism of firms dealing with commodities. If we need a new term for this historical period, then we might consider 'virtualism', because it rests on replacing consumers with virtual consumers.

Postmodernism and Virtualism

Most social scientists would be sympathetic to a story that chose as its villains such classic targets as neo-classical economics, auditing and management theory. For my story to have any bite, the third candidate should be a much less congenial or stereotyped manifestation of this historical trend. In this section, therefore my argument will turn against those social scientists whose antipathy to the quantitative and the managerial would be unequivocal and who see themselves as inhabiting the opposite end of the academic spectrum.

During the same period that economists have been gaining power and auditing has expanded, social scientists such as human geographers and sociologists increasingly have been concerned with consumption. The literature on this topic, once conspicuous by its absence, is now almost impossible to keep track of. The term that has characterised the new style and content of such writing is 'postmodernism'. This has many connotations, but I refer to those that roughly follow Jameson's original *New Left Review* article (1984). Growth has been prodigious. A search in my own library (University College London) reveals 321 titles, most published during the 1990s. A characteristic of these works is that they claim that we have entered into a new era, to which they attribute what have become a familiar series of properties. These rarely derive from any study of actual populations, but come rather from the constant repetition of the works of key gurus who are supposed to have told us how the world now is, such as Foucault, Deleuze and Guttari, Baudrillard, Lyotard and so forth.

Just as the World Bank claims to operate on behalf of the poor and auditing claims to operate on behalf of the consumer, so postmodernists claim to operate on behalf of the radical angels. In anthropology they claim to give voice to local people against the authority of academics. In feminism and multi-culturalism they are heralded as the voice of pluralism struggling against grand narratives that were really just attempts to control through assertions of rationalism. Postmodernist writers are scathing about the mass population, deluded individualists who merely serve as signs to capitalist commodities. However, there is always a place for heroines and heroes at the margins, for the transgressive forces that return to some special role advocated by a long history of critics from Nietzsche through to Bataille, whose violence and dissonance confirm a claim to authenticity that separates them from the common humanity who follow the herd.

Postmodernists, however, represent the quintessence of what they purport to describe. The crux of their case is that modern society has lost its authenticity and grounding in the traditions of the world. It has become instead an endless circuit of commodity signs that represent mere superficiality in that they depend mainly on the constant reiteration of references to each other. I can not see how any ethnographic encounter with actual people could generate such a failure of empathy with human practice. The only area of social life that does seem to live up to these postmodernist claims is the literature on postmodernism itself, which consists largely of an endless circuit of cross-citations in which each author can cite hundreds of others now making the same claims about the postmodern world. These claims commonly are based on the analysis of media, advertising and other textual forms, but without any grounding in the careful study of the society they claim to represent. In short, I would define postmodernism as the branch of social analysis that proclaimed the advent of a new superficiality and managed simultaneously to constitute itself as the prime example of what it proclaimed.

I want to suggest that this literature shows the same process of virtual replacement of the consumer that characterises neo-classical economics and auditing. As evidence to support this conjecture I picked two of the 'guru' figures who are quoted widely by postmodernists among the social sciences, and three titles from the same arena. I deal with the social sciences rather than literature and the humanities, because the latter two make fewer pretensions to represent the world in some concrete relation. I proceeded to look at how these volumes treat the concept of the consumer or consumer society.

To start with the two gurus. First is Zygmunt Bauman, whose influence is strongest within sociology but is by no means restricted to that discipline, as he is cited throughout the literature on postmodernism. The most pertinent of his books is his *Intimations of Postmodernity*. Bauman places consumption centre stage in his discussion of the postmodern. He says that the idea of consumer freedom 'now takes over the crucial role of the link which fastens together the life-worlds of the individual agents and the purposeful rationality of the system' (1992: 49). In the concluding interview in the book, Bauman again points to the rise of consumption as the source of modern identity and as crucial for understanding the significance of postmodernity. I would not balk at his claim that consumption has become central to contemporary life-worlds, a claim I have pushed just as far (for example, Miller 1995). However, the passage I have just quoted, with its reliance on classic sociological terminology, raises the suspicion that Bauman is less interested in the nature of consumer society than in using it as a device to re-configure the abstract paradigms of sociological categorisation. Such a suspicion is borne out when one tries to discover what Bauman means by consumption. Despite the massive effect it is now supposed to have, his description returns to well-worn clichés. Consumption gives free reign to 'the pleasure principle' and is a sign of many new pressures to spend, including symbolic rivalry, merchandising and the needs of self-construction through acquisition. Where Bauman differs from other post-modernist writers is that he says that this amounts to a stable new era, which justifies the traditional sociological concern with systems and life-worlds. By contrast, other writers proclaim postmodernism as the end of systemic connections between different elements of identity and society. Bauman's argument rests upon assertions about the centrality of consumption, but the only reference to any actual study of consumption is a footnote to Bourdieu's *Distinction* (1984).

More widely quoted than Bauman is Baudrillard. He is one of the two or three key figures in establishing the concept of postmodernism, since Jameson's essay on the new superficiality of late capitalism is in many respects a re-cycling of concepts that Baudrillard had presented more than a decade earlier. Consumption is evidently central for Baudrillard, as most of his writings return to the central discussion of consumption in his early work. Much of that work (Baudrillard 1975, 1981) rested on a deft re-casting of Marx's critique of exchange value in terms of Baudrillard's own critique of use value. Baudrillard says that where commodities once signified human or social attributes, today society is the signified of commodity values created by capitalism. Pleasure, desire and gratification become major components of this new system. In his later work, Baudrillard elaborates and extends this new superficiality, pointing to different ways that what had once been representation has now become various forms of hyper-reality and simulacra.

To investigate the wider legacy of such writings I selected three further books, one each from anthropology, geography and sociology. I picked the first book I found in my college library that incorporated a link between the postmodern and consumption. The anthropology book was *Hybrids of Modernity* (P. Harvey 1996). It is a study of Expo'92, and includes a critical discussion of more traditional styles of anthropology from a postmodern perspective. The most relevant chapter is 'Hybrid Subjects: Citizens as Consumers', which views consumption mainly in terms of Baudrillard's writings. There are twelve references to Baudrillard, including six direct quotations, though other postmodernist gurus are well represented. As this suggests, Harvey deals with consumption primarily as the manipulation of signs by commerce and states. The description of exhibitions, which makes up much of the chapter, is based on the author's observations, which she describes as 'interpretative possibilities which interest me, and which can become adequate descriptions when framed in particular theoretical contexts' (1996: 165). In contrast to the author's experiences, references to visitors, the actual consumers of the exhibitions, are rare in this chapter and in the book as a whole. At one point Harvey follows a long passage from Baudrillard with the following statement: 'This abstract declaration on the nature of consumption is the kind of statement that annoys the anthropologists of a more empiricist bent' (1996: 155). Harvey is correct. Her chapter on consumption, in which consumers are almost entirely absent, is a good example of postmodernism as virtualism.

The geography example was a collection edited by Benko and Strohmayer (1997). In their Introduction, they relate the rise of the postmodern to the rise of both enterprise and consumption as primary modes of life. Thus, 'once cultural works are divorced from the historical context in which they appeared, their value can only be defined by the *market*' (1997: 16). The chapters in the collection generally portray consumers as purely bad or purely heroic. In one chapter, 'Postmodern Becomings: From the Space of Form to the Space of Potentiality', women under postmodernism are found to have become

> vacuous spaces of desire that must be satisfied by consumption . . . As consumer she is seen to participate in the realization of capitalist commodities, putting them to their final, unproductive uses: under the influence of capitalist advertising and mood manipulation she translates her sexual desires into needs which must be satisfied by consumption (Gibson-Graham 1997: 212, 213).

On the other hand, in 'Imagining the Nomad: Mobility and the Postmodern Primitive', we are told, following de Certeau, that consumers are now the heroic tacticians denying total strategic control (Cresswell 1997: 368).

The final book, in sociology, was the collection *Theories of Modernity and Postmodernity* (Turner 1990). In one chapter, typical of many, the evidence for the relationship between the postmodern and consumption comes from treating the film 'Wall Street' as a text. Commoditisation is here revealed as the creation of illusion, 'since the real has become a commodity that is transformed into a thing with a market value, all that is purchased are the illusions of things and the money they cost' (Denzin 1990: 37). Baudrillard's language inspired many of the other contributors to this book. For example, in a chapter on Habermas we are told that when 'consumer capitalism overripens' and 'semiurgy replaces production, the world increasingly becomes hyperreal and posits a realm of infinite and imploded possibilities' (Ashley 1990: 100), while another chapter tells us that citizenship is now dead since 'contemporary society killed the Enlightenment's modern individual, first by commodification, then by communication' (Wexler 1990: 165). And again, the evidence is references to Baudrillard, Jameson and Lyotard.

I am concerned about the postmodernism these authors and books represent because I am not convinced that the contemporary world is postmodern at all, because I am sceptical about the foundations of postmodernist ideals in anthropology (see Lindholm 1997), and particularly because I am sceptical about the representation of consumption in this literature. In my own ethnographic work on consumption in Trinidad and Britain, I have seen no real evidence that most people's relationship with consumption is less authentic or more superficial than their relationship with production. (Indeed, in Trinidad there is much to suggest the reverse.) Pleasure is of limited relevance to much consumption; the core factors that determine desire and purchase have surprisingly little to do with the logic of capitalism (Miller 1994, 1997, 1998), points that are invisible to academics who simply read off their view of consumption from their model of capitalism. Very few of the people I encountered in my research on consumption appear to be particularly superficial, nor do I find it meaningful to describe their relationship to the world as more superficial than the relationship of those I met when undertaking more conventional anthropological work in villages in India and in the Solomon Islands. In the absence of sustained ethnographic research to support postmodernist arguments, I must treat its theories as entirely misguided. Like business, consumption as a practice is highly grounded and contextual. On the other hand, the one place where we find a fine example of postmodernism, with its endless cycle of self-referential signs divorced from that which they purport to represent, is in the theory of postmodernism itself. Its degree of abstraction also makes that theory an excellent example of virtualism.

Some critics of Baudrillard see as his saving grace his recognition that he is himself a typical symptom of this new condition (Rojek and Turner 1993: xii). We can, however, go a great deal further and see writers such as Baudrillard and Bauman as the cause rather than the symptom. It is the body of postmodernist writing that becomes the only evidence that sustains the hundreds of subsequent volumes that explain how the new consumer society is best characterised as postmodern. Consumption is certainly central to the analysis of this new age, but once again appearances may deceive. What postmodernists produced was not an empathetic understanding of consumption as a complex human practice that is part of the struggle for human welfare within capitalism. Instead, they produced a rhetoric, based on the homogenising 'consumer society' and 'consumer culture', that simply stood for the consumer, who in turn was reduced to a symbol of superficial difference. Rather than descriptions and analyses of actual consumption, we find in postmodernism an academic model of the virtual consumer that comes to displace actual consumers and their practices.[5]

5. One can see a similar movement in the way the original ethnographic foundations of Stuart Hall's marvellously innovative and critical cultural studies at Birmingham quickly became its opposite, decontextualised texts in which academics read off the nature of the consumer society from what

So it is that in this narrative the social scientists are not the grand heroes and heroines who have stood up against the rise of economics and the virtual consumers. They are simply a weaker, parallel academic movement that reflects the very same trajectory, equally expressive of the movement from capitalism to virtualism. Baudrillard and Bauman provide the same service to the social sciences that economists provide to government and that auditors provide to institutions. They create a meta-level of abstraction within which consumer interests can be replaced by models of virtual consumers. The major difference between the discourse of postmodernism and my two previous examples is not that it is more or less daft, but that it has substantially less power. Outside the arts and the universities, it is unlikely that this discourse has made much difference to people or beasts. Economics may have its roots in a set of academic concerns that are just as esoteric, but when it is taken up as the elimination of welfare or farming subsidies, then its impact on people and beasts becomes vast and growing.

Conclusion

Dialectical stories absorb rather than supplant their antecedents, so that symptoms of virtualism are easy to see as continuities with capitalism, as more abstract forms of macro-capitalism. An example would be the increase in abstract or virtual versions of capital itself, the extraordinary new forms of esoteric finance capital that have been studied by geographers such as Nigel Thrift and David Harvey (Corbridge, Martin and Thrift 1994; D. Harvey 1989). The rise in power of financiers and the new forms of the control of capital have more to do with continuities in the tendencies that were identified in the classic models of capitalism than with the principles of virtualism as established here.[6] This is not to say that virtualism can not add to our understanding of these processes: for example, of the ways that pension funds intended to serve as the basis for consumption amongst the elderly become instrumental in the rise of capital to more abstract levels, a rise that can, ironically, destroy the urban environment of the elderly in whose names such pension funds are invested (Davis 1990). But I would not pretend that understanding the higher levels of derivatives and bond markets has much to do with the logic of consumption.

---

became set models. This had nothing in common with the original cultural studies, which set itself the task of an empathetic experience of moments of consumption, socialisation and oppression.

6. There are clear parallels, however. The kind of abstraction of quotas as commodities that Helgason and Pálsson document for Iceland in their chapter may not quite reach the esoteric forms of derivatives found in modern financial markets. However, their status as overly-abstract forms derived from actual production processes, and the problematic consequences of that abstraction, are similar to complex derivatives and the consequences of their tendency to spiral out of any clear relationship to the currencies and shares from which they were originally derived.

The critique of virtualism presented in this chapter is both similar to and different from the critique of capitalism that appears in some of the chapters in this collection. As such, this chapter is not intended merely to conclude the volume as a whole. Instead, I take the contributions to this collection as an important grounding for this abstract critique. For example, Nelson points out arenas in which economics and finance receive counter-colonisation from the social world. I do not think that such examples are incompatible with the overarching tendencies that can be discerned in virtualism. Rather, the rest of the volume provides the caveats and cautions that allow such a larger argument to be presented in a context that prevents it being seen as merely a glib assertion with pretensions to encompassing all trends within one.

So, while the narrative that underlies virtualism in this chapter is intended to be surprisingly encompassing, I certainly do not mean it to be all-encompassing. There are other stories that can be written about contemporary capitalism that would complement and cross-cut that told here. Furthermore, there are regions of the world that are at different stages in this story or are part of quite different stories. We co-exist with some plantation-based societies where Marxism is much more relevant for understanding the present predicament than is virtualism. Similarly, the argument I have presented here, as it centres on the fetishisation of the consumer, sheds little useful light upon the rise of an international capitalist class that Sklair describes. This is so even though his argument provides a major contribution to understanding virtualism, because it describes a way that capitalist abstraction becomes embodied in the de-contextualisation of people.

Nevertheless, a story is worth telling if it links together a group of characters who would otherwise appear as relatively autonomous, and if it demonstrates that their fates have been closely linked because they manifest a larger theme. This is the claim made by the narrative unfolded here. The story started with established forms of capitalism, and then told of the various ways that capitalism as a force for abstraction from humanity had been tamed. In this taming, consumption played a conspicuous role in creating new particularity and localisms. The story went on to suggest that new forms of abstraction have arisen subsequently. We do not discern these at first, since they arise under the guise of consumer authority, the very medium that had transformed and tamed capitalism. In the three examples presented here, academic economics, auditing and postmodernism, consumers and consumer culture remain central, but in each case virtual consumers replace actual ones.

In making these points I am not suggesting that abstraction is merely a property of representation. Many of the examples of the abstraction of class, finance and economic processes presented in this collection speak to substantial properties in the world, not merely representations that lack substance. The major difference between my final example of the postmodern and the examples of economists and auditors is that the latter two have the power to manifest their 'formalist' view by changing the world, whether business or health service, to match their models.

In the case of the postmodernist theorists, some have suggested that they reflect the particular niche of the self-reflexive intellectual of the modern middle class (for the evidence from Britain, see Savage *et al.* 1992: 127–132). But in any event, my criticism of postmodernists is not that they raise the spectre of abstraction – a project that this essay clearly shares. Rather, it is that postmodernism is based in large measure upon a misreading of the experience of consumption, that theorists abstract in a way that reinforces abstraction as virtualism. They replace consumption as human experience with the virtual figure of the postmodernist consumer. As such, they contribute to a consequence of economics and auditing, a general experience of alienation from what is viewed as an abstract and distant world. That is a world in which the economy, the institutions of business and government and the self-indulgent dissonance of the intellectual class all contribute to that state of unhappy consciousness wherein the citizens feel unable to recognise or re-appropriate those forces that have been constructed in their name. In particular, I have stressed the irony by which these forces are experienced as oppressive precisely because they legitimate themselves in the name of the actual practice of consumption, a practice that had been emerging as the primary means by which citizens struggled to confront the previous manifestations of these abstractions (see Miller 1987).

It also follows from a dialectical perspective that all new forms of abstraction contain positive potentials some time in the future. So my argument is not opposed to abstraction itself. Such a stance would be extraordinarily hypocritical given that grand narratives are characterised by their own abstraction by comparison with more parochial tales. In emulation of Simmel's (1978) view of the rise of money as abstraction, one would welcome all new forms of abstraction because of their potential contribution towards understanding the processes they address, even including economics: managing a welfare state without economists is probably not imaginable. The stance taken here relates, then, only to historical moments in a story. All new forms of abstraction are to be welcomed if they can be recognised as human constructions and can be re-appropriated as part of the enhancement of human self-understanding and cultural development. The narrative only suggests that, at this particular moment, we should be fearful that these forces will continue to increase their power to mould the world to make it conform to the abstract shapes dictated by their internal logic. If this happens, we will see an even greater negation of progressive movements and forces, and their replacement with increasingly oppressive rhetorics and practices. It is to help us to see and think about these forces more clearly, as something distinct from the object of earlier critiques, that we have suggested 'virtualism' as a replacement for 'capitalism' to summarise this phase in history.

The critique of virtualism, like the critique of capitalism, is a grand project. However, it is important to remember that, within a dialectical tradition, an eagle-eyed attempt to determine the changing landscape of history and to discern the shape of the woods must be founded on the experience of wandering amongst the trees, with all the sensual delight and satisfaction to be found in ethnographic stumbling around the leaves and flowers of the undergrowth, in the mud and mire of everyday lives. But the telling of narrative, a commitment to Ricoeur's (1984–88) sense of empathy with human experience in time, has to be grand as well as modest. It is an equal part of the academic responsibility to knowledge, and in particular within a commitment to rationalism as the foundation for the critical use of knowledge. At that level, many little streams that may otherwise seem quite isolated one from another may be discerned as constituting that larger flow in history that we need to comprehend and challenge before we are overwhelmed in its flood.

References

Ashley, D. 1990. Habermas and the Completion of 'The Project of Modernity'. In Bryan Turner (ed.), *Theories of Modernity and Postmodernity*, pp. 88–107. London: Sage.

Baudrillard, Jean 1975. *The Mirror of Production*. St Louis: Telos Press.

—— 1981. *For a Critique of the Political Economy of the Sign*. St Louis: Telos Press.

Bauman, Zygmunt 1992. *Intimations of Postmodernity*. London: Routledge.

Benko, Georges, and Ulf Strohmayer (eds) 1997. *Space and Social Theory: Interpreting Modernity and Postmodernity*. Oxford: Basil Blackwell.

Bourdieu, Pierre 1984. *Distinction: A Social Critique of the Judgement of Taste*. London: Routledge & Kegan Paul.

Carrier, James G. (ed.) 1997. *Meanings of the Market: The Free Market in Western Culture*. Oxford: Berg.

Corbridge, Stuart, Ron Martin and Nigel Thrift (eds) 1994. *Money, Power and Space*. Oxford: Basil Blackwell.

Cresswell, T. 1997. Imagining the Nomad: Mobility and the Postmodern Primitive. In Georges Benko and Ulf Strohmayer (eds), *Space and Social Theory: Interpreting Modernity and Postmodernity*, pp. 360–379. Oxford: Basil Blackwell.

Davis, Mike 1990. *City of Quartz*. London: Verso.

Denzin, N. 1990. Reading 'Wall Street': Postmodern Contradictions in the American Social Structure. In Bryan Turner (ed.), *Theories of Modernity and Postmodernity*, pp. 31–44. London: Sage.

Dilley, Roy (ed.) 1992. *Contesting Markets: Analyses of Ideology, Discourse and Practice*. Edinburgh: Edinburgh University Press.

Ekins, Paul, and Manfred Max-Neef (eds) 1992. *Real-Life Economics: Understanding Wealth Creation*. London: Routledge.

Fardon, Richard (ed.) 1990. *Localizing Strategies: Regional Traditions in Ethnographic Writing*. Edinburgh: Scottish Academic Press.

Fine, Ben 1995. From Political Economy to Consumption. In Daniel Miller (ed.), *Acknowledging Consumption*, pp. 127–163. London: Routledge.

Fine, Ben, and Ellen Leopold 1993. *The World of Consumption*. London: Routledge.

George, Susan, and Fabrizio Sabelli 1994. *Faith and Credit*. London Penguin.

Gibson-Graham, J. 1997. Postmodern Becomings: From the Space of Form to the Space of Potentiality. In Georges Benko and Ulf Strohmayer (eds), *Space and Social Theory: Interpreting Modernity and Postmodernity*, pp. 306–323. Oxford: Basil Blackwell.

Gledhill, John 1994. *Power and Its Disguises*. London: Pluto Press.

Gudeman, Stephen 1998. The New Captains of Information. *Anthropology Today* 14(1): 1–3.

Hamsun, Knut 1921. *Hunger*. New York: Knopf.

Harvey, David 1989. *The Condition of Postmodernity*. Oxford: Basil Blackwell.

—— 1996. *Justice, Nature and the Geography of Difference*. Oxford: Basil Blackwell.

Harvey, Penelope 1996. *Hybrids of Modernity*. London: Routledge.

Jameson, Fredric 1984. Postmodernism, the Cultural Logic of Late Capitalism. *New Left Review* 146: 53–92.

Keat, Russell, Nigel Whiteley and Nicholas Abercrombie (eds) 1994. *The Authority of the Consumer*. London: Routledge

Lawson, T. 1997. *Economics and Reality*. London: Routledge.

Lindholm, Charles 1997. Logical and Moral Problems of Postmodernism. *Journal of the Royal Anthropological Institute* 3: 747–760.

McCloskey, D. 1985. *The Rhetoric of Economics*. Madison: University of Wisconsin Press.

MacLennan, Carol 1997. Democracy under the Influence: Cost–Benefit Analysis in the United States. In James G. Carrier (ed.), *Meanings of the Market: The Free Market in Western Culture*, pp. 195–224. Oxford: Berg.

Mayer, Thomas 1993. *Truth versus Precision in Economics*. Aldershot: Edward Elgar.

Miller, Daniel 1987. *Material Culture and Mass Consumption*. Oxford: Basil Blackwell.

—— 1988. Appropriating the State on the Council Estate. *Man* 23: 353–372.

—— 1994. *Modernity: An Ethnographic Approach*. Oxford: Berg.

—— 1995. Introduction. In D. Miller (ed.), *Acknowledging Consumption*, pp. 1–57 London: Routledge.

—— 1997. *Capitalism: An Ethnographic Approach*. Oxford: Berg.

—— 1998. *A Theory of Shopping*. Cambridge: Polity Press.

Montagna, Paul 1990. Accounting Rationality and Financial Legitimation. In Sharon Zukin and Paul DiMaggio (eds), *Structures of Capital*, pp. 227–260. Cambridge: Cambridge University Press.

O'Shea, James, and Charles Madigan 1997. *Dangerous Company: The Consulting Powerhouses and the Businesses They Save and Ruin*. London: Nicholas Brearley.

Power, Michael 1994. *The Audit Explosion*. London: Demos.

—— 1997. *The Audit Society*. Oxford: Oxford University Press.

Radnitzky, Gerald, and Peter Bernholz (eds) 1987. *Economic Imperialism*. New York: Paragon House.

Ricoeur, Paul 1984–1988. *Time and Narrative*. Chicago: University of Chicago Press.

Rojek, Chris, and Bryan Turner 1993. *Forget Baudrillard*. London: Routledge.

Rose, Nicholas 1996. The Death of the Social? Re-Figuring the Territory of Government. *Economy and Society* 25: 327–356.

Salaman, Graeme 1997. Culturing Production. In Paul DuGay (ed.), *Production of Culture/Cultures of Production*, pp. 235–272. London: Sage.

Savage, Mike, James Barlow, Peter Dickens and Tony Fielding 1992. *Property, Bureaucracy and Culture*. London: Routledge.

Simmel, Georg 1978. *The Philosophy of Money*. (Edited by David Frisby; translated by Tom Bottomore and David Frisby.) London: Routledge & Kegan Paul

Sloman, John 1994. *Economics*. New York: Harvester-Wheatsheaf.

Smart, Alan 1997. Oriental Despotism and Sugar-Coated Bullets: Representations of the Market in China. In James G. Carrier (ed.), *Meanings of the Market: The Free Market in Western Culture*, pp. 195–225. Oxford: Berg.

Stewart, Frances 1995. *Adjustment and Poverty: Options and Choices*. London: Routledge.

Stiglitz, Joseph 1993 *Economics*. New York: W. W. Norton and Co.

Strathern, Marilyn 1997. 'Improving Ratings': Audit in the British University System. *European Review* 5: 305–321.

Thrift, Nigel 1997. The Rise of Soft Capitalism. *Cultural Values* 1: 29–57.

Tommasi, Mariano, and Kathryn Ierulli (eds) 1995. *The New Economics of Human Behaviour*. Cambridge: Cambridge University Press.

Turner, Bryan (ed.) 1990. *Theories of Modernity and Postmodernity*. London: Sage.

Walsh, Kieron 1994. Citizens, Charters and Contracts. In Russell Keat, Nigel Whiteley and Nicholas Abercrombie (eds), *The Authority of the Consumer*, pp. 189–206. London: Routledge.

Wexler, P. 1990. Citizenship in the Semiotic Society. In Bryan Turner (ed.), *Theories of Modernity and Postmodernity*, pp. 164–175. London: Sage.

Zelizer, Viviana 1985. *Pricing the Priceless Child*. New York: Basic Books.

Notes on Contributors

James G. Carrier teaches anthropology at the University of Durham. He has done fieldwork in Papua New Guinea and historical research on exchange and circulation in Western societies. His most recent books are *Gifts and Commodities: Exchange and Western Capitalism since 1700* (London, Routledge, 1994), *Occidentalism: Images of the West* (Oxford, Oxford University Press, 1995, editor) and *Meanings of the Market: The Free Market in Western Culture* (Oxford, Berg, 1997, editor).

Ben Fine is Professor of Economics and Director of the Centre for Economic Policy for Southern Africa (CEPSA) at the School of Oriental and African Studies, University of London. His recent books include *The World of Consumption* (London, Routledge, 1993, with Ellen Leopold), *Consumption in the Age of Affluence: The World of Food* (London, Routledge, 1996, with Michael Heasman and Judith Wright), and *The Political Economy of South Africa: From Minerals–Energy Complex to Industrialisation* (London, Hurst, 1997, with Zavareh Rustomjee). He has just completed a book on diet, health and information to be published by Routledge.

Agnar Helgason is currently completing a D. Phil. degree at the Institute of Biological Anthropology, University of Oxford. His previous research has focused on public reactions to the commoditisation of fishing rights in Iceland (*Journal of the Royal Anthropological Institute* 1997, with Gísli Pálsson). He is currently working on the genetic and demographic history of Icelanders, in addition to undertaking research on public reactions to bodily commodities in Iceland and the United Kingdom.

Philip McMichael is Professor of Rural and Development Sociology and Director of the International Political Economy Program at Cornell University. His publications include *Settlers and the Agrarian Question: Foundations of Capitalism in Colonial Australia* (Cambridge, Cambridge University Press, 1984), *The Global Restructuring of Food Systems* (Ithaca, NY, Cornell, 1994, editor), *Food and Agrarian Orders in the World Economy* (Westport, Conn., Greenwood, 1995, editor) and *Development and Social Change: A Global Perspective* (Thousand Oaks, Cal., Pine Forge, 1996).

Daniel Miller is Professor of Anthropology at University College London. His recent books include *A Theory of Shopping* (Cambridge, Polity and Ithaca, NY, Cornell University Press, 1998, with others), *Shopping, Place and Identity* (London, Routledge, 1998, editor), *Material Cultures* (London, UCL Press and Chicago, University of Chicago Press, 1998) and *Capitalism: An Ethnographic Approach* (Oxford, Berg, 1997).

Julie A. Nelson is Associate Professor in the Department of Economics and Graduate School of International Economics and Finance at Brandeis University. She is the author of *Feminism, Objectivity, and Economics* (London, Routledge, 1996), co-editor of *Beyond Economic Man: Feminist Theory and Economics* (Chicago, University of Chicago Press, 1993), and author of articles on the economics of household (in the *Journal of Political Economy, Econometrica* and other journals).

Gísli Pálsson is Professor of Anthropology, University of Iceland, Reykjavik, and (formerly) Research Fellow at the Swedish Collegium for Advanced Study in the Social Sciences, Uppsala. He has published a number of articles on fishing, practical skills and environmental issues. Among his books are *The Textual Life of Savants: Ethnography, Iceland and the Linguistic Turn* (Reading, Harwood Academic, 1995) and *Nature and Society: Anthropological Perspectives* (London, Routledge, 1996, co-edited with Philippe Descola).

Leslie Sklair teaches in the Sociology Department at the London School of Economics. Recent publications include *Sociology of the Global System* (second edition, Baltimore, Johns Hopkins University Press and Englewood Cliffs, NJ, Prentice-Hall, 1995) and 'Globalization and the Corporations: The Case of the California *Fortune* Global 500' (*International Journal of Urban and Regional Research* 1998).

Nigel Thrift is a Professor of Geography in the School of Geographical Sciences, University of Bristol. His main interests are in social and cultural theory, time and new forms of capitalism. His most recent publications are *Mapping the Subject* (London, Routledge, 1995, co-edited with Steve Pile), *Spatial Formations* (London, Sage, 1996), *Money/Space* (London, Routledge, 1997, with Andrew Leyshon) and *Consumption, Place and Identity* (London, Routledge, 1998, with Daniel Miller, Peter Jackson, Beverley Holbrook and Michael Rowlands).

Index